DIALOGUES OF PLATO

Translated from the Greek by Benjamin Jowett
Supplementary materials written by
Cory Reed
Series edited by Cynthia Brantley Johnson

SIMON & SCHUSTER PAPERBACKS
NEW YORK   LONDON   TORONTO   SYDNEY

Simon & Schuster Paperbacks
A Division of Simon & Schuster, Inc.
1230 Avenue of the Americas
New York, NY 10020

Copyright 1950, © 2010 by Simon & Schuster, Inc.
Supplementary materials copyright © 2001, 2010 by Simon & Schuster, Inc.

This Simon & Schuster paperback edition December 2010

SIMON & SCHUSTER PAPERBACKS and colophon are registered trademarks of Simon & Schuster, Inc.

For information about special discounts for bulk purchases, please contact Simon & Schuster Special Sales at 1-866-506-1949 or business@simonandschuster.com.

The Simon & Schuster Speakers Bureau can bring authors to your live event. For more information or to book an event, contact the Simon & Schuster Speakers Bureau at 1-866-248-3049 or visit our website at www.simonspeakers.com.

Cover art by Robert Hunt

Manufactured in the United States of America

20   19   18   17   16

ISBN: 978-1-4391-6948-3

CONTENTS

INTRODUCTION

Dialogues of Plato:
THE BIRTH OF PHILOSOPHY

For more than two centuries, writers, philosophers, and statesmen throughout the world have celebrated Plato as one of history's greatest thinkers. In his dialogues (399–360 BCE), Plato explores the great ideas of life—love, death, search for immortality—and essentially what it means to be human. His dialogues are also full of biting social criticism. He rails at hypocrites, challenging politicians, teachers, and other leaders to rethink their morality and ethics. Unleashing the dramatic potential in the literary form of the dialogue, Plato creates lively debates among different points of view that invite the reader to join the discussion.

Though Plato's dialogues are serious, they also provide entertaining discourse. They tell the story of his controversial teacher, Socrates (c. 469–399 BCE), an independent thinker and nonconformist who is arrested on trumped-up charges of corruption and is tried, convicted, and executed by his political enemies. *Meno* and *Euthyphro* find Socrates at the height of his career, as he questions authority and decries hypocrisy. The trilogy of *Apology, Crito,* and *Phaedo* takes the reader from Socrates' trial to his prison cell, for serious discussions on justice, loyalty, death, and the immortality of the soul. *Symposium,* one of Plato's undisputed masterpieces, presents Socrates as a guest at a dinner party, joining his friends in food, drink, and a delightful night of speeches about love that are comic, sentimental, and inspirational. Set in ancient Athens during a period of political turmoil, *Dialogues of Plato* depicts Socrates as a vivid, imperfect human being, both funny and solemn, who challenges the leaders of Athenian society to think critically about their strongest convictions.

On a deeper level, Plato's dialogues draw a distinction between the physical world that can deceive us and an ideal spirit world, which inspires us to strive for truth and goodness. Plato emphasizes a spiritual reward that awaits the faithful after a worldly life of trials and tribulations. Plato's works not only influenced the foundations of Christianity, but also the development of philosophy from the time of his pupil Aristotle (384–322 BCE) until the present day. With his focus on debate as a process for discovering the truth, Plato's philosophy can be applied to a wide spectrum of ethical issues, including torture, war, and the role of government in a democratic society. *Dialogues of Plato* is among the first works of literature to ask the most pointed questions about human existence, questions that we continue to attempt to answer each day.

The Life and Work of Plato

Very little is known about Plato's life, and the sources that mention him are incomplete and unreliable. Even his date of birth is uncertain. He was born sometime around 427 BCE, the fourth child of an aristocratic

Athenian family whose lineage claimed well-known ancestors like the Athenian lawgiver Solon, and even the god Poseidon. His family probably resided on the island of Aegina, about fifteen miles from Athens. Plato's father died around the time of his birth, which later inspired the even more fantastic legend that the god Apollo himself was Plato's real father. Plato's stepfather was a close friend of the Athenian statesman Pericles, and the family's political connections may explain why the young Plato aspired to a career in public service.

Plato's early education included training in gymnastics, the arts, mathematics, and history. Traditionally, male children of noble families were placed with older tutors who instructed them in virtue and practical matters. Although he may have had other teachers first, Plato met Socrates between the ages of fifteen and twenty. Plato entered adulthood during the last stages of the Peloponnesian War between Athens and Sparta, and it is possible that he served in the military. His brothers, Adeimantus and Glaucon, distinguished themselves in the war, and two of his uncles, Critias and Charmides, formed part of the elite Oligarchy of the Thirty, the antidemocratic government that ruled Athens after its defeat. Despite his family's involvement in Athenian politics, or perhaps because of it, Plato gave up his plan for a public career and instead became a dedicated pupil to Socrates, pursuing a life as a philosopher. Plato later cast his heroic brothers and controversial uncles as characters in a number of his dialogues.

Perhaps the most significant event that defined Plato's adult life was the trial and execution of his mentor, Socrates, in 399 BCE. During the political instability that followed the Peloponnesian War, Athenian democracy collapsed (in 404 BCE), only to be restored a year later after a battle that claimed the lives of Plato's uncles. A general amnesty was issued to stop acts of political revenge. Socrates, however, could not escape criticism for his previous associations with the enemies of the new government; when the amnesty prevented Athenian leaders from charging him with political crimes, they accused him of sacrilege against the gods and corrupting the youth of Athens. Plato attended the trial, which he recounts in *Apology*. He dramatizes Socrates' last days awaiting execution in *Crito* and *Phaedo*.

In the years after Socrates' death, Plato began writing his early dialogues, including *Meno, Euthyphro, Apology*, and *Crito*, featuring his teacher as the protagonist. The dialogue form allowed him to dramatize Socrates' method, called dialectic, in which he used a series of questions to challenge his interlocutor's preconceived assumptions and illogical reasoning. Like many of Socrates' followers, he moved away from Athens, settling for a time in Megara, near the border with Sparta. Even as his fame as a philosopher spread, he was never far removed from political intrigue. He was invited several times to Sicily to tutor kings Dionysius I and II of Syracuse, where he established a close friendship with the elder king's brother-in-law, Dion. His experience as a royal tutor was a mixed blessing. In 384 BCE, Dionysius I grew angry with Plato and sold him into slavery. He was freed shortly thereafter and returned to Athens. Some twenty years later, Dionysius II accused his uncle, Dion, of plotting with Plato against him. Dion was banished to Athens and Plato was held under house arrest before being allowed to join the exiled Dion. A few years later, Dion would successfully overthrow his nephew only to be assassinated in 354 BCE.

Upon his return to Athens from his first voyage to Sicily, Plato founded the Academy, a center for advanced study that taught mathematics, political theory, and philosophy through Plato's dialectical method of questions and answers. Plato composed his middle dialogues, including *Phaedo, Symposium,* and his masterpiece, *The Republic,* during these years. His dialogues played an important role in the Academy's instruction, and the school continued to draw talented Athenian youth until at least 79 BCE, some three hundred years after Plato founded it. Plato's most famous student, Aristotle, arrived at the Academy in 367 BCE. Plato continued to write his dialogues until his death in 347 BCE.

Historical and Literary Context of *Dialogues of Plato*

The Rise and Fall of Ancient Athens

Plato lived during a time of military and political turmoil as Athen's stature as a great power declined. Ancient Greece was divided into independent city-states, each of which included a primary city and the rural areas surrounding it. More than a generation before Plato's birth, Athens emerged as the most powerful of these by forming the Delian League, a coalition of states organized to repel the forces of Persia, which had invaded Greece in 480 BCE. Athens eventually turned the alliance into its own empire. Athens boasted a stable, democratic government, had a constitution that protected the rights of citizens of all social classes, and adult male citizens could vote and participate in public assemblies, although the military and political leaders tended to come from the aristocracy. Under the rule of the celebrated statesman Pericles (461–429 BCE),

Athens entered a so-called Golden Age of culture that extended Athenian influence throughout the region. Pericles constructed the Parthenon, the great temple to the goddess Athena, and his architects, sculptors, and artists transformed Athens into a beautiful, flourishing city. Some of the greatest works of ancient Greek literature date from this period, including the tragedies of Sophocles and the comic dramas of Aristophanes. It is also the time of the birth of Greek philosophy and the teachings of Socrates, which Plato would later dramatize in his dialogues.

The outbreak of the Peloponnesian War, a twenty-seven-year conflict between Athens and Sparta, began the period of Athens' decline. For centuries, Sparta had maintained a militaristic society and saw Athenian power as a threat to its own security. During the last decade of Pericles' government, conflicts between the two powers escalated. In 431, full war broke out between Athens and Sparta, and the death of Pericles in 429 effectively ended the Golden Age of Athens.

The long war drained Athenian resources and threatened democracy. The Peace of Nicias, signed in 421 BCE, brought a temporary end to the fighting, but the conflict was renewed after Athens invaded the island of Melos (which had remained neutral in the war) and attacked Spartan allies in Sicily. The great general Alcibiades was chosen to lead the Sicilian campaign but was abruptly recalled to Athens on charges of sacrilege. Athens suffered defeat in Sicily, and when Sparta renewed the war, Alcibiades was again put in charge of the Athenian fleet. As Plato wrote in his *Apology*, Socrates himself also fought in the Peloponnesian War, and his friendship with the controversial Alcibiades, who appears as a drunken soldier in *Symposium*, may have played a role in the charges that were levied against him at his trial and led to his execution.

Though Alcibiades led his fleet to many victories, the war turned against Athens after Sparta's new general, Lysander, led a final drive offensive. A devastated Athens surrendered to Sparta in 404 BCE, and the humiliating aftermath of the Peloponnesian War significantly altered Athenian society and its political system. Pro-Sparta forces and aristocrats gave power to an elite governing class, called the Oligarchy of the Thirty. This small, privileged group became known as tyrants for their cruel policies and abuse of authority. Plato's two uncles Critias and Charmides were members of the Thirty. In 403 BCE, democracy was restored, and it is believed that Socrates' personal association with Plato's uncles may have compelled his arrest under the new government.

The restored democracy would last for the rest of Plato's life. Although he probably saw the new Athenian democracy as a return to political stability, he could not know that Athenian power would be eclipsed by the arrival of Alexander the Great from the northern region of Macedonia, who conquered most of Greece a generation after Plato's death.

Greek Literature in the Time of Plato

Many of the roots of Western civilization as we know it today can be traced to the tremendous literary, cultural, and philosophical production of ancient Greece. The Greek literary tradition begins with the epic poems of Homer, the *Iliad* and the *Odyssey*, dated to the eighth century BCE, which told the legendary stories of the Trojan War and its heroes. It is likely that a series of poets contributed to these works, perhaps over centuries, but they had taken their final form approximately a century before Plato's birth. Homer became one of the cornerstones of Athenian education, and Plato quotes him frequently in his dialogues.

The literary tradition begun by Homer flourished in the age of Pericles and culminated in the great dramas of Sophocles, Euripides, Aristophanes, and others during Plato's lifetime. Prizes were awarded for the best plays at festivals honoring Dionysus, the god of wine and celebration. Sophocles, author of the tragedy *Oedipus the King*, was awarded more prizes than any other dramatist, but Euripides won first prize for *The Bacchae*, although it was performed after his death. Aristophanes defined the genre of comedy with plays like *The Clouds*, in which he caricatured Socrates. Agathon composed prize-winning tragedies, although none of his plays survive today. Plato comments on all of these authors in his dialogues and casts Agathon as the host of the banquet in *Symposium*, which Aristophanes attends as a guest. As a literary form, the Platonic dialogue owes much to the poetic and dramatic traditions of ancient Greece. Like classical tragedies, Plato's dialogues use debate among characters as a way of presenting different sides of moral arguments. Like comedy, the Platonic dialogues portray characters drawn from contemporary society, who employ irony and humor in their discussions.

Plato, Socrates, and the Origins of Greek Philosophy

Philosophy and science, as we know them, were not separate disciplines in ancient Greece; many of the philosophers before the time of Socrates and Plato were trying to understand different kinds of scientific, mathematical, and practical problems as well as metaphysical questions.

Some of the famous philosophers before Socrates include Pythagoras, known for his studies on mathematics and religion, Heracleitus, who believed that the world was in a state of perpetual flux, Parmenides, who applied logic to philosophical reasoning, and Anaxagoras, who taught that the mind brought order to the chaos of the universe. Although there was not yet a formal, unified discipline of philosophy, these traditions of critical thinking influenced Plato through the teachings of Socrates.

Most of what we know about Socrates comes from Plato himself and a few others who wrote about him. The modern reader cannot be sure how much of Plato's portrayal of Socrates corresponds to the historical man and how much is a literary character created by Plato as a mouthpiece for his own philosophy. Still, it is apparent that Socrates was Plato's most important influence, and the Socratic method of using questions and answers to discover truth forms the foundation of Plato's dialogues. In the time of Socrates, professional teachers known as sophists made their living instructing the youth of Athens in moral, political, and practical knowledge. Socrates distinguished himself from the sophists by challenging their knowledge of the subjects they taught. Through the method he called dialectic, he would approach a person claiming to be an expert and ask him a series of pointed questions to find flaws in his arguments to reveal his ignorance. Socrates is famous for claiming that the Oracle of Delphi, speaking for the god Apollo, proclaimed him the wisest man in Athens. Socrates maintained that his only wisdom was in knowing his own ignorance. The Platonic dialogue is, in effect, a dramatization of the Socratic dialectic at work. Together, Socrates and Plato are credited with transforming philosophy from the diverse kinds of inquiry of the pre-Socratic thinkers into a unified discipline with its own aims and methods.

CHRONOLOGY OF
PLATO'S LIFE AND WORK

427 BCE   Plato is born on Aegina, an island near Athens, within a few years of this date. Plato's father dies around the time of his birth.

408–409 BCE   Plato's brothers, Adeimantus and Glaucon, distinguish themselves in the Peloponnesian War.

403 BCE   Plato's uncles, Critias and Charmides, members of the Oligarchy of the Thirty, are killed in the battle of Munychia.

399 BCE   Plato attends the trial of Socrates.

399–387 BCE   Plato is at work writing his early dialogues, including *Meno, Euthyphro, Apology,* and *Crito.*

396 BCE   Plato moves to Megara when many of Socrates' followers leave Athens.

385 BCE   Plato travels to Syracuse at the invitation of Dionysius I. There he befriends and tutors Dion, the king's brother-in-law.

385–383 BCE   Plato distributes drafts of his early dialogues, including Book I of *Republic.*

384 BCE	Dionysius is angered with Plato's instruction; Plato is sold into slavery.
383 BCE	Plato returns from Sicily and founds the Academy.
380–360 BCE	Plato writes his middle dialogues, including *Phaedo* and *Symposium,* and completes *Republic.*
367 BCE	Aristotle arrives at the Academy.
367 BCE	Death of Dionysius I of Syracuse.
366 BCE	Dion persuades the young Dionysius II to invite Plato to tutor him at Syracuse.
365–361 BCE	Plato and Dion both live in Athens.
361 BCE	Plato makes a third trip to Syracuse, summoned by Dionysius II.
360 BCE	He returns to Athens where he would remain for the rest of his life.
357 BCE	Dion attacks Syracuse to overthrow his nephew, Dionysius II.
354 BCE	Assassination of Dion.
355–347 BCE	Plato writes his later dialogues, including *Laws,* which would circulate after his death.
347 BCE	Plato dies.

HISTORICAL CONTEXT OF
DIALOGUES OF PLATO

480 BCE	Warriors from throughout the Greek city-states defeat the Persian invasion at the Battle of Salamis.
ca. 469 BCE	Socrates is born.
465 BCE	Xerxes I, King of Persia, is murdered by his head bodyguard.
460 BCE	First Peloponnesian War begins with Sparta leading the Peloponnesian League against the Delian League, led by Athens.
445 BCE	First Peloponnesian War ends with a treaty called the Thirty Years' Peace.
431 BCE	After little more than a decade, the cease-fire ends and the Second Peloponnesian War begins.
429 BCE	The death of Pericles marks the end of the Golden Age of Athens.
423 BCE	Aristophanes' play *The Clouds*, which lampoons Socrates in particular and Athenian intellectual society in general, is first performed at the Greater Dionysia festival.

413 BCE	Syracuse destroys the military apparatus of the Athenian empire with Sparta's assistance.
404 BCE	A brutal, Spartan-backed oligarchy known as "the Thirty" overthrows Athenian democracy.
403 BCE	The Battle of Munychia, a coup led by Thrasybulus, restores democracy to Athens. Critias, a leader of the Thirty and a relative of Plato, is killed.
399 BCE	Socrates is put to death by the new leadership after being charged with corrupting the youth of Athens and rejecting the state religion.
386 BCE	Aristophanes dies.
384 BCE	Aristotle is born.
359 BCE	King Philip II of Macedon ascends to the throne.
347 BCE	After Plato's death, Aristotle leaves Athens and the Academy, eventually serving as tutor to King Philip II's son, Alexander.
338 BCE	The Greek city-states are dissolved under the hegemony of King Philip II.
336 BCE	Philip II of Macedon is murdered by one of his bodyguards.
336 BCE	Alexander the Great, son of King Philip II and student of Aristotle, ascends to the throne.
335 BCE	Aristotle returns to Athens to found the Lyceum.
323 BCE	After capturing India and humiliating Persia, Alexander the Great dies in the palace of Nebuchadnezzar II in Babylon after a banquet organized by his friend Medius.
322 BCE	Aristotle dies in Chalcis.

DIALOGUES OF PLATO

EUTHYPHRO

Persons of the Dialogue
SOCRATES, EUTHYPHRO

Scene
THE PORCH OF THE KING ARCHON

Euthyphro: Why have you left the Lyceum,[1] Socrates? and what are you doing in the Porch of the King Archon?[2] Surely you cannot be concerned in a suit before the King, like myself?

Socrates: Not in a suit, Euthyphro; impeachment is the word which the Athenians use.

Euth.: What! I suppose that some one has been prosecuting you, for I cannot believe that you are the prosecutor of another.

Soc.: Certainly not.

Euth.: Then some one else has been prosecuting you?

Soc.: Yes.

Euth.: And who is he?

Soc.: A young man who is little known, Euthyphro; and I hardly know him: his name is Meletus,[3] *Euthyphro and Socrates meet at the porch of the King Archon. Both have legal business on hand.*

and he is of the deme[4] of Pitthis. Perhaps you may remember his appearance; he has a beak, and long straight hair, and a beard which is ill grown.

Euth.: No, I do not remember him, Socrates. But what is the charge which he brings against you?

Soc.: What is the charge? Well, a very serious charge, which shows a good deal of character in the young man, and for which he is *Meletus has brought a charge against Socrates.*

certainly not to be despised. He says he knows how the youth are corrupted and who are their corruptors. I fancy that he must be a wise man, and seeing that I am the reverse of a wise man, he has found me out, and is going to accuse me of corrupting his

5

young friends. And of this our mother the state is to be the judge. Of all our political men he is the only one who seems to me to begin in the right
d   way, with the cultivation of virtue in youth; like a
3a   good husbandman, he makes the young shoots his first care, and clears away us who are the destroyers of them. This is only the first step; he will afterwards attend to the elder branches; and if he goes on as he has begun, he will be a very great public benefactor.

Euth.: I hope that he may; but I rather fear, Socrates, that the opposite will turn out to be the truth. My opinion is that in attacking you he is simply aiming a blow at the foundation of the state. But in what way does he say that you corrupt the young?

b   *Soc.:* He brings a wonderful ac-   *The nature*
cusation against me, which at first   *of the charge*
hearing excites surprise: he says   *against*
that I am a poet or maker of gods,   *Socrates.*
and that I invent new gods and deny the existence of old ones; this is the ground of his indictment.

Euth.: I understand, Socrates; he means to attack you about the familiar sign which occasionally, as you say, comes to you. He thinks that you are a neologian,[5] and he is going to have you up before
c   the court for this. He knows that such a charge is readily received by the world, as I myself know too well; for when I speak in the assembly about divine things, and foretell the future to them, they laugh at me and think me a madman. Yet every word that I say is true. But they are jealous of us all; and we must be brave and go at them.

Soc.: Their laughter, friend Euthyphro, is not

a matter of much consequence. For a man may be thought wise; but the Athenians, I suspect, do not much trouble themselves about him until he begins to impart his wisdom to others, and then for some reason or other, perhaps, as you say, from jealousy, they are angry. d

Euth.: I am never likely to try their temper in this way.

Soc.: I dare say not, for you are reserved in your behaviour, and seldom impart your wisdom. But I have a benevolent habit of pouring out myself to everybody, and would even pay for a listener, and I am afraid that the Athenians may think me too talkative. Now if, as I was saying, they would only laugh at me, as you say that they laugh at you, the time might pass gaily enough in the court; but perhaps they may be in earnest, and then what the end will be you soothsayers only can predict. e

Euth.: I dare say that the affair will end in nothing, Socrates, and that you will win your cause; and I think that I shall win my own.

Soc.: And what is your suit, Euthyphro? are you the pursuer or the defendant?

Euth.: I am the pursuer.

Soc.: Of whom?

Euth.: You will think me mad when I tell you. 4a

Soc.: Why, has the fugitive wings?

Euth.: Nay, he is not very volatile at his time of life.

Soc.: Who is he?

Euth.: My father.

Soc.: Your father! my good man?

Euth.: Yes.

Soc.: And of what is he accused?

Euth.: Of murder, Socrates.

Soc.: By the powers, Euthy- *The irony of*
phro! how little does the common *Socrates.*
herd know of the nature of right and truth. A man

b must be an extraordinary man, and have made
great strides in wisdom, before he could have seen
his way to bring such an action.

Euth.: Indeed, Socrates, he must.

Soc.: I suppose that the man *Euthyphro is*
whom your father murdered was *under a sacred*
one of your relatives—clearly he *obligation to*
was; for if he had been a stranger *prosecute a*
you would never have thought of *homicide, even*
prosecuting him. *if the murderer*
is his own
Euth.: I am amused, Socrates, *father.*
at your making a distinction between one who
is a relation and one who is not a relation; for
surely the pollution is the same in either case, if
you knowingly associate with the murderer when
you ought to clear yourself and him by proceeding against him. The real question is whether the
murdered man has been justly slain. If justly, then
your duty is to let the matter alone; but if unjustly,
then even if the murderer lives under the same

c roof with you and eats at the same table, proceed
against him. Now the man who is dead was a poor
dependant of mine who worked for us as a field
labourer on our farm in Naxos, and one day in a
fit of drunken passion he got into a quarrel with
one of our domestic servants and slew him. My father bound him hand and foot and threw him into
a ditch, and then sent to Athens to ask of a diviner
what he should do with him. Meanwhile he never

d attended to him and took no care about him, for

he regarded him as a murderer; and thought that no great harm would be done even if he did die. Now this was just what happened. For such was the effect of cold and hunger and chains upon him, that before the messenger returned from the diviner, he was dead. And my father and family are angry with me for taking the part of the murderer and prosecuting my father. They say that he did not kill him, and that if he did, the dead man was but a murderer, and I ought not to take any notice, for that a son is impious who prosecutes a father. Which shows, Socrates, how little they know what e the gods think about piety and impiety.

Soc.: Good heavens, Euthyphro! and is your knowledge of religion and of things pious and impious so very exact, that, supposing the circumstances to be as you state them, you are not afraid lest you too may be doing an impious thing in bringing an action against your father?

Euth.: The best of Euthyphro, and that which distinguishes him, Socrates, from other men, is his exact knowledge of all such matters. What should I 5a be good for without it?

Soc.: Rare friend! I think that I cannot do better than be your disciple. Then before the trial with Meletus comes on I shall challenge him, and say that I have always had a great interest in religious questions, and now, as he charges me with rash imaginations and innovations in religion, I have become your disciple. You, Meletus, as I shall say to him, acknowledge Euthyphro to be a great theologian, and

Socrates, who is accused of false theology, thinks that he cannot do better than become the disciple of so great a theologian as Euthyphro.

b

sound in his opinions; and if you approve of him you ought to approve of me, and not have me into court; but if you disapprove, you should begin by indicting him who is my teacher, and who will be the ruin, not of the young, but of the old; that is to say, of myself whom he instructs, and of his old father whom he admonishes and chastises. And if Meletus refuses to listen to me, but will go on, and will not shift the indictment from me to you, I cannot do better than repeat this challenge in the court.

c   *Euth.:* Yes, indeed, Socrates; and if he attempts to indict me I am mistaken if I do not find a flaw in him; the court shall have a great deal more to say to him than to me.

    Soc.: And I, my dear friend,   *He asks, "What* knowing this, am desirous of be- *is piety?"* coming your disciple. For I observe that no one appears to notice you—not even this Meletus; but his sharp eyes have found me out at once, and he has

d indicted me for impiety. And therefore, I adjure you to tell me the nature of piety and impiety, which you said that you knew so well, and of murder, and of other offences against the gods. What are they? Is not piety in every action always the same? and impiety, again—is it not always the opposite of piety, and also the same with itself, having, as impiety, one notion which includes whatever is impious?

    Euth.: To be sure, Socrates.

    Soc.: And what is piety, and what is impiety?

    Euth.: Piety is doing as I am   *Piety is doing*
e doing; that is to say, prosecuting *as I am doing:* any one who is guilty of murder, *like Zeus, I am* sacrilege, or of any similar crime— *proceeding* whether he be your   father or *against my*   *father.*

mother, or whoever he may be—that makes no difference; and not to prosecute them is impiety. And please to consider, Socrates, what a notable proof I will give you of the truth of my words, a proof which I have already given to others:—of the principle, I mean, that the impious, whoever he may be, ought not to go unpunished. For do not men regard Zeus as the best and most righteous of the gods?—and yet they admit that he bound his father (Cronos) because he wickedly devoured his sons, and that he too had punished his own father (Uranus) for a similar reason, in a nameless manner. And yet when I proceed against my father, they are angry with me. So inconsistent are they in their way of talking when the gods are concerned, and when I am concerned.

6a

Soc.: May not this be the reason, Euthyphro, why I am charged with impiety—that I cannot away with these stories about the gods? *Does Euthyphro believe these amazing stories about the gods?* and therefore I suppose that people think me wrong. But, as you who are well informed about them approve of them, I cannot do better than assent to your superior wisdom. What else can I say, confessing as I do, that I know nothing about them? Tell me, for the love of Zeus, whether you really believe that they are true.

b

Euth.: Yes, Socrates; and things more wonderful still, of which the world is in ignorance.

Soc.: And do you really believe that the gods fought with one another, and had dire quarrels, battles, and the like, as the poets say, and as you may see represented in the works of great artists? The temples are full of them; and notably the robe

c

of Athene,[6] which is carried up to the Acropolis at the great Panathenaea,[7] is embroidered with them. Are all these tales of the gods true, Euthyphro?

Euth.: Yes, Socrates; and, as I was saying, I can tell you, if you would like to hear them, many other things about the gods which would quite amaze you. *Yes, and things more amazing.*

Soc.: I dare say; and you shall tell me them at some other time when I have leisure. But just at present I would rather hear from you a more precise answer, which you have not as yet given, my friend, to the question, What is 'piety'? When asked, you only replied, Doing as you do, charging your father with murder.

Euth.: And what I said was true, Socrates.

Soc.: No doubt, Euthyphro; but you would admit that there are many other pious acts?

Euth.: There are.

Soc.: Remember that I did not ask you to give me two or three examples of piety, but to explain the general idea which makes all pious things to be pious. Do you not recollect that there was one idea which made the impious impious, and the pious pious?

Euth.: I remember.

Soc.: Tell me what is the nature of this idea, and then I shall have a standard to which I may look, and by which I may measure actions, whether yours or those of any one else, and then I shall be able to say that such and such an action is pious, such another impious.

Euth.: I will tell you, if you like.

Soc.: I should very much like.

Euth.: Piety, then, is that which is dear to the gods, and impiety is that which is not dear to them.

Soc.: Very good, Euthyphro; you have now   7a
given me the sort of answer which I wanted. But
whether what you say is true or not I cannot as yet
tell, although I make no doubt that you will prove
the truth of your words.

Euth.: Of course.

Soc.: Come, then, and let us   *A more correct*
examine what we are saying. That   *definition: piety*
thing or person which is dear to   *is that which is*
the gods is pious, and that thing   *dear to the gods.*
or person which is hateful to the gods is impious,
these two being the extreme opposites of one another. Was not that said?

Euth.: It was.

Soc.: And well said?

Euth.: Yes, Socrates, I thought so; it was cer-   b
tainly said.

Soc.: And further, Euthyphro, the gods were admitted to have enmities and hatreds and differences?

Euth.: Yes, that was also said.

Soc.: And what sort of differ-   *Differences*
ence creates enmity and anger?   *about numbers*
Suppose for example that you and   *and figures*
I, my good friend, differ about a   *create no ill will*   c
number; do differences of this   *because they*
sort make us enemies and set us at   *can be settled*
variance with one another? Do we   *by a sum or*
not go at once to arithmetic, and   *by a weighing*
put an end to them by a sum?   *machine, but*
                                   enmities about
Euth.: True.   *the just and*
                 unjust are the
Soc.: Or suppose that we dif-   *occasions of*
fer about magnitudes, do we not   *quarrels, both*
quickly end the differences by   *among gods and*
measuring?   *men.*

Euth.: Very true.

Soc.: And we end a controversy about heavy and light by resorting to a weighing machine?

Euth.: To be sure.

Soc.: But what differences are there which cannot be thus decided, and which therefore make us angry and set us at enmity with one another? I dare say the answer does not occur to you at the moment, and therefore I will suggest that these enmities arise when the matters of difference are the just and unjust, good and evil, honourable and dishonourable. Are not these the points about which men differ, and about which when we are unable satisfactorily to decide our differences, you and I and all of us quarrel, when we do quarrel?

Euth.: Yes, Socrates, the nature of the differences about which we quarrel is such as you describe.

Soc.: And the quarrels of the gods, noble Euthyphro, when they occur, are of a like nature?

Euth.: Certainly they are.

Soc.: They have differences of opinion, as you say, about good and evil, just and unjust, honourable and dishonourable: there would have been no quarrels among them, if there had been no such differences—would there now?

Euth.: You are quite right.

Soc.: Does not every man love that which he deems noble and just and good, and hate the opposite of them?

Men and gods alike love the things that they deem noble and just, but they are not agreed what these are.

Euth.: Very true.

Soc.: But, as you say, people regard the same things, some as just and others as unjust,—about these they dis-

pute; and so there arise wars and fightings among   8a
them.

Euth.: Very true.

Soc.: Then the same things are hated by the
gods and loved by the gods, and are both hateful
and dear to them?

Euth.: True.

Soc.: And upon this view the same things, Euthyphro, will be pious and also impious?

Euth.: So I should suppose.

Soc.: Then, my friend, I remark with surprise
that you have not answered the question which I
asked. For I certainly did not ask you to tell me
what action is both pious and impious: but now
it would seem that what is loved by the gods is
also hated by them. And therefore, Euthyphro,
in thus chastising your father you may very likely   b
be doing what is agreeable to Zeus but disagree-
able to Cronos or Uranus, and what is acceptable
to Hephaestus[8] but unacceptable to Here,[9] and
there may be other gods who have similar differences of opinion.

Euth.: But I believe, Socrates, that all the gods
would be agreed as to the propriety of punishing a
murderer: there would be no difference of opinion
about that.

Soc.: Well, but speaking of men, Euthyphro, did   c
you ever hear any one arguing that a murderer or
any sort of evil-doer ought to be let off?

Euth.: I should rather say that these are the
questions which they are always arguing, especially
in courts of law: they commit all sorts of crimes,
and there is nothing which they will not do or say
in their own defence.

Soc.: But do they admit their guilt, Euthyphro, and yet say that they ought not to be punished?

Euth.: No; they do not.

Soc.: Then there are some things which they do not venture to say and do: for they do not venture to argue that the guilty are to be unpunished, but

d they deny their guilt, do they not?

Euth.: Yes.

Soc.: Then they do not argue that the evil-doer should not be punished, but they argue about the fact of who the evil-doer is, and what he did and when?

Euth.: True.

Soc.: And the gods are in the same case, if as you assert they quarrel about just and unjust, and some of them say while others

e deny that injustice is done among them. For surely neither God nor man will ever venture to say that the doer of injustice is not to be punished?

Euth.: That is true, Socrates, in the main.

Neither God nor man will say that the doer of evil is not to be punished, but they are doubtful about particular acts. What proof is there that all the gods approve of the prosecution of your father?

Soc.: But they join issue about the particulars—gods and men alike; and, if they dispute at all, they dispute about some act which is called in question, and which by some is affirmed to be just, by others to be unjust. Is not that true?

Euth.: Quite true.

9a *Soc.:* Well then, my dear friend Euthyphro, do tell me, for my better instruction and information, what proof have you that in the opinion of all the gods a servant who is guilty of murder, and is put in

chains by the master of the dead man, and dies because he is put in chains before he who bound him can learn from the interpreters of the gods what he ought to do with him, dies unjustly; and that on behalf of such an one a son ought to proceed against his father and accuse him of murder. How   b
would you show that all the gods absolutely agree in approving of his act? Prove to me that they do, and I will applaud your wisdom as long as I live.

Euth.: It will be a difficult task; but I could make the matter very clear indeed to you.

Soc.: I understand; you mean to say that I am not so quick of apprehension as the judges: for to them you will be sure to prove that the act is unjust, and hateful to the gods.

Euth.: Yes indeed, Socrates; at least if they will listen to me.

Soc.: But they will be sure to listen if they find   c
that you are a good speaker. There was a notion that came into my mind while you were speaking; I said to myself: 'Well, and what if Euthyphro does prove to me that all the gods regarded the death of the serf as unjust, how do I know anything more of the nature of piety and impiety? for granting that this action may be hateful to the gods, still piety and impiety are not adequately defined by these distinctions, for that which is hateful to the gods has been shown to be also pleasing and dear to them.' And therefore, Euthyphro, I do not ask you to prove this; I will suppose, if you *Let us say then*
like, that all the gods condemn *that what all the*
and abominate such an action. *gods approve is*   d
But I will amend the definition so *pious and holy.*
far as to say that what all the gods hate is impious,

and what they love pious or holy; and what some of them love and others hate is both or neither. Shall this be our definition of piety and impiety?

Euth.: Why not, Socrates?

Soc.: Why not! certainly, as far as I am concerned, Euthyphro, there is no reason why not. But whether this admission will greatly assist you in the task of instructing me as you promised, is a matter for you to consider.

e   *Euth.:* Yes, I should say that what all the gods love is pious and holy, and the opposite which they all hate, impious.

Soc.: Ought we to enquire into the truth of this, Euthyphro, or simply to accept the mere statement on our own authority and that of others? What do you say?

Euth.: We should enquire; and I believe that the statement will stand the test of enquiry.

Soc.: We shall know better, my good friend, in a little while. The point which I should first wish to understand is whether the pious *But does the state follow the act, or the act the state?*

10a

or holy is beloved by the gods because it is holy, or holy because it is beloved of the gods.

Euth.: I do not understand your meaning, Socrates.

Soc.: I will endeavour to explain: we, speak of carrying and we speak of being carried, of leading and being led, seeing and being seen. You know that in all such cases there is a difference, and you know also in what the difference lies?

Euth.: I think that I understand.

Soc.: And is not that which is beloved distinct from that which loves?

Euth.: Certainly.

Soc.: Well; and now tell me, is that which is car-   b
ried in this state of carrying because it is carried, or
for some other reason?

Euth.: No; that is the reason.

Soc.: And the same is true of what is led and of
what is seen?

Euth.: True.

Soc.: And a thing is not seen because it is visible,
but conversely, visible because it is seen; nor is a
thing led because it is in the state of being led, or
carried because it is in the state of being carried,
but the converse of this. And now I think, Euthyphro, that my meaning will be intelligible; and my
meaning is, that any state of action or passion im-   c
plies previous action or passion. It does not become
because it is becoming, but it is in a state of becoming because it becomes; neither does it suffer
because it is in a state of suffering, but it is in a state
of suffering because it suffers. Do you not agree?

Euth.: Yes.

Soc.: Is not that which is loved in some state either of becoming or suffering?

Euth.: Yes.

Soc.: And the same holds as in   *The latter is the*
the previous instances; the state   *truer account,*
of being loved follows the act of   *and therefore*
being loved, and not the act the   *we can only*
state.   *say that what*
                                     is loved by all
Euth.: Certainly.   *the gods is in a*

Soc.: And what do you say of   *state to be loved*   d
piety, Euthyphro: is not piety, ac-   *by them; but*
cording to your definition, loved   *holiness has a*
by all the gods?   *wider meaning*
                                     than this.

Euth.: Yes.

Soc.: Because it is pious or holy, or for some other reason?

Euth.: No, that is the reason.

Soc.: It is loved because it is holy, not holy because it is loved?

Euth.: Yes.

Soc.: And that which is dear to the gods is loved by them, and is in a state to be loved of them because it is loved of them?

Euth.: Certainly.

Soc.: Then that which is dear to the gods, Euthyphro, is not holy, nor is that which is holy loved of God, as you affirm; but they are two different things.

Euth.: How do you mean, Socrates?

e   *Soc.*: I mean to say that the holy has been acknowledged by us to be loved of God because it is holy, not to be holy because it is loved.

Euth.: Yes.

Soc.: But that which is dear to the gods is dear to them because it is loved by them, not loved by them because it is dear to them.

Euth.: True.

Soc.: But, friend Euthyphro, if that which is holy is the same with that which is dear to God, and is loved because it is holy, then that which is
11a dear to God would have been loved as being dear to God; but if that which is dear to God is dear to him because loved by him, then that which is holy would have been holy because loved by him. But now you see that the reverse is the case, and that they are quite different from one another. For one (theophiles) is of a kind to be loved cause it is

loved, and the other (osion) is loved because it is of a kind to be loved.[10] Thus you appear to me, Euthyphro, when I ask you what is the essence of holiness, to offer an attribute only, and not the essence—the attribute of being loved by all the gods. But you still refuse to explain to me the nature of holiness. And therefore, if you please, I will ask you not to hide your treasure, but to tell me once more what holiness or piety really is, whether dear to the gods or not (for that is a matter about which we will not quarrel); and what is impiety?

What is the essential meaning of holiness or piety?

Euth.: I really do not know, Socrates, how to express what I mean. For somehow or other our arguments, on whatever ground we rest them, seem to turn round and walk away from us.

Soc.: Your words, Euthyphro, are like the handiwork of my ancestor Daedalus;[11] and if I were the sayer or propounder of them, you might say that my arguments walk away and will not remain fixed where they are placed because I am a descendant of his. But now, since these notions are your own, you must find some other gibe, for they certainly, as you yourself allow, show an inclination to be on the move.

Euth.: Nay, Socrates, I shall still say that you are the Daedalus who sets arguments in motion; not I, certainly, but you make them move or go round, for they would never have stirred, as far as I am concerned.

Soc.: Then I must be a greater than Daedalus: for whereas he only made his own inventions to move, I move those of other people as well. And

the beauty of it is, that I would rather not. For I
e would give the wisdom of Daedalus, and the wealth
of Tantalus,[12] to be able to detain them and keep
them fixed. But enough of this. As I perceive that
you are lazy, I will myself endeavour to show you
how you might instruct me in the nature of piety;
and I hope that you will not grudge your labour.
Tell me, then—Is not that which is pious necessarily just?

Euth.: Yes.

Soc.: And is, then, all which is   *All which is*
just pious? or, is that which is pious   *pious is just:*
all just, but that which is just, only   *is therefore all*
12a in part and not all, pious?   *which is just*
                                           pious?
Euth.: I do not understand you,
Socrates.

Soc.: And yet I know that you are as much wiser
than I am, as you are younger. But, as I was saying, revered friend, the abundance of your wisdom
makes you lazy. Please to exert yourself, for there
is no real difficulty in understanding me. What I
mean I may explain by an illustration of what I do
not mean. The poet (Stasinus)[13] sings—

'Of Zeus, the author and creator of all these
   things,
You will not tell: for where there is fear there is
   also reverence.'

b Now I disagree with this poet. Shall I tell you in
what respect?

Euth.: By all means.

Soc.: I should not say that where there is fear
there is also reverence; for I am sure that many

persons fear poverty and disease, and the like evils,
but I do not perceive that they *We may say,*
reverence the objects of their fear. *e.g., that*
wherever there
    Euth.: Very true. *is reverence*
    Soc.: But where reverence is, *there will be*
there is fear; for he who has a feel- *fear, but not*
ing of reverence and shame about *that wherever*
the commission of any action, fears *there is fear* c
and is afraid of an ill reputation. *there will be*
reverence.
    Euth.: No doubt.

    Soc.: Then we are wrong in saying that where
there is fear there is also reverence; and we should
say, where there is reverence there is also fear. But
there is not always reverence where there is fear;
for fear is a more extended notion, and reverence
is a part of fear, just as the odd is a part of number,
and number is a more extended notion than the
odd. I suppose that you follow me now?

    Euth.: Quite well.

    Soc.: That was the sort of question which I d
meant to raise when I asked whether the just is
always the pious, or the pious always the just; and
whether there may not be justice where there is
not piety; for justice is the more extended notion of
which piety is only a part. Do you dissent?

    Euth.: No, I think that you are quite right.

    Soc.: Then, if piety is a part of justice, I sup-
pose that we should enquire what part? If you had
pursued the enquiry in the previous cases; for instance, if you had asked me what is an even number, and what part of number the even is, I should
have had no difficulty in replying, a number which
represents a figure having two equal sides. Do you
not agree?

Euth.: Yes, I quite agree.

Soc.: In like manner, I want
e   you to tell me what part of justice
is piety or holiness, that I may be
able to tell Meletus not to do me
injustice, or indict me for impiety,

Piety or holiness is that part of justice which attends upon the gods.

as I am now adequately instructed by you in the
nature of piety or holiness, and their opposites.

Euth.: Piety or holiness, Socrates, appears to me
to be that part of justice which attends to the gods,
as there is the other part of justice which attends
to men.

13a   *Soc.:* That is good, Euthyphro; yet still there is a
little point about which I should like to have further
information. What is the meaning of 'attention'? For
attention can hardly be used in the same sense when
applied to the gods as when applied to other things.
For instance, horses are said to require attention,
and not every person is able to attend to them, but
only a person skilled in horsemanship. Is it not so?

Euth.: Certainly.

Soc.: I should suppose that the art of horsemanship is the art of attending to horses?

Euth.: Yes.

Soc.: Nor is every one qualified to attend to
dogs, but only the huntsman?

Euth.: True.

Soc.: And I should also conceive that the art of
b   the huntsman is the art of attending to dogs?

Euth.: Yes.

Soc.: As the art of the oxherd is the art of attending to oxen?

Euth.: Very true.

Soc.: In like manner holiness or piety is the art

of attending to the gods?—that would be your
meaning, Euthyphro?

Euth.: Yes.

Soc.: And is not attention always *Attention*
designed for the good or benefit of *to others is*
that to which the attention is given? *designed to*
As in the case of horses, you may *benefit and*
observe that when attended to by *improve them.*
the horseman's art they are ben- *But how are the*
efited and improved, are they not? *gods benefited*
by the holy acts
Euth.: True. *of men?*

Soc.: As the dogs are benefited by the huntsman's art, and the oxen by the art of the oxherd,
and all other things are tended or attended for   c
their good and not for their hurt?

Euth.: Certainly, not for their hurt.

Soc.: But for their good?

Euth.: Of course.

Soc.: And does piety or holiness, which has been
defined to be the art of attending to the gods, benefit or improve them? Would you say that when
you do a holy act you make any of the gods better?

Euth.: No, no; that was certainly not what I meant.

Soc.: And I, Euthyphro, never supposed that
you did. I asked you the question about the na-   d
ture of the attention, because I thought that you
did not.

Euth.: You do me justice, Socrates; that is not
the sort of attention which I mean.

Soc.: Good: but I must still ask *The attention to*
what is this attention to the gods *the gods called*
which is called piety? *piety is such as*
servants show
Euth.: It is such, Socrates, as *their masters.*
servants show to their masters.

Soc.: I understand—a sort of ministration[14] to the gods.

Euth.: Exactly.

Soc.: Medicine is also a sort of ministration or service, having in view the attainment of some object—would you not say of health?

Euth.: I should.

e *Soc.:* Again, there is an art which ministers to the ship-builder with a view to the attainment of some result?

Euth.: Yes, Socrates, with a view to the building of a ship.

Soc.: As there is an art which ministers to the house-builder with a view to the building of a house?

Euth.: Yes.

Soc.: And now tell me, my good friend, about the art which minis- ters to the gods: what work does *But in what way do men help the work of God?* that help to accomplish? For you must surely know if, as you say, you are of all men living the one who is best instructed in religion.

Euth.: And I speak the truth, Socrates.

Soc.: Tell me then, oh tell me—what is that fair work which the gods do by the help of our ministrations?

Euth.: Many and fair, Socrates, are the works which they do.

14a *Soc.:* Why, my friend, and so are those of a general. But the chief of them is easily told. Would you not say that victory in war is the chief of them?

Euth.: Certainly.

Soc.: Many and fair, too, are the works of the husbandman, if I am not mistaken; but his chief work is the production of food from the earth?

Euth.: Exactly.

Soc.: And of the many and fair things done by the gods, which is the chief or principal one?

Euth.: I have told you already, Socrates, that to   b learn all these things accurately will be very tiresome. Let me simply say that piety or holiness is learning how to please the gods in word and deed, by prayers and sacrifices. Such piety is the salvation of families and states, just as the impious, which is unpleasing to the gods, is their ruin and destruction.

Soc.: I think that you could have answered in much fewer words the chief question which I asked, Euthyphro, if you had chosen. But I see   c plainly that you are not disposed to instruct me— clearly not: else why, when we reached the point, did you turn aside? Had you only answered me I should have truly learned of you by this time the nature of piety. Now, as the asker of a question is necessarily dependent on the answerer, whither he leads I must follow; and can only ask again, what is the pious, and what is piety? Do you mean that they are a sort of science of praying and sacrificing?

Euth.: Yes, I do.

Soc.: And sacrificing is giving to the gods, and prayer is asking of the gods?

Euth.: Yes, Socrates.

Soc.: Upon this view, then, piety is a science of   d asking and giving?

Euth.: You understand me capitally, Socrates.

Soc.: Yes, my friend; the reason is that I am a votary of your science, and give my mind to it, and therefore nothing which you say will be thrown away upon me. Please then to tell me, what is the

nature of this service to the gods? Do you mean
that we prefer requests and give gifts to them?

Euth.: Yes, I do.

Soc.: Is not the right way of asking to ask of
them what we want?

Euth.: Certainly.

e   *Soc.*: And the right way of giving   *Men give to the*
is to give to them in return what   *gods, and the*
they want of us. There would be   *gods give to*
no meaning in an art which gives   *men; they do*
to any one that which he does not   *business with*
want.   *one another.*

Euth.: Very true, Socrates.

Soc.: Then piety, Euthyphro, is an art which
gods and men have of doing business with one
another?

Euth.: That is an expression which you may use,
if you like.

Soc.: But I have no particular liking for anything
but the truth. I wish, however, that you would tell
me what benefit accrues to the gods from our gifts.

5a   There is no doubt about what they give to us; for
there is no good thing which they do not give; but
how we can give any good thing to them in return
is far from being equally clear. If they give everything and we give nothing, that must be an affair of
business in which we have very greatly the advantage of them.

Euth.: And do you imagine, Socrates, that any
benefit accrues to the gods from our gifts?

Soc.: But if not, Euthyphro, what is the meaning
of gifts which are conferred by us upon the gods?

Euth.: What else, but tributes of honour; and, as
I was just now saying, what pleases them?

Soc.: Piety, then, is pleasing to the gods, but not   b
beneficial or dear to them?

Euth.: I should say that nothing could be dearer.

Soc.: Then once more the assertion is repeated
that piety is dear to the gods?

Euth.: Certainly.

Soc.: And when you say this, *Again, the*
can you wonder at your words not *argument walks*
standing firm, but walking away? *away.*
Will you accuse me of being the Daedalus who
makes them walk away, not perceiving that there
is another and far greater artist than Daedalus who
makes them go round in a circle, and he is your-   c
self; for the argument, as you will perceive, comes
round to the same point. Were we not saying that
the holy or pious was not the same with that which
is loved of the gods? Have you forgotten?

Euth.: I quite remember.

Soc.: And are you not saying that what is loved
of the gods is holy; and is not this the same as what
is dear to them—do you see?

Euth.: True.

Soc.: Then either we were wrong in our former
assertion; or, if we were right then, we are wrong
now.

Euth.: One of the two must be true.

Soc.: Then we must begin again *Nevertheless,*
and ask, What is piety? That is an *Socrates is*   d
enquiry which I shall never be *confident that*
weary of pursuing as far as in me *Euthyphro*
lies; and I entreat you not to scorn *knows the truth,*
me, but to apply your mind to the *but will not tell*
utmost, and tell me the truth. For, *him.*
if any man knows, you are he; and therefore I must

detain you, like Proteus,[15] until you tell. If you had not certainly known the nature of piety and impiety, I am confident that you would never, on behalf of a serf, have charged your aged father with murder. You would not have run such a risk of doing wrong in the sight of the gods, and you would have had too much respect for the opinions of men. I am sure, therefore, that you know the nature of piety and impiety. Speak out then, my dear Euthyphro, and do not hide your knowledge.

Euth.: Another time, Socrates; for I am in a hurry, and must go now.

Soc.: Alas! my companion, and will you leave me in despair? I was hoping that you would instruct me in the nature of piety and impiety; and then I might have cleared myself of Meletus and his indictment. I would have told him that I had been enlightened by Euthyphro, and had given up rash innovations and speculations, in which I indulged only through ignorance, and that now I am about to lead a better life.

Euthyphro is in a hurry to depart and finally leaves Socrates to his fate.

APOLOGY

Persons of the Dialogue
SOCRATES, MELETUS

Scene
IN THE COURT

Socrates: How you, O Athenians, have been affected by my accusers, I cannot tell; but I know that they almost made me forget who I was—so persuasively did they *Socrates begs to be allowed to speak in his accustomed manner.*

speak; and yet they have hardly uttered a word of truth. But of the many falsehoods told by them, there was one which quite amazed me;—I mean when they said that you should be upon your guard and not allow yourselves to be deceived by the force of my eloquence. To say this, when they were b certain to be detected as soon as I opened my lips and proved myself to be anything but a great speaker, did indeed appear to me most shameless—unless by the force of eloquence they mean the force of truth; for if such is their meaning, I admit that I am eloquent. But in how different a way from theirs! Well, as I was saying, they have scarcely spoken the truth at all; but from me you c shall hear the whole truth: not, however, delivered after their manner in a set oration duly ornamented with words and phrases. No, by heaven! but I shall use the words and arguments which occur to me at the moment; for I am confident in the justice of my cause: at my time of life I ought not to be appearing before you, O men of Athens, in the character of a juvenile orator—let no one expect it of me. And I must beg of you to grant me a favour:—If I defend myself in my accustomed manner, and you hear me using the words which I have been in the habit of using in the agora,[1] at the tables of the money-changers, or anywhere else, I would ask d　you not to be surprised, and not to interrupt me on this account. For I am more than seventy years of age, and appearing now for the first time in a court of law, I am quite a stranger to the language of the

18a　place; and therefore I would have you regard me as if I were really a stranger, whom *The judges must* you would excuse if he spoke in *excuse Socrates* his native tongue, and after the *if he defends* fashion of his country:—Am I *himself in his* making an unfair request of you? *own fashion.*

Never mind the manner, which may or may not be good; but think only of the truth of my words, and give heed to that: let the speaker speak truly and the judge decide justly.

And first, I have to reply to the older charges and to my first accusers, and then I will go on to the

b　later ones. For of old I have had many accusers, who have accused me falsely to you during many years; and I am more afraid of them than of Anytus[2] and his associates, who are dangerous, too, in their own way. But far more dangerous are the others, who began when you were children, and took possession of your minds with their falsehoods, telling of one Socrates, a wise man, who speculated about the heaven above, and searched into the

c　earth beneath, and made the worse appear the better cause. The disseminators of this tale are the accusers whom I dread; for their hearers are apt to fancy that such enquirers do not believe in the existence of the gods. And they are many, and their charges against me are of ancient date, and they were made by them in the days when you were more impressible than you are now—in childhood,

d　or it may have been in youth—and the cause when

heard went by default, for there was none to answer. And hardest of all, I do not know and cannot tell the names of my accusers; unless in the chance case of a comic poet. All who from envy and malice have persuaded you—some of them having first convinced themselves—all this class of men are most difficult to deal with; for I cannot have them up here, and cross-examine them, and therefore I must simply fight with shadows in my own defence, and argue when there is no one who answers. I will ask you then to assume with me, as I was saying, that my opponents are of two kinds; one recent,   e
the other ancient: and I hope that you will see the propriety of my answering the lat- *He has to meet* ter first, for these accusations you *two sorts of* heard long before the others, and *accusers.* much oftener.

Well, then, I must make my defence, and en-   19a
deavour to clear away in a short time a slander which has lasted a long time. May I succeed, if to succeed be for my good and yours, or likely to avail me in my cause! The task is not an easy one; I quite understand the nature of it. And so leaving the event with God, in obedience to the law I will now make my defence.

I will begin at the beginning, *There is the* and ask what is the accusation *accusation of* which has given rise to the slander *the theatres;* of me, and in fact has encouraged *which declares* Meletus to prefer this charge *that he is* against me. Well, what do the *a student*   b
slanderers say? They shall be my *of natural* prosecutors, and I will sum up their words in an *philosophy.* affidavit: "Socrates is an evil-doer, and a curious

c person, who searches into things under the earth and in heaven, and he makes the worse appear the better cause; and he teaches the aforesaid doctrines to others." Such is the nature of the accusation: it is just what you have yourselves seen in the comedy of Aristophanes,[3] who has introduced a man whom he calls Socrates, going about and saying that he walks in air, and talking a deal of nonsense concerning matters of which I do not pretend to know either much or little—not that I mean to speak disparagingly of any one who is a student of natural philosophy. I should be very sorry if Meletus could bring so grave a charge against me. But the simple truth is, O Athenians, that I have nothing to do with physical speculations. Very many of

d those here present are witnesses to the truth of this, and to them I appeal. Speak then, you who have heard me, and tell your neighbours whether any of you have ever known me hold forth in few words or in many upon such matters. . . . You hear their answer. And from what they say of this part of the charge you will be able to judge of the truth of the rest.

There is the report that he is a Sophist who receives money.

As little foundation is there for the report that I am a teacher, and take money; this accusation has no more truth in it than the other. Although, if a

e man were really able to instruct mankind, to receive money for giving instruction would, in my opinion, be an honour to him. There is Gorgias of Leontium, and Prodicus of Ceos, and Hippias of Elis,[4] who go the round of the cities, and are able to persuade the young men to leave their own citi-

20a zens by whom they might be taught for nothing,

and come to them whom they not only pay, but are thankful if they may be allowed to pay them. There is at this time a Parian philosopher residing in Athens, of whom I have heard; and I came to hear of him in this way:—I came across a *The ironical question which Socrates put to Callias.* man who has spent a world of money on the Sophists, Callias, the son of Hipponicus, and knowing that he had sons, I asked him: "Callias," I said, "if your two sons were foals or calves, there would be no difficulty in finding some one to put over them; we should hire a trainer of horses, or a farmer, b probably, who would improve and perfect them in their own proper virtue and excellence; but as they are human beings, whom are you thinking of placing over them? Is there any one who understands human and political virtue? You must have thought about the matter, for you have sons; is there any one?" "There is," he said. "Who is he?" said I; "and of what country? and what does he charge?" "Evenus the Parian,"[5] he replied; "he is the man, and his charge is five minae."[6] Happy is Evenus, I said to myself, if he really has this wisdom, and teaches at such a moderate charge. Had I the same, I should c have been very proud and conceited; but the truth is that I have no knowledge of the kind.

I dare say, Athenians, that some one among you will reply, "Yes, Socrates, but what is the origin of these accusations which are brought against you; there must have been something strange which you have been doing? All these rumours and this talk about you would never have arisen if you had been like other men: tell us, then, what is the cause of them, for we should be sorry to judge hastily of

d   you." Now I regard this as a fair challenge, and I
will endeavour to explain to you the reason why I
am called wise and have such an   *The accusations*
evil fame. Please to attend then.   *against me have*
And although some of you may   *arisen out of a*
think that I am joking, I declare   *sort of wisdom*
that I will tell you the entire truth.   *which I possess.*
Men of Athens, this reputation of mine has come
of a certain sort of wisdom which I possess. If you
ask me what kind of wisdom, I reply, wisdom such
as may perhaps be attained by man, for to that extent I am inclined to believe that I am wise;
e   whereas the persons of whom I was speaking have
a superhuman wisdom, which I may fail to describe,
because I have it not myself; and he who says that
I have, speaks falsely, and is taking away my character. And here, O men of Athens, I must beg you
not to interrupt me, even if I seem to say something extravagant. For the word which I will speak
is not mine. I will refer you to a   *My practice of*
witness who is worthy of credit;   *it arose out of a*
that witness shall be the God of   *declaration of*
Delphi[7]—he will tell you about   *the Delphian*
my wisdom, if I have any, and of   *Oracle that I*
what sort it is. You must have   *was the wisest*
known Chaerephon; he was early   *of men.*
21a   a friend of mine, and also a friend of yours, for he
shared in the recent exile of the people, and returned with you. Well, Chaerephon, as you know,
was very impetuous in all his doings, and he went
to Delphi and boldly asked the oracle to tell him
whether—as I was saying, I must beg you not to
interrupt—he asked the oracle to tell him whether
any one was wiser than I was, and the Pythian[8]

prophetess answered, that there was no man wiser. Chaerephon is dead himself; but his brother, who is in court, will confirm the truth of what I am saying.

Why do I mention this? Be-cause I am going to explain to you why I have such an evil name. When I heard the answer, I said to myself, What can the God mean? and what is the interpretation of his riddle? for I know that I have no wisdom, small or great. What then can he mean when he says that I am the wisest of men? And yet he is a god, and cannot lie; that would be against his nature. After long consideration, I thought of a method of trying the question. I reflected that if I could only find a man wiser than myself, then I might go to the god with a refutation in my hand. I should say to him, "Here is a man who is wiser than I am; but you said that I was the wisest." Accordingly I went to one who had the reputation of wisdom, and observed him—his name I need not mention; he was a politician whom I selected for examination—and the result was as follows: When I began to talk with him, I could not help think-ing that he was not really wise, although he was thought wise by many, and still wiser by himself; and thereupon I tried to explain to him that he thought himself wise, but was not really wise; and the consequence was that he hated me, and his en-mity was shared by several who were present and heard me. So I left him, saying to myself, as I went

b I went about searching after a man who was wiser than myself: at first among the politicians; then among the philosophers; and found c that I had an advantage over them, because I had no conceit of knowledge.

away: Well, although I do not suppose that either of us knows anything really beautiful and good, I am better off than he is,—for he knows nothing, and thinks that he knows; I neither know nor think that I know. In this latter particular, then, I seem to have slightly the advantage of him. Then I went to another who had still higher pretensions to wisdom, and my conclusion was exactly the same.

e

Whereupon I made another enemy of him, and of many others besides him.

Then I went to one man after another, being not unconscious of the enmity which I provoked, and I lamented and feared this: but necessity was laid upon me,—the word of God, I thought, ought to be considered first. And I said to myself, Go I must to all who appear to know, and find out the mean-

22a

ing of the oracle. And I swear to you, Athenians, by the dog I swear!—for I must tell you the truth—the result of my mission was just this: I found that the men most in repute were all but the most foolish; and that others less esteemed were really wiser and better. I will tell you the tale of my wanderings and of the "Her-culean" labours,[9] as I may call them, which I endured only to find at last the oracle irrefutable. After the politicians, I went to the

I found that the poets were the worst possible interpreters of their own writings.

b

poets; tragic, dithyrambic,[10] and all sorts. And there, I said to myself, you will be instantly detected; now you will find out that you are more ignorant than they are. Accordingly I took them some of the most elaborate passages in their own writings, and asked what was the meaning of them—thinking that they would teach me some-

thing. Will you believe me? I am almost ashamed
to confess the truth, but I must say that there is
hardly a person present who would not have talked
better about their poetry than they did themselves.
Then I knew that not by wisdom do poets write
poetry, but by a sort of genius and inspiration; they   c
are like diviners or soothsayers who also say many
fine things, but do not understand the meaning of
them. The poets appeared to me to be much in the
same case; and I further observed that upon the
strength of their poetry they believed themselves
to be the wisest of men in other things in which
they were not wise. So I departed, conceiving myself to be superior to them for the same reason that
I was superior to the politicians.

At last I went to the artisans, I   *The artisans*
was conscious that I knew nothing   *had some real*
at all, as I may say, and I was sure   *knowledge, but*   d
that they knew many fine things;   *they had also a*
and here I was not mistaken, for   *conceit that they*
they did know many things of   *knew things*
which I was ignorant, and in this   *which were*
beyond them.
they certainly were wiser than I was. But I observed that even the good artisans fell into the
same error as the poets;—because they were good
workmen they thought that they also knew all sorts
of high matters, and this defect in them overshad-
owed their wisdom; and therefore I asked myself   e
on behalf of the oracle, whether I would like to be
as I was, neither having their knowledge nor their
ignorance, or like them in both; and I made answer
to myself and to the oracle that I was better off as
I was.

This inquisition has led to my having many en-

23a   emies of the worst and most dangerous kind, and
       has given occasion also to many calumnies. And I
       am called wise, for my hearers always imagine that
       I myself possess the wisdom which   *The oracle was*
       I find wanting in others: but the   *intended to*
       truth is, O men of Athens, that   *apply, not to*
       God only is wise; and by his an-   *Socrates, but*
       swer he intends to show that the   *to all men who*
                                           know that their
       wisdom of men is worth little or   *wisdom is worth*
    b nothing; he is not speaking of   *nothing.*
       Socrates, he is only using my name by way of illus-
       tration, as if he said, He, O men, is the wisest, who,
       like Socrates, knows that his wisdom is in truth
       worth nothing. And so I go about the world obedi-
       ent to the god, and search and make enquiry into
       the wisdom of any one, whether citizen or stranger,
       who appears to be wise; and if he is not wise, then
       in vindication of the oracle I show him that he is
       not wise; and my occupation quite absorbs me, and
       I have no time to give either to any public matter
    c of interest or to any concern of my own, but I am
       in utter poverty by reason of my devotion to the
       god.
             There is another thing:—young men of the
       richer classes, who have not much   *There are*
       to do, come about me of their own   *my imitators*
       accord; they like to hear the pre- *who go about*
                                           detecting
       tenders examined, and they often   *pretenders*
       imitate me, and proceed to exam-   *and the enmity*
       ine others; there are plenty of per-*which they*
       sons, as they quickly discover, who *arouse falls*
       think that they know something,   *upon me.*
       but really know little or nothing; and then those
       who are examined by them instead of being angry

with themselves are angry with me: This con- d
founded Socrates, they say; this villainous mis-
leader of youth!—and then if somebody asks them,
Why, what evil does he practise or teach? they do
not know, and cannot tell; but in order that they
may not appear to be at a loss, they repeat the
ready-made charges which are used against all philosophers about teaching things up in the clouds
and under the earth, and having no gods, and making the worse appear the better cause; for they do
not like to confess that their pretence of knowledge has been detected—which is the truth; and as e
they are numerous and ambitious and energetic,
and are drawn up in battle array and have persua-
sive tongues, they have filled your ears with their
loud and inveterate calumnies. And this is the reason why my three accusers, Meletus and Anytus
and Lycon, have set upon me; Meletus, who has a
quarrel with me on behalf of the poets; Anytus, on 24a
behalf of the craftsmen and politicians; Lycon, on
behalf of the rhetoricians: and, as I said at the beginning, I cannot expect to get rid of such a mass of
calumny all in a moment. And this, O men of Athens, is the truth and the whole truth; I have con-
cealed nothing, I have dissembled nothing. And
yet, I know that my plainness of speech makes
them hate me, and what is their hatred but a proof
that I am speaking the truth? Hence has arisen the
prejudice against me; and this is the reason of it, as b
you will find out either in this or in any future
enquiry.

I have said enough in my de-   *The second class*
fence against the first class of   *of accusers.*
my accusers; I turn to the second class. They are

headed by Meletus, that good man and true lover of his country, as he calls himself. Against these, too, I must try to make a defence:—Let their affidavit be read: it contains something of this kind: It says that Socrates is a doer of evil, who corrupts the youth; and who does not believe in the gods of

c the State, but has other new divinities of his own. Such is the charge; and now let us examine the particular counts. He says that I am a doer of evil, and corrupt the youth; but I say, O men of Athens, that Meletus is a doer of evil, in that he pretends to be in earnest when he is only in jest, and is so eager to bring men to trial from a pretended zeal and interest about matters in which he really never had the smallest interest. And the truth of this I will endeavour to prove to you.

Come hither, Meletus, and let me ask a ques-

d tion of you. You think a great deal about the improvement of youth?

Yes, I do.

Tell the judges, then, who is their improver; for you must know, as you have taken the pains to discover their corrupter, and are citing and accusing me before them. Speak, then, and tell the judges who their improver is.—Observe, Meletus, that you are silent, and have nothing to *All men are* say. But is not this rather disgrace- *discovered to* ful, and a very considerable proof *be improvers of* of what I was saying, that you have *youth with the* no interest in the matter? Speak *single exception* up, friend, and tell us who their *of Socrates.* improver is.

The laws.

e But that, my good sir, is not my meaning. I want

to know who the person is, who, in the first place, knows the laws.

The judges, Socrates, who are present in court.

What, do you mean to say, Meletus, that they are able to instruct and improve youth?

Certainly they are.

What, all of them, or some only and not others?

All of them.

By the goddess Here, that is good news! There are plenty of improvers, then. And what do you say of the audience,—do they improve them?

Yes, they do.

And the senators?

Yes, the senators improve them.

But perhaps the members of the assembly corrupt them?—or do they improve them?

They improve them.

Then every Athenian improves and elevates them; all with the exception of myself; and I alone am their corrupter? Is that what you affirm?

That is what I stoutly affirm.

I am very unfortunate if you are right. But suppose I ask you a question: How about horses? Does one man do them harm and all the world good? Is not the exact opposite the truth? One man is *But this rather unfortunate fact does not accord with the analogy of the animals.* b

able to do them good, or at least not many;—the trainer of horses, that is to say, does them good, and others who have to do with them rather injure them? Is not that true, Meletus, of horses, or of any other animals? Most assuredly it is; whether you and Anytus say yes or no. Happy indeed would be the condition of youth if they had one corrupter

c only, and all the rest of the world were their improvers. But you, Meletus, have sufficiently shown
that you never had a thought about the young: your
carelessness is seen in your not caring about the
very things which you bring against me.

And now, Meletus, I will ask you another
question—by Zeus I will: Which is better, to live
among bad citizens, or among good ones? Answer,
friend, I say; the question is one which may be easily answered. Do not the good do their neighbours
good, and the bad do them evil?

Certainly.

d And is there any one who would   *When I do harm*
rather be injured than benefited   *to my neighbour*
by those who live with him? An-   *I must do harm*
swer, my good friend, the law re-   *to myself:*
quires you to answer—does any   *and therefore*
one like to be injured?   *I cannot be*
                                    supposed to
Certainly not.   *injure them*
And when you accuse me of cor-   *intentionally.*
rupting and deteriorating the youth, do you allege
that I corrupt them intentionally or unintentionally?

Intentionally, I say.

But you have just admitted that the good do
their neighbours good, and the evil do them evil.
Now, is that a truth which your superior wisdom
e has recognized thus early in life, and am I, at my
age, in such darkness and ignorance as not to know
that if a man with whom I have to live is corrupted
by me, I am very likely to be harmed by him; and
yet I corrupt him, and intentionally, too—so you
26a say, although neither I nor any other human being
is ever likely to be convinced by you. But either I
do not corrupt them, or I corrupt them uninten-

tionally; and on either view of the case you lie. If my offence is unintentional, the law has no cognizance of unintentional offences: you ought to have taken me privately, and warned and admonished me; for if I had been better advised, I should have left off doing what I only did unintentionally—no doubt I should; but you would have nothing to say to me and refused to teach me. And now you bring me up in this court, which is a place not of instruction, but of punishment.

It will be very clear to you, Athenians, as I was saying, that Meletus has no care at all, great or small, about the matter. But still I should like to know, Meletus, in what I am affirmed to corrupt the young. I suppose you mean, as I infer from your indictment, that I teach them not to acknowledge the gods which the State acknowledges, but some other new divinities or spiritual agencies in their stead. These are the lessons by which I corrupt the youth, as you say.

Yes, that I say emphatically.

Then, by the gods, Meletus, of whom we are speaking, tell me and the court, in somewhat plainer terms, what you mean! For I do not as yet understand whether you affirm that I teach other men to acknowledge some gods, and therefore that I do believe in gods, and am not an entire atheist—this you do not lay to my charge,— but only you say that they are not the same gods which the city recognizes—the charge is that they are different gods. Or, do you mean that I am an atheist simply, and a teacher of atheism?

Socrates is declared by Meletus to be an atheist and to corrupt the religion of the young.

I mean the latter—that you are a complete atheist.

What an extraordinary statement! Why do you
d   think so, Meletus? Do you mean that I do not believe in the godhead of the sun or moon, like other
men?

I assure you, judges, that he does not: for he
says that the sun is stone, and the moon earth.

Friend Meletus, you think that   *Meletus has*
you are accusing Anaxagoras: and   *confounded*
you have but a bad opinion of the   *Socrates with*
judges, if you fancy them illiterate   *Anaxagoras,*
to such a degree as not to know that these doctrines are found in the books of Anaxagoras the
Clazomenian,[11] which are full of them. And so, for-
sooth, the youth are said to be taught them by
e   Socrates, when there are not unfrequently exhibi-
tions of them at the theatre[12] (price of admission
one drachma[13] at the most); and they might pay
their money, and laugh at Socrates if he pretends
to father these extraordinary views. And so, Meletus, you really think that I do not believe in any
god?

I swear by Zeus that you be-   *and he has*
lieve absolutely in none at all.   *contradicted*
Nobody will believe you, Mel-   *himself in the*
etus, and I am pretty sure that you   *indictment.*
do not believe yourself. I cannot help thinking,
men of Athens, that Meletus is reckless and im-
pudent, and that he has written this indictment in
27a   a spirit of mere wantonness and youthful bravado.
Has he not compounded a riddle, thinking to try
me? He said to himself:—I shall see whether the
wise Socrates will discover my facetious contradic-

tion, or whether I shall be able to deceive him and the rest of them. For he certainly does appear to me to contradict himself in the indictment as much as if he said that Socrates is guilty of not believing in the gods, and yet of believing in them—but this is not like a person who is in earnest.

I should like you, O men of Athens, to join me in examining what I conceive to be his inconsistency; and do you, Meletus, answer. And I must b remind the audience of my request that they would not make a disturbance if I speak in my accustomed manner:

Did ever man, Meletus, believe in the existence of human things, and not of human beings? ... I wish, men of Athens, that he would answer, and not be always

How can Socrates believe in divine agencies and not believe in gods?

trying to get up an interruption. Did ever any man believe in horsemanship, and not in horses? or in flute-playing, and not in flute-players? No, my friend; I will answer to you and to the court, as you refuse to answer for yourself. There is no man who ever did. But now please to answer the next c question: Can a man believe in spiritual and divine agencies, and not in spirits or demigods?

He cannot.

How lucky I am to have extracted that answer, by the assistance of the court! But then you swear in the indictment that I teach and believe in divine or spiritual agencies (new or old, no matter for that); at any rate, I believe in spiritual agencies,—so you say and swear in the affidavit; and yet if I believe in divine beings, how can I help believing in spirits or demigods;—must I

not? To be sure I must; and therefore I may assume that your silence gives consent. Now what
d   are spirits or demigods? are they not either gods
or the sons of gods?

Certainly they are.

But this is what I call the facetious riddle invented by you: the demigods or spirits are gods,
and you say first that I do not believe in gods, and
then again that I do believe in gods; that is, if I
believe in demigods. For if the demigods are the
illegitimate sons of gods, whether by the nymphs
or by any other mothers, of whom they are said to
be the sons—what human being will ever believe
e   that there are no gods if they are the sons of gods?
You might as well affirm the existence of mules,
and deny that of horses and asses. Such nonsense,
Meletus, could only have been intended by you
to make trial of me. You have put this into the indictment because you had nothing real of which
to accuse me.[14] But no one who has a particle of
understanding will ever be convinced by you that
28a the same men can believe in divine and superhuman things, and yet not believe that there are gods
and demigods and heroes.

I have said enough in answer to the charge of
Meletus: any elaborate defence is unnecessary;
but I know only too well how many are the enmities which I have incurred, and this is what will
be my destruction if I am destroyed;—not Meletus, nor yet Anytus, but the envy and detraction
of the world, which has been the death of many
b   good men, and will probably be the death of many
more; there is no danger of my being the last of
them.

Some one will say: And are you *Let no man fear* not ashamed, Socrates, of a course *death or fear* of life which is likely to bring you *anything but* to an untimely end? To him I may *disgrace.* fairly answer: There you are mistaken: a man who is good for anything ought not to calculate the chance of living or dying; he ought only to consider whether in doing anything he is doing right or wrong—acting the part of a good man or of a bad. Whereas, upon your view, the heroes who fell at   c Troy were not good for much, and the son of The-tis[15] above all, who altogether despised danger in comparison with disgrace; and when he was so eager to slay Hector, his goddess mother said to him, that if he avenged his companion Patroclus, and slew Hector, he would die himself—"Fate," she said, in these or the like words, "waits for you next after Hector"; he, receiving this warning, ut-terly despised danger and death, and instead of fearing them, feared rather to live in dishonour,   d and not to avenge his friend. "Let me die forth-with," he replies, "and be avenged of my enemy, rather than abide here by the beaked ships, a laughing-stock and a burden of the earth." Had Achilles any thought of death and danger? For wherever a man's place is, whether the place which he has chosen or that in which he has been placed by a commander, there he ought to remain in the hour of danger; he should not think of death or of anything but of disgrace. And this, O men of Ath-ens, is a true saying.

Strange, indeed, would be my conduct, O men of Athens, if I, who, when I was ordered by the   e generals whom you chose to command me at Pot-

idaea and Amphipolis and Delium,[16] remained
where they placed me, like any other man, facing
death—if now, when, as I conceive and imagine,
God orders me to fulfil the philosopher's mission
of searching into myself and other *Socrates, who*
men, I were to desert my post *has often faced*
through fear of death, or any other *death in battle,*
will not make
29a fear; that would indeed be strange, *any condition in*
and I might justly be arraigned in *order to save his*
court for denying the existence of *own life; for he*
the gods, if I disobeyed the oracle *does not know*
because I was afraid of death, fan- *whether death*
cying that I was wise when I was *is a good or an*
evil.
not wise. For the fear of death is
indeed the pretence of wisdom, and not real wisdom, being a pretence of knowing the unknown;
and no one knows whether death, which men in
b their fear apprehend to be the greatest evil, may
not be the greatest good. Is not this ignorance of a
disgraceful sort, the ignorance which is the conceit
that a man knows what he does not know? And in
this respect only I believe myself to differ from
men in general, and may perhaps claim to be wiser
than they are:—that whereas I know but little of
the world below, I do not suppose that I know: but
I do know that injustice and disobedience to a bet-
c ter, whether God or man, is evil and dishonourable, and I will never fear or avoid a possible good
rather than a certain evil. And therefore if you let
me go now, and are not convinced by Anytus, who
said that since I had been prosecuted I must be put
to death; (or if not that I ought never to have been
prosecuted at all); and that if I escape now, your
sons will all be utterly ruined by listening to my

words—if you say to me, Socrates, this time we will
not mind Anytus, and you shall be let off, but upon
one condition, that you are not to enquire and
speculate in this way any more, and that if you are   d
caught doing so again you shall die;—if this was the
condition on which you let me go, I should reply;
Men of Athens, I honour and love you; but I shall
obey God rather than you, and while I have life
and strength I shall never cease from the practice
and teaching of philosophy, ex-   *He must always*
horting any one whom I meet and   *be a preacher of*
saying to him after my manner: *philosophy.*
You, my friend,—a citizen of the great and mighty
and wise city of Athens,—are you not ashamed of   e
heaping up the greatest amount of money and
honour and reputation, and caring so little about
wisdom and truth and the greatest improvement of
the soul, which you never regard or heed at all?
And if the person with whom I am arguing, says:
Yes, but I do care; then I do not leave him or let
him go at once; but I proceed to interrogate and
examine and cross-examine him, and if I think that
he has no virtue in him, but only says that he has, I   30a
reproach him with undervaluing the greater, and
overvaluing the less. And I shall repeat the same
words to every one whom I meet, young and old,
citizen and alien, but especially to the citizens, inasmuch as they are my brethren. For know that
this is the command of God; and I believe that no
greater good has ever happened   *"Necessity is*
in the State than my service to the   *laid upon me:*
God. For I do nothing but go   *'I must obey*
about persuading you all, old and   *God rather than*
young alike, not to take thought   *man.'"*   b

for your persons or your properties, but first and chiefly to care about the greatest improvement of the soul. I tell you that virtue is not given by money, but that from virtue comes money and every other good of man, public as well as private. This is my teaching, and if this is the doctrine which corrupts the youth, I am a mischievous person. But if any one says that this is not my teaching, he is speaking an untruth. Wherefore, O men of Athens, I say to you, do as Anytus bids or not as Anytus bids, and c either acquit me or not; but whichever you do, understand that I shall never alter my ways, not even if I have to die many times.

Men of Athens, do not interrupt, but hear me; there was an understanding between us that you should hear me to the end: I have something more to say, at which you may be inclined to cry out; but I believe that to hear me will be good for you, and therefore I beg that you will not cry out. I would have you know, that if you kill such an one as I am, you will injure yourselves more than you will injure d me. Nothing will injure me, not Meletus nor yet Anytus—they cannot, for a bad man is not permitted to injure a better than himself.   *Neither you nor* I do not deny that Anytus may,   *Meletus can* perhaps, kill him, or drive him   *ever injure me.* into exile, or deprive him of civil rights; and he may imagine, and others may imagine, that he is inflicting a great injury upon him: but there I do not agree. For the evil of doing as he is doing—the evil of unjustly taking away the life of another—is greater far.

And now, Athenians, I am not going to argue for my own sake, as you may think, but for yours, that

you may not sin against the God by condemning
me, who am his gift to you. For if you kill me you
will not easily find a successor to me, who, if I may
use such a ludicrous figure of speech, am a sort of
gadfly,[17] given to the State by God; *I am the gadfly*
and the state is a great and noble *of the Athenian*
steed who is tardy in his motions *people, given*
owing to his very size, and re- *to them by*
quires to be stirred into life. I am *will never have*
that gadfly which God has at- *another if they*
tached to the State, and all day *kill me.*
long and in all places am always fastening upon
you, arousing and persuading and reproaching
you. You will not easily find another like me, and
therefore I would advise you to spare me. I dare
say that you may feel out of temper (like a person
who is suddenly awakened from sleep), and you
think that you might easily strike me dead as Anytus advises, and then you would sleep on for the
remainder of your lives, unless God in his care of
you sent you another gadfly. When I say that I am
given to you by God, the proof of my mission is
this:—if I had been like other men, I should not
have neglected all my own concerns or patiently
seen the neglect of them during all these years,
and have been doing yours, coming to you individually like a father or elder brother, exhorting
you to regard virtue; such conduct, I say, would be
unlike human nature. If I had gained anything, or
if my exhortations had been paid, there would have
been some sense in my doing so; but now, as you
will perceive, not even the impudence of my accusers dares to say that I have ever exacted or
sought pay of any one; of that they have no witness.

And I have a sufficient witness to the truth of what I say—my poverty.

Some one may wonder why I go about in private giving advice and busying myself with the concerns of others, but do not venture to come forward in public and advise the State. I will tell you why. You have heard me speak at sundry times and in divers[18] places of an oracle or sign which comes to me, and is the divinity

d which Meletus ridicules in the indictment. This sign, which is a kind of voice, first began to come to me when I was a child; it always forbids but never commands me to do anything which I am going to do. This

The internal sign always forbade him to engage in politics; and if he had done so, he would have perished long ago.

is what deters me from being a politician. And rightly, as I think. For I am certain, O men of Athens, that if I had engaged in politics, I should have perished long

e ago, and done no good either to you or to myself. And do not be offended at my telling you the truth: for the truth is, that no man who goes to war with you

32a or any other multitude, honestly striving against the many lawless and unrighteous deeds which are done in a state, will save his life; he who will fight for the right, if he would live even for a brief space, must have a private station and not a public one.

I can give you convincing evidence of what I say, not words only, but what you value far more—actions. Let me relate to you a passage of my own life which will prove to you that I should never have yielded to injustice from any fear of death and that "as I should

He had shown that he would sooner die than commit injustice at the trial of the generals and under the tyranny of the Thirty.

have refused to yield" I must have died at once. I will tell you a tale of the courts, not very interesting perhaps, but nevertheless true. The only office   b of State which I ever held, O men of Athens, was that of senator: the tribe Antiochis, which is my tribe, had the presidency at the trial of the generals who had not taken up the bodies of the slain after the battle of Arginusae; and you proposed to try them in a body, contrary to law, as you all thought afterwards; but at the time I was the only one of the Prytanes[19] who was opposed to the illegality, and I gave my vote against you; and when the orators threatened to impeach and arrest me, and you called and shouted, I made up my mind that I would run the risk, having law and justice with   c me, rather than take part in your injustice because I feared imprisonment and death. This happened in the days of the democracy. But when the oligarchy of the Thirty[20] was in power, they sent for me and four others into the rotunda, and bade us bring Leon the Salaminian from Salamis, as they wanted to put him to death. This was a specimen of the sort of commands which they were always giving with the view of implicating as many as possible in   d their crimes; and then I showed, not in word only but in deed, that, if I may be allowed to use such an expression, I cared not a straw for death, and that my great and only care was lest I should do an unrighteous or unholy thing. For the strong arm of that oppressive power did not frighten me into doing wrong; and when we came out of the rotunda the other four went to Salamis and fetched Leon, but I went quietly home. For which I might have lost my life, had not the power of the Thirty shortly

e   afterwards come to an end. And many will witness
to my words.

Now, do you really imagine that I could have
survived all these years, if I had led a public life,
supposing that like a good man I had always maintained the right and had made justice, as I ought,
the first thing? No, indeed, men of Athens, neither
I nor any other man. But I have been always the
33a same in all my actions, public as well as private,
and never have I yielded any base   *He is always*
compliance to those who are slan-   *talking to the*
derously termed my disciples, or   *citizens, but he*
to any other. Not that I have any   *teaches nothing;*
regular disciples. But if any one   *he takes no*
likes to come and hear me while I   *pay and has no*
am pursuing my mission, whether   *secrets.*
he be young or old, he is not excluded. Nor do I
b   converse only with those who pay; but any one,
whether he be rich or poor, may ask and answer
me and listen to my words; and whether he turns
out to be a bad man or a good one, neither result
can be justly imputed to me; for I never taught or
professed to teach him anything. And if any one
says that he has ever learned or heard anything
from me in private which all the world has not
heard, let me tell you that he is lying.

But I shall be asked, Why do people delight in
continually conversing with you? I have told you
c   already, Athenians, the whole truth about this matter: they like to hear the cross-examination of the
pretenders to wisdom; there is amusement in it.
Now, this duty of cross-examining[21] other men has
been imposed upon me by God; and has been sig-
nified to me by oracles, visions, and in every way in

which the will of divine power was ever intimated
to any one. This is true, O Athenians; or, if not true,
would be soon refuted. If I am or have been cor-   d
rupting the youth, those of them who are now
grown up and have become sensible that I gave
them bad advice in the days of their youth should
come forward as accusers, and take their revenge;
or if they do not like to come themselves, some of
their relatives, fathers, brothers, or other kinsmen,
should say what evil their families have suffered at
my hands. Now is their time. Many of them I see in
the court.[22] There is Crito, who is of the same age
and of the same deme with my-   *The parents
self, and there is Critobulus his   and kinsmen of   e
son, whom I also see. Then again   those whom he
there is Lysanias of Sphettus, who is supposed to
is the father of Aeschines—he is   have corrupted
present; and also there is Anti-   do not come
phon of Cephisus, who is the fa-   forward and
ther of Epigenes; and there are   testify against
                                    him.*
the brothers of several who have associated with
me. There is Nicostratus the son of Theosdotides,
and the brother of Theodotus (now Theodotus
himself is dead, and therefore he, at any rate, will
not seek to stop him); and there is Paralus the son
of Demodocus, who had a brother Theages; and   34a
Adeimantus the son of Ariston, whose brother
Plato is present; and Aeantodorus, who is the
brother of Apollodorus, whom I also see. I might
mention a great many others, some of whom Meletus should have produced as witnesses in the
course of his speech; and let him still produce
them, if he has forgotten—I will make way for him.
And let him say, if he has any testimony of the sort

which he can produce. Nay, Athenians, the very opposite is the truth. For all these are ready to wit-
b ness on behalf of the corrupter, of the injurer of their kindred, as Meletus and Anytus call me; not the corrupted youth only—there might have been a motive for that—but their uncorrupted elder relatives. Why should they too support me with their testimony? Why, indeed, except for the sake of truth and justice, and because they know that I am speaking the truth, and that Meletus is a liar.

Well, Athenians, this and the like of this is all the defence which I have to offer. Yet a word more.
c Perhaps there may be some one who is offended at me, when he calls to mind how he himself on a similar, or even a less serious occasion, prayed and entreated the judges with many tears, and how he produced his children in court, which was a moving spectacle, together with a host of relations and friends; whereas I, who am probably in danger of my life, will do none of these things. The contrast may occur to his mind, and he may be set against
d me, and vote in anger because he is displeased at me on this account. Now, if there be such a person among you,—mind, I do not say that there is,—to him I may fairly reply: My friend, I am a man, and like other men, a creature of flesh and blood, and not "of wood or stone," as Homer says; and I have a family, yes, and sons, O Athe- nians, three in number, one al- most a man, and two others who are still young; and yet I will not bring any of them hither in order to petition you for an acquittal. And why not? Not

He is flesh and blood, but he will not appeal to the pity of his judges: or make a scene in the court such as he has often witnessed.

from any self-assertion or want of respect for you.   e
Whether I am or am not afraid of death is another
question, of which I will not now speak. But, having regard to public opinion, I feel that such conduct would be discreditable to myself, and to you,
and to the whole State. One who has reached my
years, and who has a name for wisdom, ought not
to demean himself. Whether this opinion of me be
deserved or not, at any rate the world has decided   35a
that Socrates is in some way superior to other men.
And if those among you who are said to be superior
in wisdom and courage, and any other virtue, demean themselves in this way, how shameful is their
conduct! I have seen men of reputation, when they
have been condemned, behaving in the strangest
manner: they seemed to fancy that they were going
to suffer something dreadful if they died, and that
they could be immortal if you only allowed them to
live; and I think that such are a dishonour to the   b
State, and that any stranger coming in would have
said of them that the most eminent men of Athens,
to whom the Athenians themselves give honour
and command, are no better than women. And I
say that these things ought not to be done by those
of us who have a reputation; and if they are done,
you ought not to permit them; you ought rather to
show that you are far more disposed to condemn
the man who gets up a doleful scene and makes the
city ridiculous, than him who holds his peace.

But, setting aside the question   *This judge*
of public opinion, there seems to   *should not be*   c
be something wrong in asking a   *influenced by*
    his feelings, but
favour of a judge, and thus pro-   *convinced by*
curing an acquittal, instead of in-   *reason.*

forming and convincing him. For his duty is, not to make a present of justice, but to give judgment; and he has sworn that he will judge according to the laws, and not according to his own good pleasure; and we ought not to encourage you, nor should you allow yourselves to be encouraged, in this habit of

d perjury—there can be no piety in that. Do not then require me to do what I consider dishonourable and impious and wrong, especially now, when I am being tried for impiety on the indictment of Meletus. For if, O men of Athens, by force of persuasion and entreaty I could overpower your oaths, then I should be teaching you to believe that there are no gods, and in defending should simply convict myself of the charge of not believing in them. But that is not so—far otherwise. For I do believe that there are gods, and in a sense higher than that in which any of my accusers believe in them. And to you and to God I commit my cause, to be determined by you as is best for you and me.

e There are many reasons why I am not grieved, O
36a men of Athens, at the vote of condemnation. I expected it, and am only surprised that the votes are so nearly equal; for I had thought that the majority against me would have been far larger; but now, had thirty votes gone over to the other side, I should have been acquitted. And I may say, I think, that I have escaped Meletus. I may say more; for without the assistance of Anytus and Lycon, any one may see that he would not have had a fifth part of the votes,[23] as the law requires, in which case he would

b have incurred a fine of a thousand drachmae.

And so he proposes death as the penalty. And

what shall I propose on my part, O men of Athens?
Clearly that which is my due. And what is my due?
What returns shall be made to the man who has
never had the wit to be idle during his whole life;
but has been careless of what the many care for—
wealth, and family interests, and military offices,
and speaking in the assembly, and magistracies,   c
and plots, and parties? Reflecting that I was really
too honest a man to be a politician   *Socrates all his*
and live, I did not go where I   *life long has*
could do no good to you or to my-   *been seeking to*
self; but where I could do the   *do the greatest*
greatest good privately to every   *good to the*
one of you, thither I went, and   *Athenians.*
sought to persuade every man among you that he
must look to himself, and seek virtue and wisdom
before he looks to his private interests, and look to
the State before he looks to the interests of the
State; and that this should be the   *Should*
order which he observes in all his   *he not be*   d
actions. What shall be done to   *rewarded with*
such an one? Doubtless some   *maintenance in*
good thing, O men of Athens, if he   *the Prytaneum?*
has his reward; and the good should be of a kind
suitable to him. What would be a reward suitable
to a poor man who is your benefactor, and who desires leisure that he may instruct you? There can
be no reward so fitting as maintenance in the Prytaneum,[24] O men of Athens, a reward which he deserves far more than the citizen who has won the
prize at Olympia in the horse or chariot race,
whether the chariots were drawn by two horses or
by many. For I am in want, and he has enough; and
he only gives you the appearance of happiness, and   e

I give you the reality. And if I am to estimate the penalty fairly, I should say that maintenance in the Prytaneum is the just return.

37a   Perhaps you think that I am braving you in what I am saying now, as in what I said before about the tears and prayers. But this is *The consciousness of innocence gives him confidence.* not so. I speak rather because I am convinced that I never intentionally wronged any one, although I cannot convince you—the time has been too short; if there were a law at Athens, as there is in other cities, that a capital cause should not be decided in

b   one day, then I believe that I should have convinced you. But I cannot in a moment refute great slanders; and, as I am convinced that I never wronged another, I will assuredly not wrong myself. I will not say to myself that I deserve any evil, or propose any penalty. Why should I? Because I am afraid of the penalty of death which Meletus proposes? When I do not know whether death is a good or an evil, why should I propose a penalty

c   which would certainly be an evil? Shall I say imprisonment? And why should I live in prison, and be the slave of the magistrate of the year—of the Eleven?[25] Or shall the penalty be a fine, and imprisonment until the fine is paid? There is the same objection. I should have to lie in prison, for money I have none, and cannot pay. And if I say exile (and this may possibly be the penalty which you will affix), I *No alternative in his own judgment preferable to death.* must indeed be blinded by the love of life, if I am so irrational as to expect that when you, who are

d   my own citizens, cannot endure my discourses and

words, and have found them so grievous and odious that you will have no more of them, others are likely to endure me. No, indeed, men of Athens, that is not very likely. And what a life should I lead, at my age, wandering from city to city, ever changing my place of exile, and always being driven out! For I am quite sure that wherever I go, there, as here, the young men will flock to me; and if I drive them away, their elders will drive me out at their request; and if I let them come, their fathers and friends will drive me out for their sakes.

e

Some one will say: Yes, Socrates, but cannot you hold your tongue, and then you may go into a foreign city, and no one will interfere with you? Now, I have great difficulty in making you understand my answer to this. For if I tell you that *For wherever* to do as you say would be a disobe- *he goes he must* dience to the God, and therefore *speak out.* that I cannot hold my tongue, you will not believe that I am serious; and if I say again that daily to discourse about virtue, and of those other things about which you hear me examining myself and others, is the greatest good of man, and that the unexamined life is not worth living, you are still less likely to believe me. Yet I say what is true, although a thing of which it is hard for me to persuade you. Also, I have never been accustomed to think that I deserve to suffer any harm. Had I money I might have estimated the offence at what I was able to pay, and not have been much the worse. But I have none, and therefore I must ask you to proportion the fine to my means. Well, perhaps I could afford a mina, and therefore I propose that penalty: Plato, Crito, Critobulus, and Apollodorus, my friends

38a

b

here, bid me say thirty minae, and they will be the sureties. Let thirty minae be the penalty; for which sum they will be ample security to you.

c Not much time will be gained, O Athenians, in return for the evil name which you will get from the detractors of the city, who will say *They will be accused of killing a wise man.*

that you killed Socrates, a wise man; for they will call me wise, even although I am not wise, when they want to reproach you. If you had waited a little while, your desire would have been fulfilled in the course of nature. For I am far advanced in years, as you may perceive, and not far from death.

d I am speaking now not to all of you, but only to those who have condemned me to death. And I *Why could they not wait a few years?*

have another thing to say to them: You think that I was convicted because I had no words of the sort which would have procured my acquittal—I mean, if I had thought fit to leave nothing undone or unsaid. Not so; the deficiency which led to my conviction was not of words—certainly not. But I had not the boldness or impudence or inclination to address you as you would have liked me to do, weeping and wailing and lamenting, and saying and doing many things which you have been accustomed to hear from others, and which, as I maintain, are unworthy of me. I thought at the time that I ought not to do anything common or mean when in danger: nor do I now repent of the style of my defence; I would rather die having spoken after my manner, than speak in your manner and live. For neither in war nor yet at law ought I or any man

e

use every way of escaping death. Often in battle   39a
there can be no doubt that if a man will throw away
his arms, and fall on his knees before his pursuers,
he may escape death; and in other dangers there
are other ways of escaping death, if a man is willing
to say and do anything. The difficulty, my friends,
is not to avoid death, but to avoid unrighteousness;
for that runs faster than death. I am old and move   b
slowly, and the slower runner has overtaken me,
and my accusers are keen and quick, and the faster
runner, who is unrighteousness, has overtaken
them. And now I depart hence condemned by you
to suffer the penalty of death,—they too go their
ways condemned by the truth to suffer the penalty
of villainy and wrong; and I must abide by my
award—let them abide by theirs. I suppose that
these things may be regarded as fated,—and I
think that they are well.

And now, O men who have condemned me, I   c
would fain prophesy to you; for I am about to die,
and in the hour of death men are gifted with pro-
phetic power. And I prophesy to you who are my
murderers, that immediately after my departure
punishment far heavier than you have inflicted on
me will surely await you. Me you have killed because you wanted to escape the *They are about*
accuser, and not to give an ac- *to slay Socrates*
count of your lives. But that will *because he*
has been their
not be as you suppose: far other- *accuser: other*   d
wise. For I say that there will be *accusers will*
more accusers of you than there *rise up and*
are now; accusers whom hitherto I *denounce*
them more
have restrained: and as they are *vehemently.*
younger they will be more incon-

siderate with you, and you will be more offended
at them. If you think that by killing men you can
prevent some one from censuring your evil lives,
you are mistaken; that is not a way of escape which
is either possible or honourable; the easiest and
the noblest way is not to be disabling others, but to
be improving yourselves. This is the prophecy
which I utter before my departure to the judges
who have condemned me.

e   Friends, who would have acquitted me, I would
like also to talk with you about the thing which has
come to pass, while the magistrates are busy, and
before I go to the place at which I must die. Stay
then a little, for we may as well talk with one an-
40a other while there is time. You are my friends, and I
should like to show you the meaning of this event
which has happened to me. O my judges—for you
I may truly call judges—I should like to tell you of
a wonderful circumstance. Hitherto the divine fac-
ulty of which the internal oracle is the source has
constantly been in the habit of op-   *He believes*
posing me even about trifles, if I   *that what is*
was going to make a slip or error   *happening to*
in any matter; and now as you see   *him will be*
there has come upon me that   *good, because*
which may be thought, and is gen-   *the internal*
erally believed to be, the last and   *oracle gives*
worst evil. But the oracle made no   *no sign of*
b   sign of opposition, either when I was leaving my   *opposition.*
house in the morning, or when I was on my way to
the court, or while I was speaking, at anything
which I was going to say; and yet I have often been
stopped in the middle of a speech, but now in
nothing I either said or did touching the matter in

hand has the oracle opposed me. What do I take to
be the explanation of this silence? I will tell you. It
is an intimation that what has happened to me is a
good, and that those of us who think that death is
an evil are in error. For the customary sign would
surely have opposed me had I been going to evil   c
and not to good.

Let us reflect in another way,   *Death either a*
and we shall see that there is great   *good or nothing:*
reason to hope that death is a good; for one of two
things—either death is a state of nothingness and
utter unconsciousness, or, as men say, there is a
change and migration of the soul from this world to
another. Now, if you suppose that there is no consciousness, but a sleep like the   *A profound*   d
sleep of him who is undisturbed   *sleep.*
even by dreams, death will be an unspeakable gain.
For if a person were to select the night in which his
sleep was undisturbed even by dreams, and were
to compare with this the other days and nights of
his life, and then were to tell us how many days and
nights he had passed in the course of his life better
and more pleasantly than this one, I think that any
man, I will not say a private man, but even the
great king will not find many such days or nights,   e
when compared with the others. Now, if death be
of such a nature, I say that to die is gain; for eternity is then only a single night. But if death is the
journey to another place, and there, as men say, all
the dead abide, what good, O my friends and
judges, can be greater than this? If indeed, when
the pilgrim arrives in the world below, he is deliv-   41a
ered from the professors of justice in this world,
and finds the true judges who are said to give judg-

ment there, Minos and Rhadamanthus and Aeacus and Triptolemus, and other sons of God who were righteous in their own life, that pilgrimage will be worth making. What would not a man give if he might converse with Orpheus and Musaeus and Hesiod and Homer?

b   Nay, if this be true, let me die again and again. I myself, too, shall have a wonderful interest in there meeting and conversing with Palamedes, and Ajax the son of Telamon, and any other ancient hero who has suffered death through an unjust judgment; and there will be no small pleasure, as I think, in comparing my own sufferings with theirs. Above all, I shall then be able to continue my search into true and false knowledge; as in this world, so also in the next; and I shall find out who is wise, and who pretends to be wise, and

c   is not. What would not a man give, O judges, to be able to examine the leader of the great Trojan expedition; or Odysseus or Sisyphus, or numberless others, men and women too! What infinite delight would there be in conversing with them and asking them questions! In another world they do not put a man to death for asking questions: assuredly not. For besides being happier than we are, they will be immortal, if what is said is true.

Wherefore, O judges, be of good cheer about
d   death, and know of a certainty, that no evil can happen to a good man, either in life or after death. He and his are not neglected by the gods; nor has my own approaching end happened by mere chance.

How blessed to have a just judgment passed on us; to converse with Homer and Hesiod; to see the heroes of Troy, and to continue the search after knowledge in another world!

But I see clearly that the time had arrived when it was better for me to die and be released from trouble; wherefore the oracle gave no sign. For which reason, also, I am not angry with my condemners, or with my accusers; they have done me no harm, although they did not mean to do me any good; and for this I may gently blame them.

Still, I have a favour to ask of them. When my sons are grown up, I would ask you, O my friends, *Do to my sons as I have done to you.* e

to punish them; and I would have you trouble them, as I have troubled you, if they seem to care about riches, or anything, more than about virtue; or if they pretend to be something when they are really nothing,—then reprove them, as I have reproved you, for not caring about that for which they ought to care, and thinking that they are something when they are really nothing. And if you do this, both I and my sons will have received 42a justice at your hands.

The hour of departure has arrived, and we go our ways—I to die, and you to live. Which is better God only knows.

CRITO

Persons of the Dialogue
SOCRATES, CRITO

Scene
THE PRISON OF SOCRATES

Socrates.: Why have you come at this hour, Crito? It must be quite early?   43a

Crito.: Yes, certainly.

Soc. What is the exact time?

Cr.: The dawn is breaking.

Soc.: I wonder that the keeper of the prison would let you in.

Cr.: He knows me, because I often come, Socrates; moreover, I have done him a kindness.

Crito appears at break of dawn in the prison of Socrates, whom he finds asleep.

Soc.: And are you only just arrived?

Cr.: No, I came some time ago.

Soc.: Then why did you sit and say nothing, in-   b
stead of at once awakening me?

Cr.: I should not have liked myself, Socrates, to be in such great trouble and unrest as you are—indeed I should not: I have been watching with amazement your peaceful slumbers; and for that reason I did not awake you, because I wished to minimize the pain. I have always thought you to be of a happy disposition; but never did I see anything like the easy, tranquil manner in which you bear this calamity.

Soc.: Why, Crito, when a man has reached my age he ought not to be repining at the approach of death.

Cr.: And yet other old men find themselves   c
in similar misfortunes, and age does not prevent them from repining.

Soc.: That is true. But you have not told me why you come at this early hour.

Cr.: I come to bring you a mes-   *The ship*
sage which is sad and painful; not,   *from Delos is*
as I believe, to yourself, but to all   *expected.*

of us who are your friends, and saddest of all to me.

Soc.: What? Has the ship come from Delos,1 on

d the arrival of which I am to die?

Cr.: No, the ship has not actually arrived, but she will probably be here to-day, as persons who have come from Sunium tell me that they left her there; and therefore tomorrow, Socrates, will be the last day of your life.

Soc.: Very well, Crito; if such is the will of God, I am willing; but my belief is that there will be a delay of a day.

44a *Cr.:* Why do you think so?

Soc.: I will tell you. I am to die on the day after the arrival of the ship.

Cr.: Yes; that is what the authorities say.

Soc.: But I do not think that the ship will be here until to-morrow; this I infer from a vision which I had last night, or rather only just now, when you fortunately allowed me to sleep.

A vision of a fair woman who prophesies in the language of Homer that Socrates will die on the third day.

Cr.: And what was the nature of the vision?

Soc.: There appeared to me the likeness of a

b woman, fair and comely, clothed in bright raiment, who called to me and said: O Socrates,

> "The third day hence to fertile Phthia shalt thou
> go."2

Cr.: What a singular dream, Socrates!

Soc.: There can be no doubt about the meaning, Crito, I think.

Cr.: Yes; the meaning is only too clear. But, oh! my beloved Socrates, let me entreat you once more to take my advice and escape. For if you die I shall not only lose a friend who can never be replaced, but there is another evil: people who do not know you and me will believe that I might have saved you if I had been willing to give money, but that I did not care. Now, can there be a worse disgrace c
than this—that I should be thought to value money more than the life of a friend? For the many will not be persuaded that I wanted you to escape, and that you refused.

Soc.: But why, my dear Crito, should we care about the opinion of the many? Good men, and they are the only persons who are worth considering, will think of these things truly as they occurred.

Crito by a variety of arguments tries to induce Socrates to make his escape. The means will be easily provided and without danger to any one.

Cr.: But you see, Socrates, that d
the opinion of the many must be regarded, for what is now happening shows that they can do the greatest evil to any one who has lost their good opinion.

Soc.: I only wish it were so, Crito; and that the many could do the greatest evil; for then they would also be able to do the greatest good—and what a fine thing this would be! But in reality they can do neither; for they cannot make a man either wise or foolish; and whatever they do is the result of chance.

Cr.: Well, I will not dispute with you; but please e
to tell me, Socrates, whether you are not acting out of regard to me and your other friends: are you not afraid that if you escape from prison we may get

into trouble with the informers for having stolen you away, and lose either the whole or a great part of our property; or that even a worse evil may hap-

45a pen to us? Now, if you fear on our account, be at ease; for in order to save you, we ought surely to run this, or even a greater risk; be persuaded, then, and do as I say.

Soc.: Yes, Crito, that is one fear which you mention, but by no means the only one.

Cr.: Fear not—there are persons who are willing to get you out of prison at no great cost; and as for the informers, they are far from being exorbitant in

b their demands—a little money will satisfy them. My means, which are certainly ample, are at your service, and if you have a scruple about spending all mine, here are strangers who will give you the use of theirs; and one of them, Simmias the Theban,[3] has brought a large sum of money for this very purpose; and Cebes and many others are prepared to spend their money in helping you to escape. I say, therefore, do not hesitate on our account, and do not say, as you did in the court, that you will have a difficulty in knowing what to do with yourself anywhere else.

c For men will love you in other places to which you may go, and not in Athens only; there are friends of mine in Thessaly, if you like to go to them, who will value and protect you, and no Thessalian will give you any trouble. Nor can I think that you are at all justified, Socrates, in betraying *He is not* your own life when you might be *justified in* saved; in acting thus you are play- *throwing away* ing into the hands of your enemies, *his life; he will* who are hurrying on your destruc- *be deserting his* tion. And further I should say that *will bring*

you are deserting your own chil- *the reproach of*
dren; for you might bring them *cowardice on his*
up and educate them; instead of *friends.* d
which you go away and leave them, and they will
have to take their chance; and if they do not meet
with the usual fate of orphans, there will be small
thanks to you. No man should bring children into
the world who is unwilling to persevere to the end in
their nurture and education. But you appear to be
choosing the easier part, not the better and manlier,
which would have been more becoming in one who
professes to care for virtue in all his actions, like
yourself. And, indeed, I am ashamed not only of you,
but of us who are your friends, when I reflect that e
the whole business will be attributed entirely to our
want of courage. The trial need never have come on,
or might have been managed differently; and this
last act, or crowning folly, will seem to have occurred
through our negligence and cowardice, who might
have saved you, if we had been good for anything; 46a
and you might have saved yourself, for there was no
difficulty at all. See now, Socrates, how sad and discreditable are the consequences, both to us and
you. Make up your mind, then, or rather have your
mind already made up, for the time of deliberation
is over, and there is only one thing to be done, which
must be done this very night, and if we delay at all
will be no longer practicable or possible; I beseech
you therefore, Socrates, be persuaded by me, and
do as I say.

Soc.: Dear Crito, your zeal is invaluable, if a b
right one; but if wrong, the greater the zeal the
greater the danger; and therefore we ought to consider whether I shall or shall not do as you say. For

I am and always have been one of those natures who must be guided by reason, whatever the reason may be which upon reflection ap- *Socrates is one of those who must be guided by reason.*

c pears to me to be the best; and now that this chance has befallen me, I cannot repudiate my own words: the principles which I have hitherto honoured and revered I still honour, and unless we can at once find other and better principles, I am certain not to agree with you; no, not even if the power of the multitude could inflict many more imprisonments, confiscations, deaths, frightening us like children with hobgoblin terrors. What will be the fairest way of considering the question? Shall I return to your old argument about the opinions of men?—we

d were saying that some of them are to be regarded, and others not. Now, were we right in maintaining this before I was condemned? And has the argument which was once good now proved to be talk for the sake of talking—mere childish nonsense? That is what I want to consider with your help, Crito:—whether, under my present circumstances, the argument appears to be in any way different or not; and is to be allowed by me or disallowed. That argument, which, as I believe, is maintained by many persons of authority, was to the effect, as I

e was saying, that the opinions of some men are to be regarded, and of other men not to be regarded.

47a Now you, Crito, are not going to die to-morrow—at least, there is no human probability of this—and therefore you are disinterested and not liable to be deceived by the circumstances in which you are placed. Tell me, then, whether I am right in saying that some opinions, and the opinions of some men only, are to be valued, *Ought he to* and that other opinions, and the *follow the* opinions of other men, are not to *opinion of the* be valued. I ask you whether I was *many or of the* right in maintaining this? *wise or of the unwise?*

Cr.: Certainly.

Soc.: The good are to be regarded, and not the bad?

Cr.: Yes.

Soc.: And the opinions of the wise are good, and the opinions of the unwise are evil?

Cr.: Certainly.

Soc.: And what was said about another matter?   b Is the pupil who devotes himself to the practice of gymnastic supposed to attend to the praise and blame and opinion of every man, or of one man only—his physician or trainer, whoever he may be?

Cr.: Of one man only.

Soc.: And he ought to fear the censure and welcome the praise of that one only, and not of the many?

Cr.: Clearly so.

Soc.: And he ought to act and train, and eat and drink in the way which seems good to his single master who has understanding, rather than according to the opinion of all other men put together?

Cr.: True.

Soc.: And if he disobeys and disregards the   c opinion and approval of the one, and regards the opinion of the many who have no understanding, will he not suffer evil?

Cr.: Certainly he will.

Soc.: And what will the evil be, whither tending and what affecting, in the disobedient person?

Cr.: Clearly, affecting the body; that is what is destroyed by the evil.

Soc.: Very good; and is not this true, Crito, of other things which we need not separately enumerate? In questions of just and un-   *The opinion of the one wise man is to be followed.*
just, fair and foul, good and evil, which are the subjects of our present consultation, ought we to follow the opinion of the many and to fear them;
d   or the opinion of the one man who has understanding? ought we not to fear and reverence him more than all the rest of the world: and if we desert him shall we not destroy and injure that principle in us which may be assumed to be improved by justice and deteriorated by injustice;—there is such a principle?

Cr.: Certainly there is, Socrates.

Soc.: Take a parallel instance:—if, acting under the advice of those who have no understanding, we destroy that which is improved by health and is de-
e   teriorated by disease, would life be worth having? And that which has been destroyed is—the body?

Cr.: Yes.

Soc.: Could we live, having an evil and corrupted body?

Cr.: Certainly not.

Soc.: And will life be worth having, if that higher part of man be destroyed, which is improved by justice and depraved by injustice? Do we suppose
48a   that principle, whatever it may be in man, which has to do with justice and injustice, to be inferior to the body?

Cr.: Certainly not.

Soc.: More honourable than the body?

Cr.: Far more.

Soc.: Then, my friend, we must *No matter what* not regard what the many say of *the many say* us: but what he, the one man who *of us.* has understanding of just and unjust, will say, and what the truth will say. And therefore you begin in error when you advise that we should regard the opinion of the many about just and unjust, good and evil, honourable and dishonourable.—"Well," some one will say, "But the many can kill us."

Cr.: Yes, Socrates; that will clearly be the answer.   b

Soc.: And it is true; but still I *Not life, but a* find with surprise that the old ar- *good life, to be* gument is unshaken as ever. And I *chiefly valued.* should like to know whether I may say the same of another proposition—that not life, but a good life, is to be chiefly valued?

Cr.: Yes, that also remains unshaken.

Soc.: And a good life is equivalent to a just and honourable one—that holds also?

Cr.: Yes, it does.

Soc.: From these premises I proceed to argue the question whether I ought or ought not to try to escape without the consent of the Athenians: and if   c I am clearly right in escaping, then I will make the attempt; but if not, I will abstain. The other consid- erations which you mention, of money and loss of character and the duty of educating one's children, are, I fear, only the doctrines of the multitude, who would be as ready to restore people to life, if they were able, as they are to put them *Admitting these* to death—and with as little reason. *principles, ought* But now, since the argument has *I to try and* thus far prevailed, the only ques- *escape or not?*

d tion which remains to be considered is, whether we shall do rightly either in escaping or in suffering others to aid in our escape and paying them in money and thanks, or whether in reality we shall not do rightly; and if the latter, then death or any other calamity which may ensue on my remaining here must not be allowed to enter into the calculation.

Cr.: I think that you are right, Socrates; how then shall we proceed?

Soc.: Let us consider the matter together, and
e do you either refute me if you can, and I will be convinced; or else cease, my dear friend, from repeating to me that I ought to escape against the wishes of the Athenians: for I highly value your attempts to persuade me to do so, but I may not be persuaded against my own better judgment. And
49a now please to consider my first position, and try how you can best answer me.

Cr.: I will.

Soc.: Are we to say that we are never intentionally to do wrong, or that in one way we ought and in another way we ought not to *May we sometimes do evil that good may come?* do wrong, or is doing wrong always evil and dishonourable, as I was just now saying, and as has been already acknowledged by us? Are all our former admissions which were made within a few days to be thrown away? And have we, at our age,
b been earnestly discoursing with one another all our life long only to discover that we are no better than children? Or, in spite of the opinion of the many, and in spite of consequences whether better or worse, shall we insist on the truth of what was then said, that injustice is always an evil and

dishonour to him who acts unjustly? Shall we say so or not?

Cr.: Yes.

Soc.: Then we must do no wrong?

Cr.: Certainly not.

Soc.: Nor when injured injure in return, as the many imagine; for we must injure no one at all?

Cr.: Clearly not.

Soc.: Again, Crito, may we do evil?

Cr.: Surely not, Socrates.

Soc.: And what of doing evil in return for evil, which is the morality of the many—is that just or not?   *May we render evil for evil?*

Cr.: Not just.

Soc.: For doing evil to another is the same as injuring him?

Cr.: Very true.

Soc.: Then we ought not to retaliate or render evil for evil to any one, whatever evil we may have suffered from him. But I would have you consider, Crito, whether you really mean what you are saying. For this opinion has never been held, and never will be held, by any considerable number of persons; and those who are agreed and those who are not agreed upon this point have no common ground, and can only despise one another when they see how widely they differ. Tell me, then, whether you agree with and assent to my first principle, that neither injury nor retaliation nor warding off evil by evil is ever right. And shall that be the premise of our argument? Or do you decline and dissent from this? For so I have ever thought, and con-   *Or is evil always to be deemed evil? Are you of the same mind as formerly about all this?*

tinue to think; but, if you are of another opinion, let me hear what you have to say. If, however, you remain of the same mind as formerly, I will proceed to the next step.

Crito assents.

Cr.: You may proceed, for I have not changed my mind.

Soc.: Then I will go on to the next point, which may be put in the form of a question:—Ought a man to do what he admits to be right, or ought he to betray the right?

Cr.: He ought to do what he thinks right.

Then ought Socrates to desert or not?

Soc.: But if this is true, what is the application? In leaving the
50a prison against the will of the Athenians, do I wrong any? or rather do I not wrong those whom I ought least to wrong? Do I not desert the principles which were acknowledged by us to be just—what do you say?

Cr.: I cannot tell, Socrates; for I do not know.

The Laws come and argue with him.—Can a State exist in which law is set aside?

Soc.: Then consider the matter in this way:—Imagine that I am about to play truant (you may call the proceeding by any name which you like), and the laws and
b the government come and interrogate me: "Tell us, Socrates," they say; "what are you about? are you not going by an act of yours to overturn us—the laws, and the whole state, as far as in you lies? Do you imagine that a state can subsist and not be overthrown, in which the decisions of law have no power, but are set aside and trampled upon by individuals?" What will be our answer, Crito, to these and the like words? Any one, and especially a rhetorician, will have a good deal to say

on behalf of the law which requires a sentence to
be carried out. He will argue that this law should
not be set aside; and shall we reply, "Yes; but the   c
state has injured us and given an unjust sentence."
Suppose I say that?

Cr.: Very good, Socrates.

Soc.: "And was that our agreement with you?"
the law would answer; "or were you to abide by the
sentence of the state?" And if I were to express my
astonishment at their words, the   *Has he any fault*
law would probably add: "Answer,   *to find with*
Socrates, instead of opening your   *them?*
eyes—you are in the habit of asking and answering   d
questions. Tell us,—What complaint have you to
make against us which justifies you in attempting
to destroy us and the state? In the first place did we
not bring you into existence? Your father married
your mother by our aid and begat you. Say whether
you have any objection to urge against those of us
who regulate marriage?" None, I should reply. "Or
against those of us who after birth regulate the
nurture and education of children, in which you
also were trained? Were not the laws, which have
the charge of education, right in commanding your
father to train you in music and gymnastic?" Right,   e
I should reply. "Well, then, since you were brought
into the world and nurtured and educated by us,
can you deny in the first place that you are our
child and slave, as your fathers were before you?
And if this is true, you are not on   *No man has any*
equal terms with us; nor can you   *right to strike*
think that you have a right to do to   *a blow at his*
us what we are doing to you.   *country any*
Would you have any right to strike   *more than at his*
                                       father or mother.

or revile or do any other evil to your father or your
master, if you had one, because you have been
struck or reviled by him, or received some other
51a   evil at his hands?—you would not say this? And because we think right to destroy you, do you think
that you have any right to destroy us in return, and
your country as far as in you lies? Will you, O pro-
fessor of true virtue, pretend that you are justified
in this? Has a philosopher like you failed to discover that our country is more to be valued and
higher and holier far than mother or father or any
ancestor, and more to be regarded in the eyes of
b   the gods and of men of understanding? also to be
soothed, and gently and reverently entreated when
angry, even more than a father, and either to be
persuaded, or if not persuaded, to be obeyed? And
when we are punished by her, whether with imprisonment or stripes, the punishment is to be endured in silence; and if she lead us to wounds or
death in battle, thither we follow as is right; neither
may any one yield or retreat or leave his rank, but
whether in battle or in a court of law, or in any
other place, he must do what his city and his country order him; or he must change their view of
what is just: and if he may do no violence to his fa-
c   ther or mother, much less may he do violence to
his country." What answer shall we make to this,
Crito? Do the laws speak truly, or do they not?

Cr.: I think that they do.

Soc.: Then the laws will say: "Consider, Socrates,
if we are speaking truly that in your present attempt you are going to do us an injury. For, having
brought you into the world, and nurtured and edu-
d   cated you, and given you and every other citizen a

share in every good which we had to give, we further proclaim to any Athenian by the liberty which we allow him, that if he does not like us when he has become of age and has seen the ways of the city, and made our acquaintance, he may go where he pleases and take his goods with him. None of us laws will forbid him or interfere with him. Any one who does not like us and the city, and who wants to emigrate to a colony or to any other city, may go where he likes, retaining his property. *The Laws argue that he has made an implied agreement with them which he is not at liberty to break at his pleasure.* e

But he who has experience of the manner in which we order justice and administer the State, and still remains, has entered into an implied contract that he will do as we command him. And he who disobeys us is, as we maintain, thrice wrong; first, because in disobeying us he is disobeying his parents; secondly, because we are the authors of his education; thirdly, because he has made an agreement with us that he will duly obey our commands; and he neither obeys them nor convinces us that our commands are unjust; and we do not rudely impose them, but give him the alternative of obeying or convincing us;—that is what we offer, and he does neither. 52a

"These are the sort of accusations to which, as we were saying, you, Socrates, will be exposed if you accomplish your intentions; you, above all other Athenians." Suppose now I ask, why I rather than anybody else? they will justly retort upon me that I above all other men have acknowledged the agreement. "There is clear proof," they will say, "Socrates, that we and the city were not displeas- b ing to you. Of all Athenians you have been the most constant resident in the city, which, as you never leave, you may be supposed to love. For you never went out of the city either to see the games, except once when you went to the Isthmus,[4] or to any other place unless when you were on military service; nor did you travel as other men do. Nor had you any curiosity to know other States or their

c laws: your affections did not go beyond us and our State; we were your special favourites, and you acquiesced in our government of you; and here in this city you begat your children, which is a proof of your satisfaction. Moreover, you might in the course of the trial, if you had liked, have fixed the penalty at banishment; the State which refuses to let you go now would have let you go then. But you pretended that you preferred death to exile, and that you were not unwilling to die. And now you

d have forgotten these fine sentiments, and pay no respect to us, the laws, of whom you are the destroyer; and are doing what only a miserable slave would do, running away and turning your back upon the compacts and agreements which you made as a citizen. And, first of all, answer this very question: Are we right in saying that you agreed to be governed according to us in deed, and not in word only? Is that true or not?" How shall we answer, Crito? Must we not assent?

Cr.: We cannot help it, Socrates.

Soc.: Then will they not say: *This agreement*
e "You, Socrates, are breaking the *he is now going* covenants and agreements which *to break.* you made with us at your leisure, not in any haste or under any compulsion or deception, but after

you have had seventy years to think of them, during which time you were at liberty to leave the city, if we were not to your mind, or if our covenants appeared to you to be unfair. You had your choice, and might have gone either to Lacedaemon[5] or Crete, both which States are often praised by you for their good government, or to some other Hellenic[6] or foreign State. Whereas you, above all other Athenians, seemed to be so fond of the State, or, in other words, of us, her laws (and who would care about a State which has no laws?), that you never stirred out of her; the halt, the blind, the maimed were not more stationary in her than you were. And now you run away and forsake your agreements. Not so, Socrates, if you will take our advice; do not make yourself ridiculous by escaping out of the city.

53a

"For just consider, if you transgress and err in this sort of way, what good will you do either to yourself or to your friends? That your friends will be driven into *If he does he will injure his friends and will disgrace himself.*

b

exile and deprived of citizenship, or will lose their property, is tolerably certain; and you yourself, if you fly to one of the neighbouring cities, as, for example, Thebes or Megara, both of which are well governed, will come to them as an enemy, Socrates, and their government will be against you, and all patriotic citizens will cast an evil eye upon you as a subverter of the laws, and you will confirm in the minds of the judges the justice of their own condemnation of you. For he who is a corrupter of the laws is more than likely to be a corrupter of the young and foolish portion of mankind. Will

c

you then flee from well-ordered cities and virtuous men? and is existence worth having on these
terms? Or will you go to them without shame, and
talk to them, Socrates? And what will you say to
them? What you say here about virtue and justice
and institutions and laws being the best things
among men? Would that be decent of you? Surely

d   not. But if you go away from well-governed States
to Crito's friends in Thessaly, where there is great
disorder and licence, they will be charmed to hear
the tale of your escape from prison, set off with
ludicrous particulars of the manner in which you
were wrapped in a goatskin or some other disguise,
and metamorphosed as the manner is of runaways;
but will there be no one to remind you that in your
old age you were not ashamed to violate the most
sacred laws from a miserable desire of a little more

e   life? Perhaps not, if you keep them in a good temper; but if they are out of temper you will hear
many degrading things; you will live, but how?—as
the flatterer of all men, and the servant of all men;
and doing what?—eating and drinking in Thessaly,
having gone abroad in order that you may get a dinner. And where will be your fine sentiments about

54a justice and virtue? Say that you wish to live for the
sake of your children—you want to bring them up
and educate them—will you take them into Thessaly and deprive them of Athenian citizenship? Is
this the benefit which you will confer upon them?
Or are you under the impression that they will be
better cared for and educated here if you are still
alive, although absent from them; for your friends
will take care of them? Do you fancy that if you
are an inhabitant of Thessaly they will take care

of them, and if you are an inhabitant of the other world that they will not take care of them? Nay; but if they who call themselves friends are good for anything, they will—to be sure they will.

"Listen, then, Socrates, to us who have brought you up. Think not of life and children first, and of justice afterwards, but of justice *Let him think* first, that you may be justified be- *of justice first,* fore the princes of the world *and of life* below. For neither will you nor any *afterwards.* that belong to you be happier or holier or juster in this life, or happier in another, if you do as Crito bids. Now you depart in innocence, a sufferer and not a doer of evil; a victim, not of the laws but of men. But if you go forth, returning evil for evil; and injury for injury, breaking the covenants and agreements which you have made with us, and wronging those whom you ought least of all to wrong, that is to say, yourself, your friends, your country, and us, we shall be angry with you while you live, and our brethren, the laws in the world below, will receive you as an enemy; for they will know that you have done your best to destroy us. Listen, then, to us and not to Crito."

This, dear Crito, is the voice *The mystic* which I seem to hear murmuring *voice.* in my ears, like the sound of the flute in the ears of the mystic; that voice, I say, is humming in my ears, and prevents me from hearing any other. And I know that anything more which you may say will be vain. Yet speak, if you have anything to say.

Cr.: I have nothing to say, Socrates.

Soc.: Leave me then, Crito, to fulfil the will of God, and to follow whither he leads.

MENO

Persons of the Dialogue
MENO, SOCRATES, A SLAVE OF MENO, ANYTUS

Meno: Can you tell me, Socrates, whether virtue is   70a
acquired by teaching or by practice; or if neither
by teaching nor by practice, then whether it comes
to man by nature, or in what other way?

Socrates: O Meno, there was a time when the
Thessalians[1] were famous among the other Hellenes[2] only for their riches and their riding; but
now, if I am not mistaken, they are equally famous
for their wisdom, especially at   *Meno asks*
Larisa, which is the native city of   *Socrates how*
your friend Aristippus. And this is   *virtue can*
Gorgias' doing;[3] for when he came   *be acquired.*
there, the flower of the Aleuadae,[4] *Before giving*
                                        an answer
among them your admirer Aristip-   *Socrates must*   b
pus, and the other chiefs of the   *enquire "What*
Thessalians, fell in love with his   *is virtue?"*
wisdom. And he has taught you the habit of answering questions in a grand and bold style, which
becomes those who know, and is the style in which   c
he himself answers all comers; and any Hellene
who likes may ask him anything. How different is
our lot! my dear Meno. Here at Athens there is a
dearth of the commodity, and all wisdom seems to
have emigrated from us to you. I am certain that if   71a
you were to ask any Athenian whether virtue was
natural or acquired, he would laugh in your face,
and say: 'Stranger, you have far too good an opinion of me, if you think that I can answer your question. For I literally do not know what virtue is, and
much less whether it is acquired by teaching or
not.' And I myself, Meno, living as I do in this re-   b
gion of poverty, am as poor as the rest of the world;

and I confess with shame that I know literally nothing about virtue; and when I do not know the 'quid' of anything how can I know the 'quale'?[5] How, if I knew nothing at all of Meno, could I tell if he was fair, or the opposite of fair; rich and noble, or the reverse of rich and noble? Do you think that I could?

c *Meno:* No, indeed. But are you in earnest, Socrates, in saying that you do not know what virtue is? And am I to carry back this report of you to Thessaly?

Soc.: Not only that, my dear boy, but you may say further that I have never known of any one else who did, in my judgment.

He does not know, and never met with anyone who did.

Meno: Then you have never met Gorgias when he was at Athens?

Soc.: Yes, I have.

Meno: And did you not think that he knew?

Soc.: I have not a good memory, Meno, and therefore I cannot now tell what I thought of him at the time. And I dare say that he did know, and
d that you know what he said: please, therefore, to remind me of what he said; or, if you would rather, tell me your own view; for I suspect that you and he think much alike.

Meno: Very true.

Soc.: Then as he is not here, never mind him, and do you tell me: By the gods, Meno, be generous, and tell me what you say that virtue is; for I shall be truly delighted to find that I have been mistaken, and that you and Gorgias do really have this knowledge; although I have been just saying that I have never found anybody who had.

Meno: There will be no difficulty, Socrates, in answering your question. Let us take first the virtue of a man—he should know how to administer the state, and in the administration of it to benefit

Meno describes the different kinds of virtue, but is unable to give a common notion of them.

e

his friends and harm his enemies; and he must also be careful not to suffer harm himself. A woman's virtue, if you wish to know about that, may also be easily described: her duty is to order her house, and keep what is indoors, and obey her husband. Every age, every condition of life, young or old, male or female, bond or free, has a different virtue: there are virtues numberless, and no lack of definitions of them; for virtue is relative to the actions and ages of each of us in all that we do. And the same may be said of vice, Socrates.

72a

Soc.: How fortunate I am, Meno! When I ask you for one virtue, you present me with a swarm of them, which are in your keeping. Suppose that I carry on the figure of the swarm, and ask of you, What is the nature of the bee? and you answer that there are many kinds of bees, and I

Meno, not without difficulty and by help of many illustrations, is made to understand the nature of common notions.

b

reply: But do bees differ as bees, because there are many and different kinds of them; or are they not rather to be distinguished by some other quality, as for example beauty, size, or shape? How would you answer me?

Meno: I should answer that bees do not differ from one another, as bees.

Soc.: And if I went on to say: That is what I de-

c

sire to know, Meno; tell me what is the quality in which they do not differ, but are all alike;—would you be able to answer?

Meno: I should.

Soc.: And so of the virtues, however many and different they may be, they have all a common nature which makes them virtues; and on this he who

d would answer the question, 'What is virtue?' would do well to have his eye fixed: Do you understand?

Meno: I am beginning to understand; but I do not as yet take hold of the question as I could wish.

Soc.: When you say, Meno, that there is one virtue of a man, another of a woman, another of a child, and so on, does this apply only to virtue, or

e would you say the same of health, and size, and strength? Or is the nature of health always the same, whether in man or woman?

Meno: I should say that health is the same, both in man and woman.

Soc.: And is not this true of size and strength? If a woman is strong, she will be strong by reason of the same form and of the same strength subsisting in her which there is in the man. I mean to say that strength, as strength, whether of man or woman, is the same. Is there any difference?

Health and strength, and virtue and temperance and justice are the same in both men and women.

Meno: I think not.

73a *Soc.:* And will not virtue, as virtue, be the same, whether in a child or in a grown-up person, in a woman or in a man?

Meno: I cannot help feeling, Socrates, that this case is different from the others.

Soc.: But why? Were you not saying that the virtue of a man was to order a state, and the virtue of a woman was to order a house?

Meno: I did say so.

Soc.: And can either house or state or anything be well ordered without temperance and without justice?

Meno: Certainly not.

Soc.: Then they who order a state or a house   b temperately or justly order them with temperance and justice?

Meno: Certainly.

Soc.: Then both men and women, if they are to be good men and women, must have the same virtues of temperance and justice?

Meno: True.

Soc.: And can either a young man or an elder one be good, if they are intemperate and unjust?

Meno: They cannot.

Soc.: They must be temperate and just?

Meno: Yes.   c

Soc.: Then all men are good in the same way, and by participation in the same virtues?

Meno: Such is the inference.

Soc.: And they surely would not have been good in the same way, unless their virtue had been the same?

Meno: They would not.

Soc.: Then now that the sameness of all virtue has been proven, try and remember what you and Gorgias say that virtue is.

Meno: Will you have one definition of them all?

Soc.: That is what I am seeking.

Then what is virtue? Gorgias and Meno reply, "The power of governing mankind." But this cannot apply to all persons.   d

Meno: If you want to have one definition of them all, I know not what to say, but that virtue is the power of governing mankind.

Soc.: And does this definition of virtue include all virtue? Is virtue the same in a child and in a slave, Meno? Can the child govern his father, or the slave his master; and would he who governed be any longer a slave?

Meno: I think not, Socrates.

Soc.: No, indeed; there would be small reason in that. Yet once more, fair friend; according to you, virtue is 'the power of governing;' but do you not add 'justly and not unjustly'?

Meno: Yes, Socrates; I agree there; for justice is virtue.

e   *Soc.:* Would you say 'virtue,' Meno, or 'a virtue'?

Meno: What do you mean?

Soc.: I mean as I might say about anything; that a round, for example, is 'a figure' and not simply 'figure,' and I should adopt this mode of speaking, because there are other figures.[6]

Meno: Quite right; and that is just what I am saying about virtue—that there are other virtues as well as justice.

74a   *Soc.:* What are they? tell me the names of them, as I would tell you the names of the other figures if you asked me.

Meno: Courage and temperance and wisdom and magnanimity are virtues; and there are many others.

Meno names the virtues but is unable to get at the common notion of them.

Soc.: Yes, Meno; and again we are in the same case: in searching after one virtue we have found many, though not in the same way as before; but we have been unable to find the common virtue which runs through them all.

Meno: Why, Socrates, even now I am not able   b
to follow you in the attempt to get at one common notion of virtue as of other things.

Soc.: No wonder; but I will try to get nearer if I can, for you know that all things have a common notion. Suppose now that some one asked you the question which I asked before: Meno, he would say, what is figure? And if you answered 'roundness,' he would reply to you, in my way of speaking, by asking whether you would say that roundness is 'figure' or 'a figure;' and you would answer 'a figure.'

Meno: Certainly.

Soc.: And for this reason—that there are other   c
figures?

Meno: Yes.

Soc.: And if he proceeded to ask, What other figures are there? you would have told him.

Meno: I should.

Soc.: And if he similarly asked what colour is, and you answered whiteness, and the questioner rejoined, Would you say that whiteness is colour or a colour? you would reply, A colour, because there are other colours as well.

Meno: I should.

Soc.: And if he had said, Tell me what they   d
are?—you would have told him of other colours which are colours just as much as whiteness.

Meno: Yes.

Soc.: And suppose that he were   *He has a similar*
to pursue the matter in my way,   *difficulty about*
he would say: Ever and anon we   *the nature of*
are landed in particulars, but this   *Figure.*

is not what I want; tell me then, since you call them by a common name, and say that they are all figures, even when opposed to one another, what is that common nature which you designate

e as figure—which contains straight as well as round, and is no more one than the other—that would be your mode of speaking?

Meno: Yes.

Soc.: And in speaking thus, you do not mean to say that the round is round any more than straight, or the straight any more straight than round?

Meno: Certainly not.

Soc.: You only assert that the round figure is not more a figure than the straight, or the straight than the round?

Meno: Very true.

Soc.: To what then do we give the name of fig-

75a ure? Try and answer. Suppose that when a person asked you this question either about figure or colour, you were to reply, Man, I do not understand what you want, or know what you are saying; he would look rather astonished and say: Do you not understand that I am looking for the 'simile in multis'?[7] And then he might put the question in another form: Meno, he might say, what is that 'simile in multis' which you call figure, and which includes not only round and straight figures, but all? Could you not answer that question, Meno? I wish that you would try; the attempt will be good practice with a view to the answer about virtue.

b   *Meno:* I would rather that you should answer, Socrates.

Soc.: Shall I indulge you?

Meno: By all means.

Soc.: And then you will tell me about virtue?

Meno: I will.

Soc.: Then I must do my best, for there is a prize to be won.

Meno: Certainly.

Soc.: Well, I will try and explain to you what figure is. What do you say to this answer?—Figure is the only thing which always follows colour. Will you be satisfied with it, as I am sure that I should be,

Figure is defined by Socrates to be that which always follows colour.

c

if you would let me have a similar definition of virtue?

Meno: But, Socrates, it is such a simple answer.

Soc.: Why simple?

Meno: Because, according to you, figure is that which always follows colour.

(*Soc.:* Granted.)

Meno: But if a person were to say that he does not know what colour is, any more than what figure is—what sort of answer would you have given him?

Soc.: I should have told him the truth. And if he were a philosopher of the eristic[8] and antagonistic sort, I should say to him: You have my answer, and if I am wrong, your business is to take up the argument and refute me. But if we were friends, and were talking as you and I are now, I should reply in a milder strain and more in the dialectician's vein;[9] that is to say, I should not only speak the truth, but I should make use of premises which the person interrogated would be willing to admit. And this is the way in which I shall endeavour to approach you. You will acknowledge, will you not, that there is such a thing as an end, or

d

e

termination, or extremity?—all which words I use
in the same sense, although I am aware that Prodicus might draw distinctions about them: but still
you, I am sure, would speak of a thing as ended
or terminated—that is all which I am saying—not
anything very difficult.

Meno: Yes, I should; and I believe that I understand your meaning.

76a   *Soc.:* And you would speak of a surface and also
of a solid, as for example in geometry.

Meno: Yes.

Soc.: Well then, you are now in a condition to
understand my definition of figure. I define figure
to be that in which the solid ends; or, more con-
cisely, the limit of solid.

Meno: And now, Socrates, what is colour?

Soc.: You are outrageous, Meno, in thus plaguing a poor old man to give you an answer, when you
b   will not take the trouble of remembering what is
Gorgias' definition of virtue.

Meno: When you have told me what I ask, I will
tell you, Socrates.

Soc.: A man who was blindfolded has only to
hear you talking, and he would know that you are a
fair creature and have still many lovers.

Meno: Why do you think so?

Soc.: Why, because you always speak in impera-
tives: like all beauties when they are in their prime,
c   you are tyrannical; and also, as I suspect, you have
found out that I have weakness for the fair, and
therefore to humour you I must answer.

Meno: Please do.

Soc.: Would you like me to answer you after the
manner of Gorgias, which is familiar to you?

Meno: I should like nothing better.

Soc.: Do not he and you and Empedocles say that there are certain effluences of existence?[10]

Meno: Certainly.

Soc.: And passages into which and through which the effluences pass?

Meno: Exactly.

Meno, Gorgias, and Empedocles are all agreed that colour is an effluence of existence, proportioned to certain passages.

Soc.: And some of the effluences fit into the   d
passages, and some of them are too small or too large?

Meno: True.

Soc.: And there is such a thing as sight?

Meno: Yes.

Soc.: And now, as Pindar says, 'read my meaning:'—colour is an effluence of form, commensurate with sight, and palpable to sense.

Meno: That, Socrates, appears to me to be an admirable answer.

Soc.: Why, yes, because it happens to be one which you have been in the habit of hearing: and your wit will have discovered, I suspect, that you may explain in the same way the nature of sound   e
and smell, and of many other similar phenomena.

Meno: Quite true.

Soc.: The answer, Meno, was in the orthodox solemn vein, and therefore was more acceptable to you than the other answer about figure.

Meno: Yes.

Soc.: And yet, O son of Alexidemus, I cannot help thinking that the other was the better; and I am sure that you would be of the same opinion, if you would only stay and be initiated, and were not compelled, as you said yesterday, to go away before the mysteries.[11]

77a   *Meno:* But I will stay, Socrates, if you will give me many such answers.

Soc.: Well then, for my own sake as well as for yours, I will do my very best; but I am afraid that I shall not be able to give you very many as good: and now, in your turn, you are to fulfil your promise, and tell me what virtue is in the universal; and do not make a singular into a plural, as the facetious say of those who break a thing, but deliver virtue to me whole

Virtue, according to Meno, is the desire of the honourable and the good. His definition is analyzed by Socrates.

b   and sound, and not broken into a number of pieces: I have given you the pattern.

Meno: Well then, Socrates, virtue, as I take it, is when he, who desires the honourable, is able to provide it for himself; so the poet[12] says, and I say too—

'Virtue is the desire of things honourable and the power of attaining them.'

Soc.: And does he who desires the honourable also desire the good?

Meno: Certainly.

Soc.: Then are there some who desire the evil
c   and others who desire the good? Do not all men, my dear sir, desire good?

Meno: I think not.

Soc.: There are some who desire evil?

Meno: Yes.

Soc.: Do you mean that they think the evils which they desire, to be good; or do they know that they are evil and yet desire them?

Meno: Both, I think.

Soc.: And do you really imagine, Meno, that a man knows evils to be evils and desires them notwithstanding?

Meno: Certainly I do.

Soc.: And desire is of possession?

Meno: Yes, of possession.

Soc.: And does he think that the evils will do good to him who possesses them, or does he know that they will do him harm?

Men desire evil, but not what they think to be evil. d

Meno: There are some who think that the evils will do them good, and others who know that they will do them harm.

Soc.: And, in your opinion, do those who think that they will do them good know that they are evils?

Meno: Certainly not.

Soc.: Is it not obvious that those who are ignorant of their nature do not desire them; but they desire what they suppose to be goods although they are really evils; and if they are mistaken and suppose the evils to be goods they really desire goods?

Meno: Yes, in that case.

Soc.: Well, and do those who, as you say, desire evils, and think that evils are hurtful to the possessor of them, know that they will be hurt by them?

Meno: They must know it.

Soc.: And must they not suppose that those who are hurt are miserable in proportion to the hurt which is inflicted upon them?

78a

Meno: How can it be otherwise?

Soc.: But are not the miserable ill-fated?

Meno: Yes, indeed.

Soc.: And does any one desire to be miserable and ill-fated?

Meno: I should say not, Socrates.

Soc.: But if there is no one who desires to be miserable, there is no one, Meno, who desires evil; for what is misery but the desire and possession of evil?

b   *Meno:* That appears to be the truth, Socrates, and I admit that nobody desires evil.

Soc.: And yet, were you not saying just now that virtue is the desire and power of attaining good?

Meno: Yes, I did say so.

Soc.: But if this be affirmed, then the desire of good is common to all, and one man is no better than another in that respect? *The desire of good is really common to all of them.*

Meno: True.

Soc.: And if one man is not better than another in desiring good, he must be better in the power of attaining it?

Meno: Exactly.

c   *Soc.:* Then, according to your definition, virtue would appear to be the power of attaining good? *Virtue is the power of attaining good with justice.*

Meno: I entirely approve, Socrates, of the manner in which you now view this matter.

Soc.: Then let us see whether what you say is true from another point of view; for very likely you may be right:—You affirm virtue to be the power of attaining goods?

Meno: Yes.

Soc.: And the goods which you mean are such as health and wealth and the possession of gold and silver, and having office and honour in the state—those are what you would call goods?

Meno: Yes, I should include all those.

Soc.: Then, according to Meno, who is the he-   d
reditary friend of the great king, virtue is the power of getting silver and gold; and would you add that they must be gained piously, justly, or do you deem this to be of no consequence? And is any mode of acquisition, even if unjust and dishonest, equally to be deemed virtue?

Meno: Not virtue, Socrates, but vice.

Soc.: Then justice or temperance or holiness, or some other part of virtue, as would appear, must accompany the acquisition, and without them the mere acquisition of good will not be virtue.

Meno: Why, how can there be virtue without these?

Soc.: And the non-acquisition of gold and silver in a dishonest manner for oneself or another, or   e
in other words the want of them, may be equally virtue?

Meno: True.

Soc.: Then the acquisition of such goods is no more virtue than the non-acquisition and want of them, but whatever is accompanied by justice or honesty is virtue, and whatever is devoid of justice is vice.

Meno: It cannot be otherwise, in my judgment.

Soc.: And were we not saying just now that justice, temperance, and the like, were each of them a part of virtue?   *But this definition repeats the thing defined: virtue.*   79a

Meno: Yes.

Soc.: And so, Meno, this is the way in which you mock me.

Meno: Why do you say that, Socrates?

Soc.: Why, because I asked you *The power of* to deliver virtue into my hands *attaining good* whole and unbroken, and I gave *with a part of*
b you a pattern according to which *virtue.*
you were to frame your answer; and you have forgotten already, and tell me that virtue is the power of attaining good justly, or with justice; and justice you acknowledge to be a part of virtue.

Meno: Yes.

Soc.: Then it follows from your own admissions, that virtue is doing what you do with a part of virtue; for justice and the like are said by you to be parts of virtue.

Meno: What of that?

Soc.: What of that! Why, did *But if we do not* not I ask you to tell me the nature *know the nature* of virtue as a whole? And you are *of virtue as a* very far from telling me this; but *whole, how can* declare every action to be virtue *we know what a*
c which is done with a part of virtue; *part of virtue is?*
as though you had told me and I must already know the whole of virtue, and this too when frittered away into little pieces. And, therefore, my dear Meno, I fear that I must begin again and repeat the same question: What is virtue? for otherwise, I can only say, that every action done with a part of virtue is virtue; what else is the meaning of saying that every action done with justice is virtue? Ought I not to ask the question over again; for can any one who does not know virtue know a part of virtue?

Meno: No; I do not say that he can.

Soc.: Do you remember how, in the example   d
of figure, we rejected any answer given in terms
which were as yet unexplained or unadmitted?

Meno: Yes, Socrates; and we were quite right in
doing so.

Soc.: But then, my friend, do not suppose that
we can explain to any one the nature of virtue as a
whole through some unexplained portion of virtue,
or anything at all in that fashion; we should only   e
have to ask over again the old question, What is
virtue? Am I not right?

Meno: I believe that you are.

Soc.: Then begin again, and answer me, What,
according to you and your friend Gorgias, is the
definition of virtue?

Meno: O Socrates, I used to be   *Meno compares*
told, before I knew you, that you   *Socrates to a*
were always doubting yourself and   *torpedo fish*
                                     whose touch has
making others doubt; and now you   *taken away his*   80a
are casting your spells over me,   *sense and speech.*
and I am simply getting bewitched
and enchanted, and am at my wits' end. And if I
may venture to make a jest upon you, you seem to
me both in your appearance and in your power over
others to be very like the flat torpedo fish, who torpifies[13] those who come near him and touch him, as
you have now torpified me, I think. For my soul and   b
my tongue are really torpid, and I do not know how
to answer you; and though I have been delivered of
an infinite variety of speeches about virtue before
now, and to many persons—and very good ones
they were, as I thought—at this moment I cannot
even say what virtue is. And I think that you are very

wise in not voyaging and going away from home, for if you did in other places as you do in Athens, you would be cast into prison as a magician.

Soc.: You are a rogue, Meno, and had all but caught me.

Meno: What do you mean, Socrates?

c   *Soc.:* I can tell why you made a simile about me.

Meno: Why?

Soc.: In order that I might make another simile about you. For I know that all pretty young gentlemen like to have pretty similes made about them—as well they may—but I shall not return the compliment. As to my being a torpedo, if the torpedo is torpid as well as the cause of torpidity in others, then indeed I am a torpedo, but not other-

Socrates is the cause of dullness in others because he believes himself dull.

d   wise; for I perplex others, not because I am clear, but because I am utterly perplexed myself. And now I know not what virtue is, and you seem to be in the same case, although you did once perhaps know before you touched me. However, I have no objection to join with you in the enquiry.

Meno: And how will you enquire, Socrates, into that which you do not know? What will you put forth as the subject of enquiry? And if you find what you want, how will you ever know that this is the thing which you did not know?

e   *Soc.:* I know, Meno, what you mean; but just see what a tiresome dispute you are introducing. You argue that a man cannot enquire either about that which he knows, or about that which he does not

How can you enquire about what you do not know, and if you know, why should you enquire?

know; for if he knows, he has no need to enquire; and if not, he cannot; for he does not know the very subject about which he is to enquire.

Meno: Well, Socrates, and is not the argument sound?   81a

Soc.: I think not.

Meno: Why not?

Soc.: I will tell you why: I have heard from certain wise men and women who spoke of things divine that—

Meno: What did they say?

Soc.: They spoke of a glorious truth, as I conceive.

Meno: What was it? and who were they?

Soc.: Some of them were priests and priestesses, who had studied how they might be able to give a reason of their profession: there have been poets also, who spoke of these things by inspiration, like Pindar, and many others who were inspired. And they say—mark, now, and see whether *The ancient poets tell us that the soul of man is immortal and has a recollection of all that she has ever known in former states of being.*   b

their words are true—they say that the soul of man is immortal, and at one time has an end, which is termed dying, and at another time is born again, but is never destroyed. And the moral is, that a man ought to live always in perfect holiness. *'For in the ninth year Persephone sends the souls of those from whom she has received the penalty of ancient crime back again from beneath into the light of the sun above, and these are they who become noble kings and mighty men and great in wisdom and are called saintly heroes in after ages.'*[14] The soul,   c

          d

then, as being immortal, and having been born again many times, and having seen all things that exist, whether in this world or in the world below, has knowledge of them all; and it is no wonder that she should be able to call to remembrance all that she ever knew about virtue, and about everything; for as all nature is akin, and the soul has learned all things; there is no difficulty in her eliciting or as men say learning, out of a single recollection all the rest, if a man is strenuous and does not faint; for all enquiry and all learning is but recollection.[15] And therefore we ought not to listen to this sophistical argument about the impossibility of enquiry: for it

e   will make us idle; and is sweet only to the sluggard; but the other saying will make us active and inquisitive. In that confiding, I will gladly enquire with you into the nature of virtue.

Meno: Yes, Socrates; but what do you mean by saying that we do not learn, and that what we call learning is only a process of recollection? Can you teach me how this is?

Soc.: I told you, Meno, just now that you were

82a a rogue, and now you ask whether I can teach you, when I am saying that there is no teaching, but only recollection; and thus you imagine that you will involve me in a contradiction.

Meno: Indeed, Socrates, I protest that I had no such intention. I only asked the question from habit; but if you can prove to me that what you say is true, I wish that you would.

Soc.: It will be no easy matter,   *A Greek slave*
b   but I will try to please you to the   *is introduced,*
utmost of my power. Suppose that   *from whom*
you call one of your numerous at-   *certain*

tendants, that I may demonstrate on him.

Meno: Certainly. Come hither, boy.

Soc.: He is Greek, and speaks Greek, does he not?

mathematical conclusions that he has never learned are elicited by Socrates.

Meno: Yes, indeed; he was born in the house.

Soc.: Attend now to the questions which I ask him, and observe whether he learns of me or only remembers.

Meno: I will.

Soc.: Tell me, boy, do you know that a figure like this is a square?

Boy: I do.

Soc.: And you know that a square figure has these four lines equal?

c

Boy: Certainly.

Soc.: And these lines which I have drawn through the middle of the square are also equal?

Boy: Yes.

Soc.: A square may be of any size?

Boy: Certainly.

Soc.: And if one side of the figure be of two feet, and the other side be of two feet, how much will the whole be? Let me explain: if in one direction the space was of two feet, and in the other direction of one foot, the whole would be of two feet taken once?

Boy: Yes.

Soc.: But since this side is also of two feet, there are twice two feet?

Boy: There are.

Soc.: Then the square is of twice two feet?

Boy: Yes.

d   *Soc.*: And how many are twice two feet? count
and tell me.

Boy: Four, Socrates.

Soc.: And might there not be another square
twice as large as this, and having like this the lines
equal?

Boy: Yes.

Soc.: And of how many feet will that be?

Boy: Of eight feet.

Soc.: And now try and tell me the length of the
e line which forms the side of that double square:
this is two feet—what will that be?

Boy: Clearly, Socrates, it will be double.

Soc.: Do you observe, Meno,   *He is partly*
that I am not teaching the boy   *guessing.*
anything, but only asking him questions; and now
he fancies that he knows how long a line is necessary in order to produce a figure of eight square
feet; does he not?

Meno: Yes.

Soc.: And does he really know?

Meno: Certainly not.

Soc.: He only guesses that because the square is
double, the line is double.

Meno: True.

Soc.: Observe him while he recalls the steps in
regular order. (To the Boy:) Tell me, boy, do you
83a assert that a double space comes from a double
line? Remember that I am not speaking of an ob-
long, but of a figure equal every way, and twice the
size of this—that is to say of eight feet; and I want
to know whether you still say that a double square
comes from double line?

Boy: Yes.

Soc.: But does not this line become doubled if we add another such line here?

Boy: Certainly.   b

Soc.: And four such lines will make a space containing eight feet?

Boy: Yes.

Soc.: Let us describe such a figure: Would you not say that this is the figure of eight feet?

Boy: Yes.

Soc.: And are there not these four divisions in the figure, each of which is equal to the figure of four feet?

Boy: True.

Soc.: And is not that four times four?

Boy: Certainly.

Soc.: And four times is not double?

Boy: No, indeed.

Soc.: But how much?

Boy: Four times as much.

Soc.: Therefore the double line, boy, has given a   c
space, not twice, but four times as much.

Boy: True.

Soc.: Four times four are sixteen—are they not?

Boy: Yes.

Soc.: What line would give you a space of eight feet, as this gives one of sixteen feet;—do you see?

Boy: Yes.

Soc.: And the space of four feet is made from this half line?

Boy: Yes.

Soc.: Good; and is not a space of eight feet twice the size of this, and half the size of the other?

Boy: Certainly.

Soc.: Such a space, then, will be made out of a line greater than this one, and less than that one?

d   *Boy:* Yes; I think so.

Soc.: Very good; I like to hear you say what you think. And now tell me, is not this a line of two feet and that of four?

Boy: Yes.

Soc.: Then the line which forms the side of eight feet ought to be more than this line of two feet, and less than the other of four feet? *He has now learned to realize his own ignorance, and therefore will endeavour to remedy it.*

Boy: It ought.

e   *Soc.:* Try and see if you can tell me how much it will be.

Boy: Three feet.

Soc.: Then if we add a half to this line of two, that will be the line of three. Here are two and there is one; and on the other side, here are two also and there is one: and that makes the figure of which you speak?

Boy: Yes.

Soc.: But if there are three feet this way and three feet that way, the whole space will be three times three feet?

Boy: That is evident.

Soc.: And how much are three times three feet?

Boy: Nine.

Soc.: And how much is the double of four?

Boy: Eight.

Soc.: Then the figure of eight is not made out of a line of three?

Boy: No.

Soc.: But from what line?—tell me exactly; and   84a
if you would rather not reckon, try and show me
the line.

Boy: Indeed, Socrates, I do not know.

Soc.: Do you see, Meno, what advances he has
made in his power of recollection? He did not know
at first, and he does not know now, what is the side
of a figure of eight feet: but then he thought that
he knew, and answered confidently as if he knew,   b
and had no difficulty; now he has a difficulty, and
neither knows nor fancies that he knows.

Meno: True.

Soc.: Is he not better off in knowing his
ignorance?[16]

Meno: I think that he is.

Soc.: If we have made him doubt, and given
him the 'torpedo's shock,' have we done him any
harm?

Meno: I think not.

Soc.: We have certainly, as would seem, assisted
him in some degree to the discovery of the truth;   c
and now he will wish to remedy his ignorance, but
then he would have been ready to tell all the world
again and again that the double space should have
a double side.

Meno: True.

Soc.: But do you suppose that he would ever
have enquired into or learned what he fancied that
he knew, though he was really ignorant of it, until
he had fallen into perplexity under the idea that he
did not know, and had desired to know?

Meno: I think not, Socrates.

Soc.: Then he was the better for the torpedo's
touch?

Meno: I think so.

Soc.: Mark now the farther development. I shall only ask him, and not teach him, and he shall *The boy arrives at another true conclusion: which is, that the square of the diagonal is double the square of the side.*

d share the enquiry with me: and do you watch and see if you find me telling or explaining anything to him, instead of eliciting his opinion. Tell me, boy, is not this a square of four feet which I have drawn?

Boy: Yes.

Soc.: And now I add another square equal to the former one?

Boy: Yes.

Soc.: And a third, which is equal to either of them?

Boy: Yes.

Soc.: Suppose that we fill up the vacant corner?

Boy: Very good.

Soc.: Here, then, there are four equal spaces?

e   *Boy:* Yes.

Soc.: And how many times larger is this space than this other?

Boy: Four times.

Soc.: But it ought to have been twice only, as you will remember.

Boy: True.

85a *Soc.:* And does not this line, reaching from corner to corner, bisect each of these spaces?

Boy: Yes.

Soc.: And are there not here four equal lines which contain this space?

Boy: There are.

Soc.: Look and see how much this space is.

Boy: I do not understand.

Soc.: Has not each interior line cut off half of the four spaces?

Boy: Yes.

Soc.: And how many spaces are there in this section?

Boy: Four.

Soc.: And how many in this?

Boy: Two.

Soc.: And four is how many times two?

Boy: Twice.

Soc.: And this space is of how many feet?

Boy: Of eight feet.

Soc.: And from what line do you get this figure?

Boy: From this.

Soc.: That is, from the line which extends from corner to corner of the figure of four feet?

Boy: Yes.

Soc.: And that is the line which the learned call the diagonal. And if this is the proper name, then you, Meno's slave, are prepared to affirm that the double space is the square of the diagonal?

Boy: Certainly, Socrates.

Soc.: What do you say of him, Meno? Were not all these answers given out of his own head?

Meno: Yes, they were all his own.

Soc.: And yet, as we were just now saying, he did not know?

Meno: True.

Soc.: But still he had in him those notions of his—had he not?

Meno: Yes.

Soc.: Then he who does not know may still have true notions of that which he does not know?

Meno: He has.

Soc.: And at present these no-   *At present he is*
tions have just been stirred up in   *in a dream; he*
him, as in a dream; but if he were   *will soon grow*
d   frequently asked the same ques-   *clearer.*
tions, in different forms, he would know as well as
any one at last?

Meno: I dare say.

Soc.: Without any one teaching him he will recover his knowledge for himself, if he is only asked
questions?

Meno: Yes.

Soc.: And this spontaneous recovery of knowledge in him is recollection?

Meno: True.

Soc.: And this knowledge which he now has must
he not either have acquired or always possessed?

Meno: Yes.

Soc.: But if he always possessed   *Either this*
this knowledge he would always   *knowledge was*
have known; or if he has acquired   *acquired by him*
the knowledge he could not have   *in a former state*
acquired it in this life, unless he   *of existence,*
e   has been taught geometry; for he   *known to him.*
may be made to do the same with
all geometry and every other branch of knowledge.
Now, has any one ever taught him all this? You
must know about him, if, as you say, he was born
and bred in your house.

Meno: And I am certain that no one ever did
teach him.

Soc.: And yet he has the knowledge?

Meno: The fact, Socrates, is undeniable.

86a   *Soc.:* But if he did not acquire the knowledge in

this life, then he must have had and learned it at some other time?

Meno: Clearly he must.

Soc.: Which must have been the time when he was not a man?

Meno: Yes.

Soc.: And if there have been always true thoughts in him, both at the time when he was and was not a man, which only need to be awakened into knowledge by putting questions to him, his soul must have always possessed this knowledge, for he always either was or was not a man?

Meno: Obviously.

Soc.: And if the truth of all things always existed in the soul, then the soul is immortal. Wherefore be of good cheer, and try to recollect what you do not know, or rather what you do not remember. b

Meno: I feel, somehow, that I like what you are saying.

Soc.: And I, Meno, like what I am saying. Some things I have said of which I am not altogether confident. But that we shall be better and braver and less helpless if we think that we ought to enquire, *Better to enquire than to fancy that there is no such thing as enquiry and no use in it.* than we should have been if we indulged in the idle fancy that there was no knowing and no use in seeking to know what we do not know;—that is a theme upon which I am ready to fight, in word and deed, to the utmost of my power. c

Meno: There again, Socrates, your words seem to me excellent.

Soc.: Then, as we are agreed that a man should enquire about that which he does not know, shall you and I make an effort to enquire together into the nature of virtue?

Meno: By all means, Socrates. And yet I would much rather return to my original question. Whether in seeking to acquire virtue we should regard it as a thing to be taught, or as a gift of nature, or as coming to men in some other way?

Soc.: Had I the command of you as well as of myself, Meno, I would not have enquired whether virtue is given by instruction or not, until we had first ascertained 'what it is.' But as you think only of controlling me who am your slave, and never of controlling yourself,—such being your notion of freedom, I must yield to you, for you are irresistible. And therefore I have now to enquire into the qualities of a thing of which I do not as yet know the nature. At any rate, will you condescend a little, and allow the question 'Whether virtue is given by instruction, or in any other way,' to be argued upon hypothesis? As the geometrician, when he is asked whether a certain triangle is capable of being inscribed in a certain circle (Or, whether a certain area is capable of being inscribed as a triangle in a certain circle.), will reply: 'I cannot tell you as yet; but I will offer a hypothesis which may assist us in forming a conclusion: If the figure be such that when you have

Socrates cannot enquire whether virtue can be taught until he knows what virtue is, except upon an hypothesis, such as geometricians sometimes employ: e.g., can a triangle of given area be inscribed in a given circle, if when the side of it is produced, this or that consequence follows? [The hypothesis appears to be rather trivial and to have no mathematical value.]

produced a given side of it (Or, when you apply it to the given line, i.e. the diameter of the circle (autou).), the given area of the triangle falls short by an area corresponding to the part produced (Or, similar to the area so applied.), then one consequence follows, and if this is impossible then some other; and therefore I wish to assume a hypothesis before I tell you whether this triangle is capable of being inscribed in the circle':—that is a geometrical hypothesis. And we too, as we know not the nature and qualities of virtue, must ask, whether virtue is or is not taught, under a hypothesis: as thus, if virtue is of such a class of mental goods, will it be taught or not? Let the first hypothesis be that virtue is or is not knowledge,—in that case will it be taught or not? or, as we were just now saying, 'remembered'? For there is no use in disputing about the name. But is virtue taught or not? or rather, does not every one see that knowledge alone is taught?

Meno: I agree.

Soc.: Then if virtue is knowledge, virtue will be taught?

Meno: Certainly.

Soc.: Then now we have made a quick end of this question: if virtue is of such a nature, it will be taught; and if not, not?

Meno: Certainly.

Soc.: The next question is, whether virtue is knowledge or of another species?

Meno: Yes, that appears to be the question which comes next in order.

Soc.: Do we not say that virtue is a good?—This is a hypothesis which is not set aside.

Meno: Certainly.

Soc.: Now, if there be any sort of good which is distinct from knowledge, virtue may be that good; but if knowledge embraces all good, then we shall be right in thinking that virtue is knowledge?

Upon the hypothesis "that virtue is knowledge," can it be taught?

Meno: True.

Soc.: And virtue makes us good?

Meno: Yes.

e

Soc.: And if we are good, then we are profitable; for all good things are profitable?

Meno: Yes.

But is virtue knowledge? Virtue is a good and profitable: and all profitable things are either profitable or the reverse, according as they are or are not under the guidance of knowledge.

Soc.: Then virtue is profitable?

Meno: That is the only inference.

Soc.: Then now let us see what are the things which severally profit us. Health and strength, and beauty and wealth—these, and the like of these, we call profitable?

88a

Meno: True.

Soc.: And yet these things may also sometimes do us harm: would you not think so?

Meno: Yes.

Soc.: And what is the guiding principle which makes them profitable or the reverse? Are they not profitable when they are rightly used, and hurtful when they are not rightly used?

Meno: Certainly.

Soc.: Next, let us consider the goods of the soul: they are temperance, justice, courage, quickness of apprehension, memory, magnanimity, and the like?

Meno: Surely.

Soc.: And such of these as are not knowledge, but of another sort, are sometimes profitable and sometimes hurtful; as, for example, courage wanting prudence, which is only a sort of confidence? When a man has no sense he is harmed by courage, but when he has sense he is profited?

Meno: True.

Soc.: And the same may be said of temperance and quickness of apprehension; whatever things are learned or done with sense are profitable, but when done without sense they are hurtful?

Meno: Very true.

Soc.: And in general, all that the soul attempts or endures, when under the guidance of wisdom, ends in happiness; but when she is under the guidance of folly, in the opposite?

Meno: That appears to be true.

Soc.: If then virtue is a quality of the soul, and is admitted to be profitable, it must be wisdom or prudence, since none of the things *And so all virtue must be a sort of wisdom or knowledge.* of the soul are either profitable or hurtful in themselves, but they are all made profitable or hurtful by the addition of wisdom or of folly; and therefore if virtue is profitable, virtue must be a sort of wisdom or prudence?

Meno: I quite agree.

Soc.: And the other goods, such as wealth and the like, of which we were just now saying that they are sometimes good and sometimes evil, do not they also become profitable or hurtful, accordingly as the soul guides and uses them rightly or wrongly; just as the things of the soul herself are benefited when under the guidance of wisdom and harmed by folly?

Meno: True.

Soc.: And the wise soul guides them rightly, and the foolish soul wrongly.

Meno: Yes.

Soc.: And is not this universally true of human nature? All other things hang upon the soul, and 89a the things of the soul herself hang upon wisdom, if they are to be good; and so wisdom is inferred to be that which profits—and virtue, as we say, is profitable?

Meno: Certainly.

Soc.: And thus we arrive at the conclusion that virtue is either wholly or partly wisdom?

Meno: I think that what you are saying, Socrates, is very true.

Virtue is either wholly or partly wisdom.

Soc.: But if this is true, then the good are not by nature good?

Meno: I think not.

b   *Soc.:* If they had been, there would assuredly have been discerners of characters among us who would have known our future great men; and on their showing

If this is true, virtue must be taught; but then where are the teachers?

we should have adopted them, and when we had got them, we should have kept them in the citadel out of the way of harm, and set a stamp upon them far rather than upon a piece of gold, in order that no one might tamper with them; and when they grew up they would have been useful to the state?

Meno: Yes, Socrates, that would have been the right way.

Soc.: But if the good are not by nature good, are   c
they made good by instruction?

Meno: There appears to be no other alternative,
Socrates. On the supposition that virtue is knowledge; there can be no doubt that virtue is taught.

Soc.: Yes, indeed; but what if the supposition is
erroneous?

Meno: I certainly thought just now that we were
right.

Soc.: Yes, Meno; but a principle which has any
soundness should stand firm not only just now, but
always.

Meno: Well; and why are you so slow of heart to   d
believe that knowledge is virtue?

Soc.: I will try and tell you why, Meno. I do not
retract the assertion that if virtue is knowledge it
may be taught; but I fear that I have some reason
in doubting whether virtue is knowledge: for consider now and say whether virtue, and not only
virtue but anything that is taught, must not have
teachers and disciples?

Meno: Surely.

Soc.: And conversely, may not the art of which   e
neither teachers nor disciples exist be assumed to
be incapable of being taught?

Meno: True; but do you think that there are no
teachers of virtue?

Soc.: I have certainly often en-   *Can Anytus tell*
quired whether there were any,   *us who they*
and taken great pains to find them,   *are?*
and have never succeeded; and many have assisted
me in the search, and they were the persons whom
I thought the most likely to know. Here at the moment when he is wanted we fortunately have sit-

90a ting by us Anytus,[17] the very person of whom we should make enquiry; to him then let us repair. In the first place, he is the son of a wealthy and wise father, Anthemion, who acquired his wealth, not by accident or gift, like Ismenias the Theban (who has recently made himself as rich as Polycrates),[18] but by his own skill and industry, and who is a well-conditioned, modest man, not insolent, or over-bearing, or annoying; moreover, this son of his has

b received a good education, as the Athenian people certainly appear to think, for they choose him to fill the highest offices. And these are the sort of men from whom you are likely to learn whether there are any teachers of virtue, and who they are. Please, Anytus, to help me and your friend Meno in answering our question, Who are the teachers? Consider the matter thus: If we wanted Meno to

c be a good physician, to whom should we send him? Should we not send him to the physicians?

Anytus: Certainly.

Soc.: Or if we wanted him to be a good cobbler, should we not send him to the cobblers?

Anyt.: Yes.

Soc.: And so forth?

Anyt.: Yes.

Soc.: Let me trouble you with one more question. When we say that we should be right in sending

d him to the physicians if we wanted him to be a physician, do we mean that we should be right in sending him to those who profess the art, rather than to those who do not, and to those who demand payment for teaching

The arts are taught by the professors of them. And have we not heard of those who profess to teach virtue at a fixed price?

the art, and profess to teach it to any one who will come and learn? And if these were our reasons, should we not be right in sending him?

Anyt.: Yes.

Soc.: And might not the same be said of flute-playing, and of the other arts? Would a man who wanted to make another a flute-player refuse to   e
send him to those who profess to teach the art for money, and be plaguing other persons to give him instruction, who are not professed teachers and who never had a single disciple in that branch of knowledge which he wishes him to acquire— would not such conduct be the height of folly?

Anyt.: Yes, by Zeus, and of ignorance too.

Soc.: Very good. And now you are in a position to advise with me about my friend Meno. He has   91a
been telling me, Anytus, that he desires to attain that kind of wisdom and virtue by which men order the state or the house, and honour their parents, and know when to receive and when to send away citizens and strangers, as a good man should. Now,   b
to whom should he go in order that he may learn this virtue? Does not the previous argument imply clearly that we should send him to those who profess and avouch that they are the common teachers of all Hellas, and are ready to impart instruction to any one who likes, at a fixed price?

Anyt.: Whom do you mean, Socrates?

Soc.: You surely know, do you not, Anytus, that these are the people whom mankind call Sophists?

Anyt.: By Heracles,[19] Socrates, forbear! I only hope that no friend or kinsman or acquaintance of mine, whether citizen or stranger, *Anytus inveighs against the corrupting influence of the Sophists.*   c will ever be so mad as to allow himself to be corrupted by them; for they are a manifest pest and corrupting influence to those who have to do with them.

Soc.: What, Anytus? Of all the people who profess that they know how to do men good, do you mean to say that these are the only ones who not only do them no good, but positively corrupt those who are entrusted to them, and in return for this disservice have the face to demand money? Indeed, I

Why surely they cannot really be corrupters? See what fortunes they make, and what an excellent reputation many of them bear!

cannot believe you; for I know of a single man, Protagoras, who made more out of his craft than the illustrious Pheidias,[20] who created such noble works, or any ten other statuaries. How could that be? A mender of old shoes, or patcher up of clothes, who made the shoes or clothes worse than he received them, could not have remained thirty days undetected, and would very soon have starved; whereas during more than forty years, Protagoras was corrupting all Hellas, and sending his disciples from him worse than he received them, and he was never found out. For, if I am not mistaken, he was about seventy years old at his death, forty of which were spent in the practice of his profession; and during all that time he had a good reputation, which to this day he retains: and not only Protagoras, but many others are well spoken of; some who lived before him, and others who are still living. Now, when you say that they deceived and corrupted the youth, are they to be supposed to have corrupted them consciously or unconsciously? Can those who were deemed by many to be the wisest men of Hellas have been out of their minds?

Anyt.: Out of their minds! No, Socrates; the young men who gave their money to them were out of their minds, and their relations and guardians who entrusted their youth to the care of these men were still more out of their minds, and most of all, the cities who allowed them to come in, and did not drive them out, citizen and stranger alike.

The wisest men in Hellas could not have been out of their minds. No: the people who gave their money to them were out of their minds.

b

Soc.: Has any of the Sophists wronged you, Anytus? What makes you so angry with them?

Anyt.: No, indeed, neither I nor any of my belongings has ever had, nor would I suffer them to have, anything to do with them.

Soc.: Then you are entirely unacquainted with them?

Anyt.: And I have no wish to be acquainted.

Soc.: Then, my dear friend, how can you know whether a thing is good or bad of which you are wholly ignorant?

How can Anytus know that they are bad, if he does not know them at all?

c

Anyt.: Quite well; I am sure that I know what manner of men these are, whether I am acquainted with them or not.

Soc.: You must be a diviner,[21] Anytus, for I really cannot make out, judging from your own words, how, if you are not acquainted with them, you know about them. But I am not enquiring of you who are the teachers who will corrupt Meno (let them be, if you

Then who will teach Meno?

d

please, the Sophists); I only ask you to tell him who there is in this great city who will teach him how to become eminent in the virtues which I was just now describing. He is the friend of your family, and you will oblige him.

Anyt.: Why do you not tell him yourself?

Soc.: I have told him whom I supposed to be the teachers of these things; but I learn from you that

e   I am utterly at fault, and I dare say that you are right. And now I wish that you, on your part, would tell me to whom among the Athenians he should go. Whom would you name?

Anyt.: Why single out individu- *Any Athenian* als? Any Athenian gentleman,   *gentleman who* taken at random, if he will mind   *has learned* him, will do far more good to him   *of a previous* than the Sophists.   *generation of*   *gentlemen.*

Soc.: And did those gentle-men grow of themselves; and without having been taught by any one, were they nevertheless able to teach others that which they had never learned

93a   themselves?

Anyt.: I imagine that they learned of the previous generation of gentlemen. Have there not been many good men in this city?

Soc.: Yes, certainly, Anytus; and many good statesmen also there always have been and there are still, in the city of Athens. But the question is whether they were also good teachers of their own virtue;—not whether there are, or have been, good men in this part of the world, but whether

b   virtue can be taught, is the question which we have been discussing. Now, do we mean to say that the good men of our own and of other times knew how to impart to others that virtue which they had themselves; or is virtue a thing incapable of being communicated or imparted by one man to another? That is the question which I and Meno have been arguing. Look at the matter in your own way: Would you not admit that Themistocles was a good man? c

Anyt.: Certainly; no man better.

Soc.: And must not he then have been a good teacher, if any man ever was a good teacher, of his own virtue?

Anyt.: Yes certainly,—if he wanted to be so.

Soc.: But would he not have wanted? He would, at any rate, have desired to make his own son *Good men may not have been good teachers. There never was a better man than Themistocles; but he did not make much of his own son.* a good man and a gentleman; he could not have been jealous of him, or have intentionally abstained from imparting to him his own virtue. Did you never hear that he made his son Cleophantus d a famous horseman; and had him taught to stand upright on horseback and hurl a javelin, and to do many other marvellous things; and in anything which could be learned from a master he was well trained? Have you not heard from our elders of him?

Anyt.: I have.

Soc.: Then no one could say that his son showed any want of capacity?

Anyt.: Very likely not. e

Soc.: But did any one, old or young, ever say in your hearing that Cleophantus, son of Themistocles, was a wise or good man, as his father was?

Anyt.: I have certainly never heard any one say so.

Soc.: And if virtue could have been taught, would his father Themistocles have sought to train him in these minor accomplishments, and allowed him who, as you must remember, was his own son, to be no better than his neighbours in those qualities in which he himself excelled?

He had him taught accomplishments because there was no one to teach virtue.

Anyt.: Indeed, indeed, I think not.

Soc.: Here was a teacher of virtue whom you admit to be among the best men of the past. Let us take another,—Aristides, the son of Lysimachus: would you not acknowledge that he was a good man?

Anyt.: To be sure I should.

Soc.: And did not he train his son Lysimachus better than any other Athenian in all that could be done for him by the help of masters? But what has been the result? Is he a bit better than any other mortal? He is an acquaintance of yours, and you see what he is like. There is Pericles, again, magnificent in his wisdom; and he, as you are aware, had two sons, Paralus and Xanthippus.

Aristides was also a good man, and Pericles and Thucydides: they made their sons good horsemen, and wrestlers, and the like, but they did not have them taught to be good, because virtue cannot be taught.

Anyt.: I know.

Soc.: And you know, also, that he taught them to be unrivalled horsemen, and had them trained in music and gymnastics and all sorts of arts—in these respects they were on a level with the best—and

Meno: I cannot tell you, Socrates; like the rest of the world, I am in doubt, and sometimes I think that they are teachers and sometimes not.

Soc.: And are you aware that not you only and other politicians have doubts whether virtue can be taught or not, but that Theognis[23] the poet says the very same thing?   d

Meno: Where does he say so?

Soc.: In these elegiac verses:—

'Eat and drink and sit with the mighty, and make yourself agreeable to them; for from the good you will learn what is good, but if you mix with the bad you will lose the intelligence which you already have.'

Theognis implies in one passage that virtue can, and in another that it cannot, be taught.   e

Do you observe that here he seems to imply that virtue can be taught?

Meno: Clearly.

Soc.: But in some other verses he shifts about and says:—

'If understanding could be created and put into a man, then they' (who were able to perform this feat) 'would have obtained great rewards.'

And again:—

'Never would a bad son have sprung from a good sire, for he would have heard the voice of instruction; but not by teaching will you ever make a bad man into a good one.'   96a

And this, as you may remark, is a contradiction of the other.

Meno: Clearly.

Soc.: And is there anything else of which the professors are affirmed not only not to be teach- b ers of others, but to be ignorant themselves, and bad at the knowledge of that which they are professing to teach? or is there anything about which even the acknowledged 'gentle- *How can they* men' are sometimes saying that *be teachers* 'this thing can be taught,' and *if they are so* sometimes the opposite? Can you *inconsistent with* say that they are teachers in any *themselves?* true sense whose ideas are in such confusion?

Meno: I should say, certainly not.

Soc.: But if neither the Sophists nor the gentlemen are teachers, clearly there can be no other teachers?

Meno: No.

c   *Soc.:* And if there are no teachers, neither are there disciples?

Meno: Agreed.

Soc.: And we have admitted *If there are no* that a thing cannot be taught of *teachers and* which there are neither teachers *no scholars,* nor disciples? *virtue cannot be taught.*

Meno: We have.

Soc.: And there are no teachers of virtue to be found anywhere?

Meno: There are not.

Soc.: And if there are no teachers, neither are there scholars?

Meno: That, I think, is true.

Soc.: Then virtue cannot be taught?

Meno: Not if we are right in our view. But I can-   d
not believe, Socrates, that there are no good men:
And if there are, how did they come into
existence?

Soc.: I am afraid, Meno, that   *But were we*
you and I are not good for much,   *not mistaken in*
and that Gorgias has been as poor   *our view? There*
an educator of you as Prodicus   *may be another*
has been of me. Certainly we shall   *guide to good*
have to look to ourselves, and try   *action as well as*
    knowledge.
to find some one who will help in
some way or other to improve us. This I say, be-   e
cause I observe that in the previous discussion
none of us remarked that right and good action is
possible to man under other guidance than that of
knowledge (ἐπιστήμη);—and indeed if this be denied, there is no seeing how there can be any good
men at all.

Meno: How do you mean, Socrates?

Soc.: I mean that good men are necessarily use-   97a
ful or profitable. Were we not right in admitting
this? It must be so.

Meno: Yes.

Soc.: And in supposing that they will be useful
only if they are true guides to us of action—there
we were also right?

Meno: Yes.

Soc.: But when we said that a man cannot be a
good guide unless he have knowledge (φρόνησις),
this we were wrong.[24]

Meno: What do you mean by the word 'right'?

Soc.: I will explain. If a man knew the way to
Larisa, or anywhere else, and went to the place and

led others thither, would he not be a right and good guide?

Meno: Certainly.

b   *Soc.:* And a person who had a right opinion about the way, but had never been and did not know, might be a good guide also, might he not?

Meno: Certainly.

Soc.: And while he has true opinion about that which the other knows, he will be just as good a guide if he thinks the truth, as he who knows the truth?

Meno: Exactly.

Soc.: Then true opinion is as good a guide to correct action as knowledge; and that was the point *Right opinion is as good a guide to action as knowledge.*

c   which we omitted in our specu-lation about the nature of virtue, when we said that knowledge only is the guide of right action; whereas there is also right opinion.

Meno: True.

Soc.: Then right opinion is not less useful than knowledge?

Meno: The difference, Socrates, is only that he who has knowledge will always be right; but he who has right opinion will sometimes be right, and sometimes not.

Soc.: What do you mean? Can he be wrong who has right opinion, so long as he has right opinion?

Meno: I admit the cogency of your argument,

d   and therefore, Socrates, I wonder that knowledge should be preferred to right opinion—or why they should ever differ.

Soc.: And shall I explain this wonder to you?

Meno: Do tell me.

Soc.: You would not wonder if you had ever observed the images of Daedalus; but perhaps you have not got them in your country?

Meno: What have they to do with the question?

Soc.: Because they require to be fastened in order to keep them, and if they are not fastened they will play truant and run away.

Meno: Well, what of that?   e

Soc.: I mean to say that they *But right* are not very valuable possessions *opinions are apt* if they are at liberty, for they will *to walk away,* walk off like runaway slaves; but *like the images* when fastened, they are of great *of Daedalus.* value, for they are really beautiful works of art. Now this is an illustration of the nature of true opinions: while they abide with us they are beautiful and fruitful, but they run away out of the human soul, and do not remain long, and there-   98a fore they are not of much value until they are fastened by the tie of the cause; and this fastening of them, friend Meno, is recollection, as you and I have agreed to call it. But when they are bound, in the first place, they have the nature of knowledge; and, in the second place, they are abiding. And this is why knowledge is more honourable and excellent than true opinion, because fastened by a chain.

Meno: What you are saying, Socrates, seems to be very like the truth.

Soc.: I too speak rather in ignorance; I only con-   b jecture. And yet that knowledge differs from true opinion is no matter of conjecture with me. There are not many things which I profess to know, but this is most certainly one of them.

Meno: Yes, Socrates; and you are quite right in saying so.

Soc.: And am I not also right in saying that true opinion leading the way perfects action quite as well as knowledge?

Meno: There again, Socrates, I think you are right.

c   *Soc.:* Then right opinion is not a whit inferior to knowledge, or less useful in action; nor is the man who has right opinion inferior to him who has knowledge?

Meno: True.

Soc.: And surely the good man has been acknowledged by us to be useful?

Meno: Yes.

Soc.: Seeing then that men become good and useful to states, not only because they have knowledge, but because they have right opinion, and that neither knowledge nor right opinion is given to man by nature or acquired by him— (do you imagine either of them to be given by nature?

Meno: Not I.)

Soc.: Then if they are not given by nature, neither are the good by nature good?

Meno: Certainly not.

Soc.: And nature being excluded, then came the question whether virtue is acquired by teaching?

Meno: Yes.

Soc.: If virtue was wisdom (or knowledge), then, as we thought, it was taught?

Meno: Yes.

Soc.: And if it was taught it was wisdom?

Meno: Certainly.

Soc.: And if there were teachers, it might be   e
taught; and if there were no teachers, not?

Meno: True.

Soc.: But surely we acknowledged that there
were no teachers of virtue?

Meno: Yes.

Soc.: Then we acknowledged that it was not
taught, and was not wisdom?

Meno: Certainly.

Soc.: And yet we admitted that it was a good?

Meno: Yes.

Soc.: And the right guide is useful and good?

Meno: Certainly.

Soc.: And the only right guides   *If virtue and*   99a
are knowledge and true opinion—   *knowledge*
these are the guides of man; for   *cannot be*
things which happen by chance   *taught, the only*
are not under the guidance of   *right guides of*
man: but the guides of man are   *men are true*
true opinion and knowledge.   *opinions.*

Meno: I think so too.

Soc.: But if virtue is not taught, neither is virtue
knowledge.

Meno: Clearly not.

Soc.: Then of two good and useful things, one,   b
which is knowledge, has been set aside, and cannot
be supposed to be our guide in political life.

Meno: I think not.

Soc.: And therefore not by any wisdom, and
not because they were wise, did Themistocles and
those others of whom Anytus spoke govern states.
This was the reason why they were unable to make
others like themselves—because their virtue was
not grounded on knowledge.

Meno: That is probably true, Socrates.

Soc.: But if not by knowledge, the only alternative which remains is that statesmen must have guided states by right opinion, which is in politics what divination is in religion; for diviners and also prophets say many things truly, but they know not what they say.

c

Right opinion is in politics what divination is in religion; diviners, prophets, poets, statesmen, may all be called truly "divine" men.

Meno: So I believe.

Soc.: And may we not, Meno, truly call those men 'divine' who, having no understanding, yet succeed in many a grand deed and word?

Meno: Certainly.

Soc.: Then we shall also be right in calling divine those whom we were just now speaking of as diviners and prophets, including the whole tribe of poets. Yes, and statesmen above all may be said to be divine and illumined, being inspired and possessed of God, in which condition they say many grand things, not knowing what they say.

d

Meno: Yes.

Soc.: And the women too, Meno, call good men divine—do they not? and the Spartans, when they praise a good man, say 'that he is a divine man.'

Meno: And I think, Socrates, that they are right; although very likely our friend Anytus may take offence at the word.

e

Soc.: I do not care; as for Anytus, there will be another opportunity of talking with him. To sum up our enquiry—the result seems to be, if we are at all right in our view, that virtue is neither natural nor acquired, but an instinct given by God to the virtuous. Nor is the instinct accompanied by rea-

100a

son, unless there may be supposed to be among statesmen some one who is capable of educating statesmen. And if there be such an one, he may be said to be among the living what Homer says that Tiresias[25] was among the dead, 'he alone has understanding; but the rest are flitting shades'; and he and his virtue in like manner will be a reality among shadows.

Meno: That is excellent, Socrates.   b

Soc.: Then, Meno, the conclu-   *Virtue comes by* sion is that virtue comes to the vir-   *the gift of God.* tuous by the gift of God. But we shall never know the certain truth until, before asking how virtue is given, we enquire into the actual nature of virtue. I fear that I must go away, but do you, now that you are persuaded yourself, persuade our friend Anytus. And do not let him be so exasperated; if you can conciliate him, you will have done good service   c to the Athenian people.

Echecrates.: Were you yourself, Phaedo, in the prison with Socrates on the day when he drank the poison?   57a

Phaedo.: Yes, Echecrates, I was.

Ech.: I should so like to hear about his death. What did he say in his last hours? We were informed that he died by taking poison, but no one knew anything more; for no Phliasian[1] ever goes to Athens now, and it is a long time since any stranger   b
from Athens has found his way hither; so that we had no clear account.

Phaed.: Did you not hear of the proceedings at   58a
the trial?

Ech.: Yes; some one told us about the trial, and we could not understand why, having been condemned, he should have been put to death, not at the time, but long afterwards. What was the reason of this?

Phaed.: An accident, Echecrates: the stern of the ship which the Athenians sent to Delos happened to have been crowned on the day before he was tried.   *The death of Socrates was deferred by the holy season of the mission to Delos.*

Ech.: What is this ship?

Phaed.: It is the ship in which, according to Athenian tradition, Theseus went to Crete when   b
he took with him the fourteen youths, and was the saviour of them and of himself. And they are said to have vowed to Apollo at the time, that if they were saved they would send a yearly mission to Delos. Now this custom still continues, and the whole period of the voyage to and from Delos, beginning when the priest of Apollo crowns the stern

of the ship, is a holy season, during which the city
is not allowed to be polluted by public executions;
c and when the vessel is detained by contrary winds,
the time spent in going and returning is very considerable. As I was saying, the ship was crowned
on the day before the trial, and this was the reason
why Socrates lay in prison and was not put to death
until long after he was condemned.

Ech.: What was the manner of his death, Phaedo? What was said or done? And which of his
friends were with him? Or did the authorities forbid them to be present—so that he had no friends
near him when he died?

d *Phaed.:* No; there were several of them with him.

Ech.: If you have nothing to do,   *Phaedo is*
I wish that you would tell me what   *requested by*
passed, as exactly as you can.   *Echecrates to*
    give an account
Phaed.: I have nothing at all   *of the death of*
to do, and will try to gratify your   *Socrates.*
wish. To be reminded of Socrates
is always the greatest delight to me, whether I
speak myself or hear another speak of him.

Ech.: You will have listeners who are of the same
mind with you, and I hope that you will be as exact
as you can.

e *Phaed.:* I had a singular feel-   *He describes*
ing at being in his company. For   *his noble*
I could hardly believe that I was   *and fearless*
present at the death of a friend,   *demeanour.*
and therefore I did not pity him, Echecrates; he
died so fearlessly, and his words and bearing were
so noble and gracious, that to me he appeared
59a blessed. I thought that in going to the other world
he could not be without a divine call, and that he

had he no wish to make good men of them? Nay, he must have wished it. But virtue, as I suspect, could not be taught. And that you may not suppose the incompetent teachers to be only the meaner sort of Athenians and few in number; remember c again that Thucydides[22] had two sons, Melesias and Stephanus, whom, besides giving them a good education in other things, he trained in wrestling, and they were the best wrestlers in Athens: one of them he committed to the care of Xanthias, and the other of Eudorus, who had the reputation of being the most celebrated wrestlers of that day. Do you remember them?

Anyt.: I have heard of them.

Soc.: Now, can there be a doubt that Thucyd- d ides, whose children were taught things for which he had to spend money, would have taught them to be good men, which would have cost him noth- ing, if virtue could have been taught? Will you reply that he was a mean man, and had not many friends among the Athenians and allies? Nay, but he was of a great family, and a man of influence at Athens and in all Hellas, and, if virtue could have been taught, he would have found out some Athe- nian or foreigner who would have made good men of his sons, if he could not himself spare the time from cares of state. Once more, I suspect, friend e Anytus, that virtue is not a thing which can be taught?

Anyt.: Socrates, I think that you *Anytus gives an* are too ready to speak evil of men: *angry warning* and, if you will take my advice, *to Socrates.* I would recommend you to be careful. Perhaps there is no city in which it is not easier to do men 95a harm than to do them good, and this is certainly the case at Athens, as I believe that you know.

Soc.: O Meno, think that Anytus is in a rage. And he may well be in a rage, for he thinks, in the first place, that I am defaming these gentlemen; and in the second place, he is of opinion that he is one of them himself. But some day he will know what is the meaning of defamation, and if he ever does, he will forgive me. Meanwhile I will return to you, Meno; for I suppose that there are gentle-men in your region too?

Meno: Certainly there are.

Soc.: And are they willing to teach the young? and do they profess to be teachers? and do they agree that virtue is taught?

Meno: No indeed, Socrates, they are anything but agreed; you may hear them saying at one time that virtue can be taught, and then again the reverse.

The Thessalian gentry are not agreed about the possibility of teaching virtue.

Soc.: Can we call those teachers who do not acknowledge the possibility of their own vocation?

Meno: I think not, Socrates.

Soc.: And what do you think of these Sophists, who are the only professors? Do they seem to you to be teachers of virtue?

Meno: I often wonder, Socrates, that Gorgias is never heard promising to teach virtue: and when he hears others promising he only laughs at them; but thinks that men should be taught to speak.

Gorgias professes to teach rhetoric but laughs at those who pretend to teach virtue.

Soc.: Then do you not think that the Sophists are teachers?

would be happy, if any man ever was, when he arrived there; and therefore I did not pity him as
might have seemed natural at such an hour. But I
had not the pleasure which I usually feel in philosophical discourse (for philosophy was the theme
of which we spoke). I was pleased, but in the pleasure there was also a strange admixture of pain; for
I reflected that he was soon to die, and this double feeling was shared by us all; we were laughing and weeping by turns, especially the excitable   b
Apollodorus—you know the sort of man?

Ech.: Yes.

Phaed.: He was quite beside himself; and I and
all of us were greatly moved.

Ech.: Who were present?

Phaed.: Of native Athenians   *The Socratic*
there were, besides Apollodorus,   *circle:—the*
Critobulus and his father Crito,   *absence of Plato*
Hermogenes,   Epigenes,   Ae-   *is noted.*
schines, Antisthenes; likewise Ctesippus of the
deme² of Paeania, Menexenus, and some others;
Plato, if I am not mistaken, was ill.

Ech.: Were there any strangers?

Phaed.: Yes, there were; Simmias the Theban,   c
and Cebes, and Phaedondes; Euclid and Terpsion,
who came from Megara.

Ech.: And was Aristippus there, and Cleombrotus?

Phaed.: No, they were said to be in Aegina.

Ech.: Any one else?

Phaed.: I think that these were nearly all.

Ech.: Well, and what did you talk about?

Phaed.: I will begin at the be-   *The meeting at*
ginning, and endeavour to repeat   *the prison.*   d
the entire conversation. On the previous days we

had been in the habit of assembling early in the morning at the court in which the trial took place, and which is not far from the prison. There we used to wait talking with one another until the opening of the doors (for they were not opened very early); then we went in and generally passed the day with Socrates. On the last morning we assembled sooner than usual, having heard on the day before when we quitted the prison in the evening that the sacred

e ship had come from Delos; and so we arranged to meet very early at the accustomed place. On our arrival the jailer who answered the door, instead of admitting us, came out and told us to stay until he called us. "For the Eleven,"[3] he said, "are now with Socrates; they

The friends are denied admission while the Eleven are with Socrates.

are taking off his chains, and giving orders that he is to die to-day." He soon returned and said that we

60a might come in. On entering we found Socrates just released from chains, and Xanthippe,[4] whom you know, sitting by him, and holding his child in her arms. When she saw us she uttered a cry and said, as women will: "O Socrates, this is the last time that either you will converse with your friends, or they with you." Socrates turned to Crito and said: "Crito, let some one take her home." Some of Crito's people accordingly led her away, crying out and beating herself. And when she was gone, Socrates, sitting

b up on the couch, bent and rubbed his leg, saying, as he was rubbing: How singular is the thing called pleasure, and how curiously related to pain, which might be thought to be the opposite of it; for

Socrates whose chains have now been taken off, is led by the feeling of relief to remark on the curious manner

they are never present to a man at *in which*
the same instant, and yet he who *pleasure and*
pursues either is generally com- *pain are always*
pelled to take the other; their bod- *conjoined.*
ies are two, but they are joined by a single head.
And I cannot help thinking that if Aesop had re-   c
membered them, he would have made a fable
about God trying to reconcile their strife, and how,
when he could not, he fastened their heads together; and this is the reason why when one comes
the other follows: as I know by my own experience
now, when after the pain in my leg which was
caused by the chain pleasure appears to succeed.

Upon this Cebes said: I am glad, Socrates, that
you have mentioned the name of Aesop. For it re-   d
minds me of a question which has been asked by
many, and was asked of me only the day before yesterday by Evenus the poet—he will be sure to ask it
again, and therefore if you would like me to have an
answer ready for him, you may as well tell me what I
should say to him:—he wanted to know why you,
who never before wrote a line of poetry, now that you
are in prison are turning Aesop's fables into verse,
and also composing that hymn in honour of Apollo.

Tell him, Cebes, he replied, *Having been*
what is the truth—that I had no *told in a dream*
idea of rivalling him or his poems; *that he should*
to do so, as I knew, would be no *compose music,*
easy task. But I wanted to see *in order to*
whether I could purge away a *satisfy a scruple*
scruple which I felt about the *about the*
meaning of certain dreams. In the *meaning of the*
course of my life I have often had *dream he has*
intimations in dreams "that I *been writing*
verses while he
was in prison.

should compose music." The same dream came to me sometimes in one form, and sometimes in another, but always saying the same or nearly the same words: "Cultivate and make music," said the dream. And hitherto I had imagined that this was only intended to exhort and encourage me in the study of philosophy, which has been the pursuit of my life, and is the noblest and best of music.[5] The dream was bidding me do what I was already doing, in the same way that the competitor in a race is bidden by the spectators to run when he is already running. But I was not certain of this; for the dream might have meant music in the popular sense of the word, and being under sentence of death, and the festival giving me a respite, I thought that it would be safer for me to satisfy the scruple, and, in obedience to the dream, to compose a few verses before I departed. And first I made a hymn in honour of the god of the festival, and then considering that a poet, if he is really to be a poet, should not only put together words, but should invent stories, and that I have no invention, I took some fables of Aesop, which I had ready at hand and which I knew—they were the first I came upon—and turned them into verse. Tell this to Evenus, Cebes, and bid him be of good cheer; say that I would have him come after me if he be a wise man, and not tarry; and that to-day I am likely to be going, for the Athenians say that I must.

61a

b

Evenus the poet had been curious about the meaning of this behaviour of his, and Socrates gives him the explanation of it, bidding him be of good cheer, and come after him. "But he will not come."

c

Simmias said: What a message for such a man! having been a frequent companion of his I should say that, as far as I know him, he will never take your advice unless he is obliged.

Why, said Socrates,—is not Evenus a philosopher?

I think that he is, said Simmias.

Then he, or any man who has the spirit of philosophy, will be willing to die; but he will not take his own life, for that is held to be unlawful.

Here he changed his position, and put his legs off the couch on to the ground, and during the rest of the conversation he remained sitting.

Why do you say, enquired Cebes, that a man ought not to take his own life, but that the philosopher will be ready to follow the dying?

Socrates replied: And have you, Cebes and Simmias, who are the disciples of Philolaus,[6] never heard him speak of this?

Socrates replies that a philosopher like Evenus should be ready to die, though he must not take his own life.

Yes, but his language was obscure, Socrates.

My words, too, are only an echo; but there is no reason why I should not repeat what I have heard: and, indeed, as I am going to another place, it is very meet for me to be thinking and talking of the nature of the pilgrimage which I am about to make. What can I do better in the interval between this and the setting of the sun?

Then tell me, Socrates, why is suicide held to be unlawful? as I have certainly heard Philolaus, about whom you were just now asking, affirm when he was staying with us at Thebes; and there are

others who say the same, although I have never understood what was meant by any of them.

62a   Do not lose heart, replied   *This incidental*
Socrates, and the day may come   *remark leads to*
when you will understand. I sup-   *a discussion on*
pose that you wonder why, when   *suicide.*
other things which are evil may be good at certain
times and to certain persons, death is to be the only
exception, and why, when a man is better dead, he
is not permitted to be his own benefactor, but must
wait for the hand of another.

Very true, said Cebes, laughing gently and
speaking in his native Boeotian.[7]

b   I admit the appearance of in-   *Man is a*
consistency in what I am saying;   *prisoner who*
but there may not be any real   *has no right*
inconsistency after all. There is a   *to run away;*
doctrine whispered in secret that   *and he is also*
man is a prisoner who has no right   *a possession of*
to open the door and run away;   *the gods and*
this is a great mystery which I do   *must not rob his*
not quite understand. Yet I too believe that the   *masters.*
gods are our guardians, and that we men are a possession of theirs. Do you not agree?

Yes, I quite agree, said Cebes.

c   And if one of your own possessions, an ox or an
ass, for example, took the liberty of putting himself
out of the way when you had given no intimation
of your wish that he should die, would you not be
angry with him, and would you not punish him if
you could?

Certainly, replied Cebes.

Then, if we look at the matter thus, there may
be reason in saying that a man should wait, and not

take his own life until God summons him, as he is now summoning me.

Yes, Socrates, said Cebes, there *And why should* d
seems to be truth in what you say. *he wish to leave*
And yet how can you reconcile this *the best of*
seemingly true belief that God *services?*
is our guardian and we his possessions, with the willingness to die which you were just now attributing to the philosopher? That the wisest of men should be willing to leave a service in which they are ruled by the gods, who are the best of rulers, is not reasonable; for surely no wise man thinks that when set at liberty he can take better care of himself than the gods take of him. A fool may perhaps think so—he may argue that he had better run away from his master, not considering that his e duty is to remain to the end, and not to run away from the good, and that there would be no sense in his running away. The wise man will want to be ever with him who is better than himself. Now this, Socrates, is the reverse of what was just now said; for upon this view the wise man should sorrow and the fool rejoice at passing out of life.

The earnestness of Cebes seemed to please 63a
Socrates. Here, said he, turning to us, is a man who is always inquiring, and is not so easily convinced by the first thing which he hears.

And certainly, added Simmias, *You yourself,*
the objection which he is now *Socrates, are*
making does appear to me to have *too ready to run*
some force. For what can be the *away.*
meaning of a truly wise man wanting to fly away and lightly leave a master who is better than himself? And I rather imagine that Cebes is referring

to you; he thinks that you are too ready to leave
us, and too ready to leave the gods whom you acknowledge to be our good masters.

b   Yes, replied Socrates; there is reason in what
you say. And so you think that I ought to answer
your indictment as if I were in a court?

We should like you to do so, said Simmias.

Then I must try to make a more successful defence before you than I did before the judges. For
I am quite ready to admit, Sim-   *Socrates replies*
mias and Cebes, that I ought to   *that he is going*
be grieved at death, if I were not   *to other gods*
persuaded in the first place that I   *who are wise*
am going to other gods who are   *and good.*
wise and good (of which I am as certain as I can be
c   of any such matters), and secondly (though I am
not so sure of this last) to men departed, better
than those whom I leave behind; and therefore I
do not grieve as I might have done, for I have good
hope that there is yet something remaining for the
dead, and as has been said of old, some far better
thing for the good than for the evil.

But do you mean to take away your thoughts
d   with you, Socrates? said Simmias. Will you not impart them to us?—for they are a benefit in which
we too are entitled to share. Moreover, if you succeed in convincing us, that will be an answer to the
charge against yourself.

I will do my best, replied Socrates. But you must
first let me hear what Crito wants; he has long been
wishing to say something to me.

Only this, Socrates, replied Crito:—the attendant who is to give you the poison has been telling me, and he wants me to tell you, that you are

PHAEDO

Persons of the Dialogue

PHAEDO, *who is the narrator of the Dialogue to*
Echecrates of Phlius,
SOCRATES, ATTENDANT OF THE PRISON, APOLLODORUS,
SIMMIAS, CEBES, CRITO

Scene
THE PRISON OF SOCRATES

Place of the Narration
PHLIUS

not to talk much; talking, he says, increases heat, **e**
and this is apt to interfere with the action of the
poison; persons who excite themselves are sometimes obliged to take a second or even a third
dose.

Then, said Socrates, let him mind his business
and be prepared to give the poison twice or even
thrice if necessary; that is all.

I knew quite well what you would say, replied
Crito; but I was obliged to satisfy him.

Never mind him, he said.

And now, O my judges, I desire *The true*
to prove to you that the real phi- *philosopher is*
losopher has reason to be of good *always dying:—*
cheer when he is about to die, and *why then should*
he avoid the
that after death he may hope to *death which he* **64a**
obtain the greatest good in the *desires?*
other world. And how this may be,
Simmias and Cebes, I will endeavour to explain.
For I deem that the true votary of philosophy is
likely to be misunderstood by other men; they do
not perceive that he is always pursuing death and
dying; and if this be so, and he has had the desire
of death all his life long, why when his time comes
should he repine at that which he had been always
pursuing and desiring?

Simmias said laughingly: Though *"How the world* **b**
not in a laughing humour, you *will laugh when*
have made me laugh, Socrates; for *they hear this!"*
I cannot help thinking that the many when they
hear your words will say how truly you have described philosophers, and our people at home will
likewise say that the life which philosophers desire
is in reality death, and that they have found them

out to be deserving of the death which they desire.

And they are right, Simmias, in thinking so, with the exception of the words "they have found them out"; for they have not found out either what is the nature of that death which the true philosopher deserves, or how he deserves or *Yes, they do not understand the nature of death, or why the philosopher desires or deserves it.*

c desires death. But enough of them:—let us discuss the matter among ourselves. Do we believe that there is such a thing as death?

To be sure, replied Simmias.

Is it not the separation of soul and body? And to be dead is the completion of this; when the soul exists in herself, and is released from the body and the body is released from the soul, what is this but death?

Just so, he replied.

d There is another question, which will probably throw light on our present inquiry if you and I can agree about it:—Ought the philosopher to care about the pleasures—if they are to be called pleasures—of *Life is best when the soul is most freed from the concerns of the body, and is alone and by herself.*

eating and drinking?

Certainly not, answered Simmias.

And what about the pleasures of love—should he care for them?

By no means.

And will he think much of the other ways of indulging the body, for example, the acquisition of costly raiment, or sandals, or other adornments of the body? Instead of caring about them, does he not rather despise anything more than nature needs? What do you say? e

I should say that the true philosopher would despise them.

Would you not say that he is entirely concerned with the soul and not with the body? He would like, as far as he can, to get away from the body and to turn to the soul.

Quite true.

In matters of this sort philosophers, above all other men, may be observed in every sort of way to 65a dissever the soul from the communion of the body.

Very true.

Whereas, Simmias, the rest of the world are of opinion that to him who has no sense of pleasure and no part in bodily pleasure, life is not worth having; and that he who is indifferent about them is as good as dead.

That is also true.

What again shall we say of the actual acquirement of knowledge?—is the body, if invited to b share in the enquiry, a hinderer or a helper? I mean to say, have sight and hear- *The senses are* ing any truth in them? Are they *untrustworthy* not, as the poets are always telling *guides: they* us, inaccurate witnesses? and yet, *mislead the soul* if even they are inaccurate and in- *in the search for* distinct, what is to be said of the *truth.* other senses?—for you will allow that they are the best of them?

Certainly, he replied.

Then when does the soul attain truth?—for in attempting to consider anything in company with the body she is obviously deceived.

c   True.

Then must not true existence be revealed to her in thought, if at all?

Yes.

And thought is best when the mind is gathered into herself and none of these things trouble her—neither sounds nor sights nor pain nor any pleasure,—when she takes leave of the body, and has as little as possible to do with it, when she has no bodily sense or desire, but is aspiring after true being?

Certainly.

d   And in this the philosopher dishonours the body; his soul runs away from his body and desires to be alone and by herself?

And therefore the philosopher runs away from the body.

That is true.

Well, but there is another thing, Simmias: Is there or is there not an absolute justice?

Assuredly there is.

And an absolute beauty and absolute good?

Of course.

But did you ever behold any of them with your eyes?

Certainly not.

Or did you ever reach them with any other bodily sense?—and I speak not of these alone, but

Another argument. The absolute truth of justice, beauty, and other ideas is not perceived by the senses, which only introduce a disturbing element.

e   of absolute greatness, and health, and strength, and of the essence or true nature of everything. Has the reality of them ever been perceived by you through the bodily organs? or rather, is not the nearest approach to the knowledge of their several natures made by him who so orders his intellectual vision as to have the most exact conception of the essence of each thing which he considers?

Certainly.

And he attains to the purest knowledge of them who goes to each with the mind alone,[8] not introducing or intruding in the act of thought, sight or any other sense together with reason, but with the very light of the mind in her own clearness searches into the very truth of each; he who has got rid, as far as he can, of eyes and ears and, so to speak, of the whole body, these being in his opinion distracting elements which when they infect the soul hinder her from acquiring truth and knowledge— who, if not he, is likely to attain to the knowledge of true being?

66a

What you say has a wonderful truth in it, Socrates, replied Simmias.

And when real philosophers consider all these things, will they not be led to make a reflection which they will express in words something like the following? "Have we not found," they will say, "a path of thought which seems to bring us and our argument to the conclusion, that while we are in the body, and while the soul is infected with the evils of the body, our desire will not be satisfied, and our desire is of the truth? For the body is a source of endless trouble to us by reason of the mere requirement of food; and is liable also to diseases which overtake and impede us in the search after true being: it fills us full of loves, and lusts, and fears, and fancies of all kinds, and endless foolery, and in fact, as men say, takes away

The soul in herself must perceive things in themselves.

b

c

from us the power of thinking at all. Whence come wars, and fightings, and factions? whence but from
d the body and the lusts of the body? Wars are occasioned by the love of money, and money has to be acquired for the sake and service of the body; and by reason of all these impediments we have no time to give to philosophy; and, last and worst of all, even if we are at leisure and betake ourselves to some speculation, the body is always breaking in upon us, causing turmoil and confusion in our enquiries, and so amazing us that we are prevented from seeing the truth. It has been proved to us by experience that if we would have pure knowledge of anything we must be quit of the body—the soul
e in herself must behold things in themselves: and then we shall attain the wisdom which we desire, and of which we say that we are lovers; not while we live, but after death; for if while in company with the body, the soul cannot have pure knowledge, one of two things follows—either knowledge
67a is not to be attained at all, or, if at all, after death. For then, and not till then, the soul will be parted from the body and exist in herself alone. In this present life, I reckon that we make the nearest approach to knowledge when we have the least possible intercourse or communion with the body, and are not surfeited with the bodily nature, but keep ourselves pure until the hour when God himself is pleased to release us. And thus having got rid of the foolishness of the body we shall be pure and hold
b converse with the pure, and know of ourselves the clear light everywhere, which is no other than the light of truth." For the impure are not permitted to approach the pure. These are the sort of words,

Simmias, which the true lovers of knowledge cannot help saying to one another, and thinking. You
would agree; would you not?

Undoubtedly, Socrates.

But, O my friend, if this be true, there is great
reason to hope that, going whither I go, when I
have come to the end of my journey, I shall attain
that which has been the pursuit of my life. And   c
therefore I go on my way rejoicing, and not I only,
but every other man who believes that his mind
has been made ready and that he is in a manner
purified.

Certainly, replied Simmias.

And what is purification but the separation of
the soul from the body, as I was   *Purification is*
saying before; the habit of the soul   *the separation*
gathering and collecting herself   *of the soul from*
into herself from all sides out of   *the body.*
the body; the dwelling in her own place alone, as in
another life, so also in this, as far as she can;—the
release of the soul from the chains of the body?   d

Very true, he said.

And this separation and release of the soul from
the body is termed death?

To be sure, he said.

And the true philosophers, and they only, are
ever seeking to release the soul. Is not the separation and release of the soul from the body their
especial study?

That is true.

And, as I was saying at first, there would be a
ridiculous contradiction in men studying to live as   e
nearly as they can in a state of death, and yet repining when it comes upon them.

Clearly.

And the true philosophers, Simmias, are always occupied in the practice of dying, wherefore also to them least of all men is death terrible. Look at the matter thus:—if they have been in every way the enemies of the body, and are wanting to be alone with the soul, when this desire of theirs is granted, how inconsistent would they be if they trembled and repined, instead of rejoicing at their

68a departure to that place where, when they arrive, they hope to gain that which in life they desired— and this was wisdom—and at the same time to be rid of the company of their enemy. Many a man has been willing to go to the world below animated by the hope of seeing there an earthly love, or wife, or son, and conversing with them. And will he who is a true lover of wisdom, and is strongly

b persuaded in like manner that only in the world below he can *And therefore the true philosopher who has been always trying to disengage himself from the body will rejoice in death.* worthily enjoy her, still repine at death? Will he not depart with joy? Surely he will, O my friend, if he be a true philosopher. For he will have a firm conviction that there, and there only, he can find wisdom in her purity. And if this be true, he would be very absurd, as I was saying, if he were afraid of death.

He would, indeed, replied Simmias.

And when you see a man who is repining at the approach of death, is not his reluctance a sufficient

c proof that he is not a lover of wisdom, but a lover of the body, and probably at the same time a lover of either money or power, or both?

Quite so, he replied.

And is not courage, Simmias, a quality which is specially characteristic of the philosopher?

Certainly.

There is temperance again, which even by the vulgar is supposed to consist in the control and regulation of the passions, and in the sense of superiority to them—is not temperance of virtue belonging to those only who despise the body, and who pass their lives in philosophy?

He alone possesses the true secret of virtue, which in ordinary men is merely based on a calculation of lesser and greater evils.

Most assuredly.   d

For the courage and temperance of other men, if you will consider them, are really a contradiction.

How so?

Well, he said, you are aware that death is regarded by men in general as a great evil.

Very true, he said.

And do not courageous men face death because they are afraid of yet greater evils?

That is quite true.

Then all but the philosophers are courageous only from fear, and because they are afraid; and yet that a man should be courageous from fear, and because he is a coward, is surely a strange thing.

Ordinary men are courageous only from cowardice; temperate from intemperance.

Very true.   e

And are not the temperate exactly in the same case? They are temperate because they are intemperate—which might seem to be a contradiction, but is nevertheless the sort of thing which

happens with this foolish temperance. For there are pleasures which they are afraid of losing; and in their desire to keep them, they abstain from some
69a pleasures, because they are overcome by others; and although to be conquered by pleasure is called by men intemperance, to them the conquest of pleasure consists in being conquered by pleasure. And that is what I mean by saying that, in a sense, they are made temperate through intemperance.

Such appears to be the case.

Yet the exchange of one fear or *True virtue is* pleasure or pain for another fear *inseparable* or pleasure or pain, and of the *from wisdom.* greater for the less, as if they were coins, is not the exchange of virtue. O my blessed Simmias, is there not one true coin for which all things ought to be
b exchanged?—and that is wisdom; and only in exchange for this, and in company with this, is anything truly bought or sold, whether courage or temperance or justice. And is not all true virtue the companion of wisdom, no matter what fears or pleasures or other similar goods or evils may or may not attend her? But the virtue which is made up of these goods, when they are severed from wisdom and exchanged with one another, is a shadow
c of virtue only, nor is there any freedom or health or truth in her; but in the true exchange there is a purging away of all these things, and temperance, and justice, and courage, and wisdom herself are the purgation of them. The founders of the mysteries[9] would appear to have had a real meaning, and were not talking nonsense when they intimated in a figure long ago that he who passes unsanctified and uninitiated into the world below will

lie in a slough, but that he who arrives there after
initiation and purification will dwell with the gods.
For "many," as they say in the mysteries, "are the
thyrsus-bearers,[10] but few are the   *The thyrsus-*
mystics,"—meaning, as I interpret   *bearers and the*
the words, "the true philoso-   *mystics.*   d
phers." In the number of whom, during my whole
life, I have been seeking, according to my ability, to
find a place;—whether I have sought in a right way
or not, and whether I have succeeded or not, I
shall truly know in a little while, if God will, when
I myself arrive in the other world—such is my belief. And therefore I maintain that I am right, Simmias and Cebes, in not grieving or repining at
parting from you and my masters in this world, for
I believe that I shall find equally good masters and   e
friends in another world. But most men do not believe this saying; if then I succeed in convincing
you by my defence better than I did the Athenian
judges, it will be well.

Cebes answered: I agree, Socrates,   *Fears are*
in the greater part of what you say.   *entertained lest*   70a
But in what concerns the soul,   *the soul when*
men are apt to be incredulous;   *she dies should*
they fear that when she has left   *be scattered to*
the body her place may be no-   *the winds.*
where, and that on the very day of death she may
perish and come to an end—immediately on her
release from the body, issuing forth dispersed like
smoke or air and in her flight vanishing away into
nothingness. If she could only be collected into
herself after she has obtained release from the
evils of which you were speaking, there would be
good reason to hope, Socrates, that what you say   b

is true. But surely it requires a great deal of argument and many proofs to show that when the man is dead his soul yet exists, and has any force or intelligence.

True, Cebes, said Socrates; and shall I suggest that we converse a little of the probabilities of these things?

I am sure, said Cebes, that I should greatly like to know your opinion about them.

c
I reckon, said Socrates, that no one who heard me now, not even if he were one of my old enemies, *The discussion suited to the occasion.* the comic poets,[11] could accuse me of idle talking about matters in which I have no concern:—If you please, then, we will proceed with the enquiry.

Suppose we consider the question whether the souls of men after death are or are not in the world below.[12] There comes into my mind an ancient doctrine which affirms that they go from hence into the other world, and returning hither, are born again from the dead. Now, if it be true that the living come from the dead, then our souls must exist in the other world, for if not, how could

d they have been born again? And this would be conclusive, if there were any real evidence that the living are only born from the dead; but if this is not so, then other arguments will have to be adduced.

Very true, replied Cebes.

Then let us consider the whole question, not in relation to man only, but in relation to animals gen-

e erally, and to plants, and to everything of which there is generation, and the proof will be easier. Are not all things which have opposites generated out of

their opposites? I mean such things as good and evil,
just and unjust—and there are in-   *All things which*
numerable other opposites which   *have opposites*
are generated out of opposites.   *are generated*
And I want to show that in all op-   *out of opposites.*
posites there is of necessity a similar alternation; I
mean to say, for example, that anything which becomes greater must become greater after being less.

True.

And that which becomes less must have been   71a
once greater and then have become less.

Yes.

And the weaker is generated from the stronger,
and the swifter from the slower.

Very true.

And the worse is from the better, and the more
just is from the more unjust.

Of course.

And is this true of all opposites? and are we
convinced that all of them are generated out of
opposites?

Yes.

And in this universal opposition of all things, are
there not also two intermediate processes which
are ever going on, from one to the other opposite,   b
and back again; where there is a   *And there are*
greater and a less there is also an   *intermediate*
intermediate process of increase   *processes or*
and diminution, and that which   *passages into and*
grows is said to wax, and that   *out of one another,*
which decays to wane?   *such as increase*
                                      and diminution,
Yes, he said.   *division and*
And there are many other   *composition, and*
processes, such as division and   *the like.*

composition, cooling and heating, which equally involve a passage into and out of one another. And this necessarily holds of all opposites, even though not always expressed in words—they are really generated out of one another, and there is a passing or process from one to the other of them?

Very true, he replied.

c　Well, and is there not an opposite of life, as sleep is the opposite of waking?

True, he said.

And what is it?

Death, he answered.

And these, if they are opposites, are generated the one from the other, and have their two intermediate processes also?

Of course.

Now, said Socrates, I will analyze one of the two pairs of opposites which I have mentioned to you, and also its intermediate processes, and you shall analyze the other to me. One of them I term sleep, the other waking. The state of sleep is opposed to the state of waking, and out of sleeping waking is generated, and out of waking, sleeping; and

d　the process of generation is in the one case falling asleep, and in the other waking up. Do you agree?

I entirely agree.

Then suppose that you analyze life and death to me in the same manner. Is not death opposed to life?

Yes.

And they are generated one from the other?

Yes.

Life is opposed to death, as waking is to sleeping, and in like manner they are generated from one another.

What is generated from the living?

The dead.

And what from the dead?

I can only say in answer—the living.

Then the living, whether things or persons, Cebes, are generated from the dead?

That is clear, he replied.   e

Then the inference is that our souls exist in the world below?

That is true.

And one of the two processes or generations is visible—for surely the act of dying is visible?

Surely, he said.

What then is to be the result? Shall we exclude the opposite process? and shall we suppose nature to walk on one leg only? Must we not rather assign to death some corresponding process of generation?

Certainly, he replied.

And what is that process?

Return to life.

And return to life, if there be such a thing, is the birth of the dead into the world of the living?   72a

Quite true.

Then here is a new way by which we arrive at the conclusion that the living come from the dead, just as the dead come from the living; and this, if true, affords a most certain proof that the souls of the dead exist in some place out of which they come again.

Yes, Socrates, he said; the conclusion seems to flow necessarily out of our previous admissions.

And that these admissions were not unfair, Cebes, he said, may be shown, I think, as follows: b

If generation were in a straight line only, and there
were no compensation or circle in   *If there were no*
nature, no turn or return of ele-   *compensation*
ments into their opposites, then   *or return in*
you know that all things would at   *nature, all*
                                      things would
last have the same form and pass   *pass into the*
into the same state, and there   *state of death.*
would be no more generation of
them.

What do you mean? he said.

A simple thing enough, which I will illustrate by
c   the case of sleep, he replied. You know that if there
were no alternation of sleeping and waking, the
tale of the sleeping Endymion[13] would in the end
have no meaning, because all   *The sleeping*
other things would be asleep too,   *Endymion*
and he would not be distinguish-   *would be*
able from the rest. Or if there   *unmeaning*
                                      in a world of
were composition only, and no di-   *sleepers.*
vision of substances, then the
chaos of Anaxagoras[14] would come again. And in
like manner, my dear Cebes, if all things which
partook of life were to die, and after they were
dead remained in the form of death, and did not
come to life again, all would at last die, and nothing
would be alive—what other result could there be?
d   For if the living spring from any other things, and
they too die, must not all things at last be swal-
lowed up in death?

There is no escape, Socrates, said Cebes; and
to me your argument seems to be absolutely true.

Yes, he said, Cebes, it is and must be so, in my
opinion; and we have not been deluded in making
these admissions; but I am confident that there

truly is such a thing as living again, and that the living spring from the dead, and that the souls of the dead are in existence, and that the good souls have a better portion than the evil.

Cebes added: Your favourite doctrine, Socrates, that knowledge is simply recollection, if true, also necessarily implies a previous time in which we have learned *The doctrine of recollection implies a previous existence.* e

that which we now recollect. But this would be impossible unless our soul had been in some place before existing in the form of man; here then is another proof of the soul's immortality. 73a

But tell me, Cebes, said Simmias, interposing, what arguments are urged in favour of this doctrine of recollection.[15] I am not very sure at the moment that I remember them.

One excellent proof, said Cebes, is afforded by questions. If you put a question to a person in a right way, he will give a true answer of himself, but how could he *You put a question to a person, and he answers out of his own mind.*

do this unless there were knowledge and right reason already in him? And this is most clearly shown b
when he is taken to a diagram[16] or to anything of that sort.

But if, said Socrates, you are still incredulous, Simmias, I would ask you whether you may not agree with me when you look at the matter in another way;—I mean, if you are still incredulous as to whether knowledge is recollection?

Incredulous I am not, said Simmias; but I want to have this doctrine of recollection brought to my own recollection, and, from what Cebes has said, I am beginning to recollect and be convinced: but I should still like to hear what you were going to say.

c   This is what I would say, he replied:—We should agree, if I am not mistaken, that what a man recollects he must have known at some previous time.

Very true.

And what is the nature of this knowledge or recollection? I mean to ask, Whether a person who, having seen or heard or in any way perceived anything, knows not only that, but has a conception of something else which is *A person may recollect what he has never seen together with what he has seen. How is this?* the subject, not of the same but of some other kind

d   of knowledge, may not be fairly said to recollect that of which he has the conception?

What do you mean?

I mean what I may illustrate by the following instance:—The knowledge of a lyre is not the same as the knowledge of a man?

True.

And yet what is the feeling of lovers when they recognize a lyre, or a garment, or anything else which the beloved has been in the habit of using? Do not they, from knowing the lyre, form in the mind's eye an image of the youth to whom the lyre belongs? And this is recollection. In like manner any one who sees Simmias may remember Cebes; and there are endless examples of the same thing. *Recollection is the knowledge of some person or thing derived from some other person or thing which may be either like or unlike them.*

Endless, indeed, replied Simmias.

And recollection is most commonly a process of   e
recovering that which has been already forgotten
through time and inattention.

Very true, he said.

Well; and may you not also from seeing the
picture of a horse or a lyre remember a man? and
from the picture of Simmias, you may be led to
remember Cebes?

True.

Or you may also be led to the recollection of
Simmias himself?

Quite so.   74a

And in all these cases, the recollection may be
derived from things either like or unlike?

It may be.

And when the recollection is derived from like
things, then another consideration is sure to arise,
which is—whether the likeness in any degree falls
short or not of that which is recollected?

Very true, he said.

And shall we proceed a step   *The imperfect*
further, and affirm that there is   *equality of*
such a thing as equality, not of   *pieces of*
one piece of wood or stone with   *wood or stone*
another, but that, over and above   *suggests the*
this, there is absolute equality?   *perfect idea of*
Shall we say so?   *equality.*

Say so, yes, replied Simmias, and swear to it,   b
with all the confidence in life.

And do we know the nature of this absolute
essence?

To be sure, he said.

And whence did we obtain our knowledge? Did
we not see equalities of material things, such as

pieces of wood and stones, and gather from them the idea of an equality which is different from them? For you will acknowledge that there is a difference. Or look at the matter in another way:—Do not the same pieces of wood or stone appear at one time equal, and at another time unequal?

That is certain.

c   But are real equals ever unequal? or is the idea of equality the same as of inequality?

Impossible, Socrates.

Then these (so-called) equals are not the same with the idea of equality?

I should say, clearly not, Socrates.

And yet from these equals, although differing from the idea of equality, you conceived and attained that idea?

Very true, he said.

Which might be like, or might be unlike them?

Yes.

d   But that makes no difference: whenever from seeing one thing you conceived another, whether like or unlike, there must surely have been an act of recollection?

Very true.

But what would you say of equal portions of wood and stone, or other material equals? and what is the impression produced by them? Are they equals in the same sense in which absolute equality is equal? or do they fall short of this perfect equality in a measure?

Yes, he said, in a very great measure too.

And must we not allow, that *But if the*
e   when I or any one, looking at any   *material equals*

object, observes that the thing which he sees aims at being some other thing, but falls short of, and cannot be, that other thing, but is inferior, he who makes this observation must have had a previous knowledge of that to which the other, although similar, was inferior? *when compared to the ideal equality fall short of it, the ideal equality with which they are compared must be prior to them, though only known through the medium of them.*

Certainly.

And has not this been our own case in the matter of equals and of absolute equality?

Precisely.

Then we must have known equality previously   75a
to the time when we first saw the material equals, and reflected that all these apparent equals strive to attain absolute equality, but fall short of it?

Very true.

And we recognize also that this absolute equality has only been known, and can only be known, through the medium of sight or touch, or of some other of the senses, which are all alike in this respect?

Yes, Socrates, as far as the argument is concerned, one of them is the same as the other.

From the senses then is derived the knowledge   b
that all sensible things aim at an absolute equality of which they fall short?

Yes.

Then before we began to see or hear or perceive in any way, we must have had a knowledge of absolute equality, or we could not have referred to that standard the equals which are derived from the senses?—for to that they all aspire, and of that they fall short.

No other inference can be drawn from the previous statements.

And did we not see and hear and have the use of our other senses as soon as we were born?

Certainly.

c   Then we must have acquired the knowledge of equality at some previous time?

Yes.

That is to say, before we were born, I suppose?

True.

And if we acquired this knowledge before we were born, and were born having the use of it, then we also knew before we were born and at the instant of birth not only the equal or the greater or the less, but all other ideas; for we are not speaking only of equality, but of beauty, goodness, justice, holiness, and of

d   all which we stamp with the name of essence in the dialectical process,[17] both when we ask and when we answer questions. Of all this we may certainly affirm that we acquired the knowledge before birth?

We may.

But if, after having acquired, we have not forgotten what in each case we acquired, then we must always have come into life having knowledge, and shall always continue to know as long as life lasts—for knowing is the acquiring and retaining knowledge and not forgetting. Is not forgetting, Simmias, just the losing of knowledge?

e   Quite true, Socrates.

That higher sense of equality must have been known to us before we were born, was forgotten at birth, and was recovered by the use of the senses.

But if the knowledge which we acquired before birth was lost by us at birth, and if afterwards by the use of the senses we recovered what we previously knew, will not the process which we call learning be a recovering of the knowledge which is natural to us, and may not this be rightly termed recollection?

What is called learning therefore is only a recollection of ideas which we possessed in a previous state.

Very true.

So much is clear—that when we perceive some-   76a
thing, either by the help of sight, or hearing, or some other sense, from that perception we are able to obtain a notion of some other thing like or unlike which is associated with it but has been forgotten. Whence, as I was saying, one of two alternatives follows:—either we had this knowledge at birth, and continued to know through life; or, after birth, those who are said to learn only remember, and learning is simply recollection.

Yes, that is quite true, Socrates.

And which alternative, Simmias, do you prefer? Had we the knowledge at our birth, or did we rec-   b
ollect the things which we knew previously to our birth?

I cannot decide at the moment.

At any rate you can decide whether he who has knowledge will or will not be able to render an account of his knowledge? What do you say?

Certainly, he will.

But do you think that every man is able to give an account of these very matters about which we are speaking?

Would that they could, Socrates, but I rather

fear that to-morrow, at this time, there will no longer be any one alive who is able to give an account of them such as ought to be given.

c   Then you are not of opinion, Simmias, that all men know these things?

Certainly not.

They are in process of recollecting that which they learned before?

Certainly.

But when did our souls acquire this knowledge?—not since we were born as men?

Certainly not.

And therefore, previously?

Yes.

Then, Simmias, our souls must also have existed without bodies before they were *But if so, our* in the form of man, and must have *souls must have* had intelligence. *existed before*

Unless indeed you suppose, *they were in the* Socrates, that these notions are *form of man; or* given us at the very moment of *if not the souls,* birth; for this is the only time *then not the* which remains. *ideas.*

d   Yes, my friend, but if so, when do we lose them? for they are not in us when we are born—that is admitted. Do we lose them at the moment of receiving them, or, if not, at what other time?

No, Socrates, I perceive that I was unconsciously talking nonsense.

Then may we not say, Simmias, that if, as we are always repeating, there is an absolute beauty, and goodness, and an absolute essence of all things; and if

e   to this, which is now discovered to have existed in our former state, we refer all our sensations, and with this

compare them, finding these ideas to be pre-existent
and our inborn possession—then our souls must
have had a prior existence, but, if not, there would be
no force in the argument? There is the same proof
that these ideas must have existed before we were
born, as that our souls existed before we were born;
and if not the ideas, then not the souls.

Yes, Socrates; I am convinced that there is precisely the same necessity for the one as for the
other; and the argument retreats successfully to   77a
the position that the existence of the soul before
birth cannot be separated from the existence of the
essence of which you speak. For there is nothing
which to my mind is so patent as that beauty, goodness, and the other notions of which you were just
now speaking, have a most real and absolute existence; and I am satisfied with the proof.

Well, but is Cebes equally satisfied? for I must
convince him too.

I think, said Simmias, that Cebes is satisfied: although he is the most incredulous of mortals, yet I
believe that he is sufficiently convinced of the exis-   b
tence of the soul before birth. But *Simmias and*
that after death the soul will con-   *Cebes are agreed*
tinue to exist is not yet proven even   *in thinking that*
to my own satisfaction. I cannot get   *the previous*
rid of the feeling of the many to   *existence of*
which Cebes was referring—the   *the soul is*
feeling that when the man dies the   *sufficiently*
soul will be dispersed, and that this   *proved, but*
may be the extinction of her. For   *not the future*
                                          existence.
admitting that she may have been born elsewhere,
and framed out of other elements, and was in existence before entering the human body, why after

having entered in and gone out again may she not herself be destroyed and come to an end?

c   Very true, Simmias, said Cebes; about half of what was required has been proven; to wit, that our souls existed before we were born:—that the soul will exist after death as well as before birth is the other half of which the proof is still wanting, and has to be supplied; when that is given the demonstration will be complete.

But that proof, Simmias and Cebes, has been already given, said Socrates, if you put the two arguments together—I mean this and the former one, in which we admitted that everything living is born of the dead. For if the soul exists before birth, and in coming to life and being *But if the soul*
d   born can be born only from death *passes from* and dying, must she not after *death to birth,* death continue to exist, since she *she must exist* has to be born again?—Surely the *well as before* proof which you desire has been *birth.* already furnished. Still I suspect that you and Simmias would be glad to probe the argument further. Like children, you are haunted with a fear that when the soul leaves the body, the wind may really blow her away and scatter her; especially if a man should happen to die in a great storm and not when the sky is calm.

Cebes answered with a smile: Then, Socrates, you must argue us out of our fears—and yet, strictly speaking, they are not our *The fear that the* fears, but there is a child within us *soul will vanish* to whom death is a sort of hobgob- *into air must be* lin: him too we must persuade not *charmed away.* to be afraid when he is alone in the dark.

Socrates said: Let the voice of the charmer be applied daily until you have charmed away the fear.

And where shall we find a good charmer of our 78a
fears, Socrates, when you are gone?

Hellas,[18] he replied, is a large place, Cebes, and has many good men, and there are barbarous races not a few: seek for him among them all, far and wide, sparing neither pains nor money; for there is no better way of spending your money. And you must seek among yourselves too; for you will not find others better able to make the search.

The search, replied Cebes, shall certainly be made. And now, if you please, let us return to the b
point of the argument at which we digressed.

By all means, replied Socrates; what else should I please?

Very good.

Must we not, said Socrates, ask ourselves what that is which, as we imagine, is liable to be scattered, and about which we fear? and what again is that about which we have no fear? And then we may proceed further to enquire whether that which suffers dispersions is or is not of the nature of soul—our hopes and fears as to our own souls will turn upon the answers to these questions.

What is the element which is liable to be scattered? Not the simple and unchangeable, but the composite and changing.

Very true, he said.

Now the compound or composite may be sup- c
posed to be naturally capable, as of being compounded, so also of being dissolved; but that which is uncompounded, and that only, must be, if anything is, indissoluble.

Yes; I should imagine so, said Cebes.

And the uncompounded may be assumed to be the same and unchanging, whereas the compound is always changing and never the same.

I agree, he said.

d Then now let us return to the previous discussion. Is that idea or essence, which in the dialectical process we define as essence or true existence—whether essence of equality, beauty, or anything *The soul and the ideas belong to the class of the unchanging, which is also the unseen.* else—are these essences, I say, liable at times to some degree of change? or are they each of them always what they are, having the same simple self-existent and unchanging forms, not admitting of variation at all, or in any way, or at any time?

They must be always the same, Socrates, replied Cebes.

And what would you say of the many beautiful—whether men or horses or garments or any other e things which are named by the same names and may be called equal or beautiful,—are they all unchanging and the same always, or quite the reverse? May they not rather be described as almost always changing and hardly ever the same, either with themselves or with one another?

The latter, replied Cebes; they are always in a state of change.

79a And these you can touch and see and perceive with the senses, but the unchanging things you can only perceive with the mind—they are invisible and are not seen?

That is very true, he said.

Well, then, added Socrates, let us suppose that

there are two sorts of existences—one seen, the other unseen.

Let us suppose them.

The seen is the changing, and the unseen is the unchanging?

That may be also supposed.

And, further, is not one part of us body, another part soul?   b

To be sure.

And to which class is the body more alike and akin?

Clearly to the seen—no one can doubt that.

And is the soul seen or not seen?

Not by man, Socrates.

And what we mean by "seen" and "not seen" is that which is or is not visible to the eye of man?

Yes, to the eye of man.

And is the soul seen or not seen?

Not seen.

Unseen then?

Yes.

Then the soul is more like to the unseen, and the body to the seen?

That follows necessarily, Socrates.   c

And were we not saying long ago that the soul when using the body as an instrument of perception, that is to say, when using the sense of sight or hearing or some other sense (for the meaning of perceiving through the body is perceiving through the senses)— were we not saying that the soul too is then dragged by the body

The soul which is unseen, when she makes use of the bodily senses, is dragged down into the region of the changeable, and must return into herself before she can attain to true wisdom.

into the region of the changeable,[19] and wanders
and is confused; the world spins round her, and she
is like a drunkard, when she touches change?

Very true.

d   But when returning into herself she reflects,
then she passes into the other world, the region
of purity, and eternity, and immortality, and un-
changeableness, which are her kindred, and with
them she ever lives, when she is by herself and is
not let or hindered; then she ceases from her err-
ing ways, and being in communion with the unchanging is unchanging. And this state of the soul
is called wisdom?

That is well and truly said, Socrates, he replied.

And to which class is the soul more nearly alike
e   and akin, as far as may be inferred from this argument, as well as from the preceding one?

I think, Socrates, that, in the *The soul is of*
opinion of every one who follows the *the nature of the*
argument, the soul will be infinitely *unchangeable,*
more like the unchangeable—even *the body of the*
the most stupid person will not *changing; the*
deny that. *soul rules, the*
body serves; the
And the body is more like the *soul is in the*
changing? *likeness of the*
divine, the body
Yes. *of the mortal.*

80a   Yet once more consider the
matter in another light: When the soul and the body
are united, then nature orders the soul to rule and
govern, and the body to obey and serve. Now, which
of these two functions is akin to the divine? and
which to the mortal? Does not the divine appear to
you to be that which naturally orders and rules, and
the mortal to be that which is subject and servant?

True.

And which does the soul resemble?

The soul resembles the divine, and the body the mortal—there can be no doubt of that, Socrates.

Then reflect, Cebes: of all which has been said is not this the conclusion?—that the soul is in the   b
very likeness of the divine, and immortal, and intellectual, and uniform, and indissoluble, and unchangeable; and that the body is in the very likeness of the human, and mortal, and unintellectual, and multiform, and dissoluble, and changeable. Can this, my dear Cebes, be denied?

It cannot.

But if it be true, then is not the body liable to speedy dissolution? and is not the soul almost or altogether indissoluble?

Certainly.   c

And do you further observe, *Even from the* that after a man is dead, the body, *body something* or visible part of him, which is *may be learned* lying in the visible world, and is *about the soul;* called a corpse, and would natu- *for the corpse* rally be dissolved and decomposed *of a man lasts* and dissipated, is not dissolved or *for some time,* decomposed at once, but may re- *and when embalmed, in a* main for some time, nay even for *manner for ever.* a long time, if the constitution be sound at the time of death, and the season of the year favourable? For the body when shrunk and embalmed, as the manner is in Egypt, may remain almost entire through infinite ages; and even in decay, there are still some portions, such   d as the bones and ligaments, which are practically indestructible:—Do you agree?

Yes.

And is it likely that the soul, *How unlikely* which is invisible, in passing to the *then that the* place of the true Hades,[20] which *soul should at* like her is invisible, and pure, and *once pass away!* noble, and on her way to the good and wise God, whither, if God will, my soul is also soon to go,— that the soul, I repeat, if this be her nature and origin, will be blown away and destroyed immediately on quitting the body, as the many say? That can never be, my dear Simmias and Cebes. The truth
e   rather is, that the soul which is pure at departing and draws after her no bodily taint, having never voluntarily during life had connection with the body, which she is ever avoiding, herself gathered into herself;—and making such abstraction her perpetual study—which means that she has been a true disciple of philosophy; and therefore has in fact been always engaged in the practice of dying?
81a For is not philosophy the study of death?—

Certainly—

That soul, I say, herself invisible, *Rather when* departs to the invisible world—to *free from bodily* the divine and immortal and ratio- *impurity she* nal: thither arriving, she is secure *departs to the* of bliss and is released from the *seats of the* error and folly of men, their fears *blessed.* and wild passions and all other human ills, and for ever dwells, as they say of the initiated, in company with the gods. Is not this true, Cebes?

Yes, said Cebes, beyond a doubt.

b   But the soul which has been polluted, and is impure at the time of her departure, and is the companion and servant of the body always, and

is in love with and fascinated by the body and by
the desires and pleasures of the body, until she is
led to believe that the truth only exists in a bodily
form, which a man may touch and see and taste,
and use for the purposes of his lusts,—the soul,
I mean, accustomed to hate and fear and avoid
the intellectual principle, which to the bodily eye
is dark and invisible, and can be attained only by   c
philosophy;—do you suppose that such a soul will
depart pure and unalloyed?

Impossible, he replied.

She is held fast by the corporeal, which the con-
tinual association and constant care of the body
have wrought into her nature.

Very true.

And this corporeal element, *But the souls of*
my friend, is heavy and weighty *the wicked are*
and earthy, and is that element *dragged down*
of sight by which a soul is de- *by the corporeal*
element.
pressed and dragged down again   d
into the visible world, because she is afraid of the
invisible and of the world below—prowling about
tombs and sepulchres, near which, as they tell us,
are seen certain ghostly apparitions of souls which
have not departed pure, but are cloyed with sight
and therefore visible.

That is very likely, Socrates.

Yes, that is very likely, Cebes; and these must be
the souls, not of the good, but of the evil, which are
compelled to wander about such places in payment   e
of the penalty of their former evil way of life; and
they continue to wander until through the craving
after the corporeal which never leaves them they
are imprisoned finally in another body. And they

may be supposed to find their prisons in the same natures which they have had in their former lives.

What natures do you mean, Socrates?

What I mean is that men who have followed after gluttony, and wantonness, and drunkenness, and have had no thought of avoiding them, would pass into asses and animals of that sort. What do you think? *They wander into the bodies of the animals or of birds which are of a like nature with themselves.*

82a

I think such an opinion to be exceedingly probable.

And those who have chosen the portion of injustice, and tyranny, and violence, will pass into wolves, or into hawks and kites;—whither else can we suppose them to go?

Yes, said Cebes; with such natures, beyond question.

And there is no difficulty, he said, in assigning to all of them places answering to their several natures and propensities?

There is not, he said.

Some are happier than others; and the happiest both in themselves and in the place to which they go are those who have practised the civil and social virtues which are called temperance and justice, and are acquired by habit and attention without philosophy of mind.

b

Why are they the happiest?

Because they may be expected to pass into some gentle and social kind which is like their own, such as bees or wasps or ants, or back again into the form of man, and just and moderate men may be supposed to spring from them.

Very likely.

No one who has not studied philosophy and who is not entirely pure at the time of his departure is   c
allowed to enter the company of the Gods, but the lover of knowledge only. And this is the reason, Simmias and Cebes, why the true votaries of philosophy abstain from all fleshly lusts, and hold out against them and refuse to give themselves up to them,—not because they fear poverty or the ruin of their families, like the lovers of money, and the world in general; nor like the lovers of power and honour, because they dread the dishonour or disgrace of evil deeds.

No, Socrates, that would not become them, said Cebes.

No, indeed, he replied; and therefore they who   d
have any care of their own souls, and do not merely live moulding and fashioning the body, say farewell to all this; they will not walk in the ways of the blind: and when philosophy offers them purification and release from evil, they feel that they ought not to resist her influence, and whither she leads they turn and follow.

What do you mean, Socrates?

I will tell you, he said. The lov-   *The new*   e
ers of knowledge are conscious   *consciousness*
that the soul was simply fastened   *which is*
and glued to the body—until phi-   *awakened by*
losophy received her, she could   *philosophy.*
only view real existence through the bars of a prison, not in and through herself; she was wallowing in the mire of every sort of ignorance, and by reason of lust had become the principal accomplice in her own captivity. This was her original   83a

state; and then, as I was saying, and as the lovers of
knowledge are well aware, philosophy, seeing how
terrible was her confinement, of which she was
herself the cause, received and gently comforted
her and sought to release her, pointing out that the
eye and the ear and the other senses are full of deception, and persuading her to retire from them,
and abstain from all but the necessary use of them,
b   and be gathered up and collected into herself, bidding her trust in herself and her own pure apprehension of pure existence, and to mistrust whatever
comes to her through other channels and is subject
to variation; for such things are *The philosopher*
visible and tangible, but what she *considers*
sees in her own nature is intelligi- *not only the*
ble and invisible. And the soul of *consequences of*
the true philosopher thinks that *pleasures and*
she ought not to resist this deliver- *pains, but, what*
ance, and therefore abstains from *is far worse,*
pleasures and desires and pains *the false lights*
and fears, as far as she is able; re- *in which they*
show objects.
flecting that when a man has great joys or sorrows
or fears or desires, he suffers from them, not
merely the sort of evil which might be antici-
pated—as, for example, the loss of his health or
property which he has sacrificed to his lusts—but
c   an evil greater far, which is the greatest and worst
of all evils, and one of which he never thinks.

What is it, Socrates? said Cebes.

The evil is that when the feeling of pleasure or
pain is most intense, every soul of man imagines
the objects of this intense feeling to be then plain-
est and truest: but this is not so, they are really the
things of sight.

Very true.

And is not this the state in which the soul is most   d
enthralled by the body?

How so?

Why, because each pleasure and pain is a sort
of nail which nails and rivets the soul to the body,
until she becomes like the body, and believes that
to be true which the body affirms to be true; and
from agreeing with the body and having the same
delights she is obliged to have the same habits and
haunts, and is not likely ever to be pure at her departure to the world below, but is always infected   e
by the body; and so she sinks into another body
and there germinates and grows, and has therefore
no part in the communion of the divine and pure
and simple.

Most true, Socrates, answered Cebes.

And this, Cebes, is the reason why the true lovers of knowledge are temperate and brave; and not
for the reason which the world gives.

Certainly not.   84a

Certainly not! The soul of a *The soul which*
philosopher will reason in quite *has been*
another way; she will not ask phi- *emancipated*
losophy to release her in order *from pleasures*
that when released she may de- *and pains will*
liver herself up again to the thral- *not be blown*
dom[21] of pleasures and pains, *away at death.*
doing a work only to be undone again, weaving instead of unweaving her Penelope's web.[22] But she
will calm passion, and follow reason, and dwell in
the contemplation of her, beholding the true and
divine (which is not matter of opinion), and thence
deriving nourishment. Thus she seeks to live while   b

she lives, and after death she hopes to go to her own kindred and to that which is like her, and to be freed from human ills. Never fear, Simmias and Cebes, that a soul which has been thus nurtured and has had these pursuits, will at her departure from the body be scattered and blown away by the winds and be nowhere and nothing.

c   When Socrates had done speaking, for a considerable time there was silence; he himself appeared to be meditating, as most of us were, on what had been said; only Cebes and Simmias spoke a few words to one another. And *Simmias and Cebes have their doubts, but think that this is not the time to express them.* Socrates observing them asked what they thought of the argument, and whether there was anything wanting? For, said he, there are many points still open to suspicion and attack, if any one were disposed to sift the matter thoroughly. Should you be considering some other matter I say no more, but

d   if you are still in doubt do not hesitate to say exactly what you think, and let us have anything better which you can suggest; and if you think that I can be of any use, allow me to help you.

Simmias said: I must confess, Socrates, that doubts did arise in our minds, and each of us was urging and inciting the other to put the question which we wanted to have answered but which neither of us liked to ask, fearing that our importunity might be troublesome at such a time.

Socrates replied with a smile: O Simmias, what are you saying? I am not very likely to persuade *Socrates rebukes their want of confidence in him.*

e   other men that I do not regard my

present situation as a misfortune, if I cannot even persuade you that I am no worse off now than at any other time in my life. Will you not allow that I have as much of the spirit of *What is the* prophecy in me as the swans? For *meaning of the* they, when they perceive that they *swans' singing?* must die, having sung all their life long, do then 85a sing more lustily than ever, rejoicing in the thought that they are about to go away to the god whose ministers they are. But men, because they are themselves afraid of death, slanderously affirm of the swans that they sing a lament *They do not* at the last, not considering that no *lament, as men* bird sings when cold, or hungry, or *suppose, at their* in pain, not even the nightingale, *approaching* nor the swallow, nor yet the hoo- *death; but they* poe; which are said indeed to tune *rejoice because* a lay of sorrow, although I do not *they are going* believe this to be true of them any *to the God,* more than of the swans. But be- *whose servants* cause they are sacred to Apollo, *they are.* they have the gift of prophecy, and *Socrates, who is* anticipate the good things of an- *their fellow-* b other world; wherefore they sing *servant, will not* and rejoice in that day more than ever they did be- *leave the world* fore. And I, too, believing myself to be the conse- *less cheerily.* crated servant of the same God, and the fellow-servant of the swans, and thinking that I have received from my master gifts of prophecy which are not inferior to theirs, would not go out of life less merrily than the swans. Never mind then, if this be your only objection, but speak and ask anything which you like, while the eleven magistrates of Athens allow.

c　　　Very good, Socrates, said Simmias; then I will
tell you my difficulty, and Cebes will tell you his. I
feel myself (and I dare say that you have the same
feeling) how hard or rather impossible is the attainment of any certainty about questions such as
these in the present life. And yet I should deem
him a coward who did not prove what is said about
them to the uttermost, or whose heart failed him
before he had examined them on   *Simmias insists*
every side. For he should perse-   *that they must*
vere until he has achieved one of   *probe truth to*
two things: either he should dis-   *the bottom.*

d　cover, or be taught the truth about them; or, if this
be impossible, I would have him take the best and
most irrefragable of human theories, and let this
be the raft upon which he sails through life—not
without risk, as I admit, if he cannot find some
word of God which will more surely and safely
carry him. And now, as you bid me, I will venture
to question you, and then I shall not have to reproach myself hereafter with not having said at the
time what I think. For when I consider the matter,
either alone or with Cebes, the argument does certainly appear to me, Socrates, to be not sufficient.

e　　　Socrates answered: I dare say, my friend, that
you may be right, but I should like to know in what
respect the argument is insufficient.

　　　In this respect, replied Sim-   *The harmony*
86a　mias:—Suppose a person to use   *does not survive*
the same argument about har-   *the lyre; how*
mony and the lyre[23]—might he   *then can the*
not say that harmony is a thing   *soul which is*
invisible, incorporeal, perfect, di-   *also a harmony,*
vine, existing in the lyre which is   *survive the*
　　　　　　　　　　　　　　　　　　　　　body?

harmonized, but that the lyre and the strings are matter and material, composite, earthy, and akin to mortality? And when some one breaks the lyre, or cuts and rends the strings, then he who takes this view would argue as you do, and on the same analogy, that the harmony survives and has not perished—you cannot imagine, he would say, that the lyre without the strings, and the broken strings themselves which are mortal remain, and yet that the harmony, which is of heavenly and immortal nature and kindred, has perished—perished before the mortal. The harmony must still be somewhere, and the wood and strings will decay before anything can happen to that. The thought, Socrates, must have occurred to your own mind that such is our conception of the soul; and that when the body is in a manner strung and held together by the elements of hot and cold, wet and dry, then the soul is the harmony or due proportionate admixture[24] of them. But if so, whenever the strings of the body are unduly loosened or overstrained through disease or other injury, then the soul, though most divine, like other harmonies of music or of works of art, of course perishes at once; although the material remains of the body may last for a considerable time, until they are either decayed or burnt. And if any one maintains that the soul, being the harmony of the elements of the body, is first to perish in that which is called death, how shall we answer him?

Socrates looked fixedly at us as his manner was, and said with a smile: Simmias has reason on his side; and why does not some one of you who is better able than myself answer him? for there is force in his attack upon me. But perhaps, before we

answer him, we had better also hear what Cebes
e   has to say that we may gain time for reflection, and
when they have both spoken, we may either assent
to them, if there is truth in what they say, or if not,
we will maintain our position. Please to tell me
then, Cebes, he said, what was the difficulty which
troubled you?

Cebes said: I will tell you. My feeling is that the
argument is where it was, and open to the same
objections which were urged before; for I am ready
87a to admit that the existence of the soul before entering into the bodily form has been very inge-
niously, and, if I may say so, quite sufficiently
proven; but the existence of the soul after death is
still, in my judgment, unproven. Now, my objection
is not the same as that of Simmias; for I am not
disposed to deny that the soul is stronger and more
lasting than the body, being of opinion that in all
such respects the soul very far excels the body.
Well, then, says the argument to me, why do you
remain unconvinced?—When you see that the
weaker continues in existence after the man is
b   dead, will you not admit that the more lasting must
also survive during the same period of time? Now,
I will ask you to consider whether the objection,
which, like Simmias, I will express in a figure, is of
any weight. The analogy which I will adduce is that
of an old weaver, who dies, and after his death
somebody says:—He is not dead, he must be
alive;—see, there is the coat which   *A weaver*
he himself wove and wore, and   *may outlive*
which remains whole and unde-   *many coats*
cayed. And then he proceeds to   *and himself be*
                                  outlived by the
c   ask of some one who is incredu-   *last.*

lous, whether a man lasts longer, or the coat which is in use and wear; and when he is answered that a man lasts far longer, thinks that he has thus certainly demonstrated the survival of the man, who is the more lasting, because the less lasting remains. But that, Simmias, as I would beg you to remark, is a mistake; any one can see that he who talks thus is talking nonsense. For the truth is, that the weaver   d aforesaid, having woven and worn many such coats, outlived several of them; and was outlived by the last; but a man is not therefore proved to be slighter and weaker than a coat. Now the relation of the body to the soul may be expressed in a similar figure; and any one may very fairly say in like manner that the soul is lasting, *So the soul* and the body weak and short-lived *which has* in comparison. He may argue in *passed through* like manner that every soul wears *many bodies* out many bodies, especially if a *may in the end* man live many years. While he is *be worn out.* alive the body deliquesces[25] and decays, and the soul always weaves another garment and repairs   e the waste. But of course, whenever the soul perishes, she must have on her last garment, and this will survive her; and then at length, when the soul is dead, the body will show its native weakness, and quickly decompose and pass away. I would therefore rather not rely on the argument from superior   88a strength to prove the continued existence of the soul after death. For granting even more than you affirm to be possible, and acknowledging not only that the soul existed before birth, but also that the souls of some exist, and will continue to exist after death, and will be born and die again and again, and that there is a natural strength in the soul which will hold out and be born many times— nevertheless, we may be still inclined to think that she will weary in the labours of successive births, and may at last succumb in one of her deaths and

b utterly perish; and this death and dissolution of the body which brings destruction to the soul may be unknown to any of us, for no one of us can have had any experience of it: and if so, then I maintain that he who is confident about death has but a foolish confidence, unless he is able to prove that the soul is altogether immortal and imperishable. But if he cannot prove the soul's immortality, he who is about to die will always have reason to fear that when the body is disunited, the soul also may utterly perish.

c All of us, as we afterwards re- *The despair of* marked to one another, had an *the audience* unpleasant feeling at hearing what *at hearing the* they said. When we had been so *overthrow of the* firmly convinced before, now to *argument.* have our faith shaken seemed to introduce a confusion and uncertainty, not only into the previous argument, but into any future one; either we were incapable of forming a judgment, or there were no grounds of belief.

Ech.: There I feel with you—by heaven I do,

d Phaedo, and when you were speaking, I was beginning to ask myself the same question: What argument can I ever trust again? For what could be more convincing than the argument of Socrates, which has now fallen into discredit? That the soul is a harmony is a doctrine which has always had a wonderful attraction for me, and, when men-

tioned, came back to me at once, as my own original conviction. And now I must begin again and
find another argument which will assure me that
when the man is dead the soul survives. Tell me, I
implore you, how did Socrates proceed? Did he   e
appear to share the unpleasant feeling which you
mention? or did he calmly meet the attack? And
did he answer forcibly or feebly? Narrate what
passed as exactly as you can.

Phaed.: Often, Echecrates, I   *The wonderful*   89a
have wondered at Socrates, but   *manner in*
never more than on that occasion.   *which Socrates*
That he should be able to answer   *soothes his*
was nothing, but what astonished   *disappointed*
me was, first, the gentle and pleas-   *hearers and*
ant and approving manner in which   *rehabilitates the*
    argument.
he received the words of the young men, and then his
quick sense of the wound which had been inflicted
by the argument, and the readiness with which he
healed it. He might be compared to a general ral-
lying his defeated and broken army, urging them to
accompany him and return to the field of argument.

Ech.: What followed?

Phaed.: You shall hear, for I was close to him on
his right hand, seated on a sort of stool, and he on   b
a couch which was a good deal higher. He stroked
my head, and pressed the hair upon my neck—he
had a way of playing with my hair; and then he said:
To-morrow, Phaedo, I suppose that these fair locks
of yours will be severed.[26]

Yes, Socrates, I suppose that they will, I replied.

Not so, if you will take my advice.

What shall I do with them? I said.

To-day, he replied, and not to-morrow, if this

c   argument dies and we cannot bring it to life again, you and I will both shave our locks: and if I were you, and the argument got away from me, and I could not hold my ground against Simmias and Cebes, I would myself take an oath, like the Argives,[27] not to wear hair any more until I had renewed the conflict and defeated them.

Yes, I said; but Heracles himself is said not to be a match for two.

Summon me, then, he said, and I will be your Iolaus[28] until the sun goes down.

I summon you rather, I rejoined, not as Heracles summoning Iolaus, but as Iolaus might summon Heracles.

That will do as well, he said. But first let us take care that we avoid a danger.

Of what nature? I said.

d   Lest we become misologists,[29] he replied: no worse thing can happen to a man than this. For as there are misanthropists, or haters of men, there are also misologists, or haters of ideas, and both spring from the same cause, which is ignorance of the world. Misanthropy arises out of the too great confidence of inexperience;—and trust a man and think him altogether true and sound and faithful, and then in a little while he turns out to be false and knavish; and then another and another, and when this has happened several times to a man,

e   especially when it happens among those whom he deems to be his own most trusted and familiar friends, and he has often quarrelled with them, he at last hates all men, and believes that no one has

The danger of becoming haters of ideas greater than of becoming haters of men.

any good in him at all. You must have observed this trait of character?

I have.

And is not the feeling discreditable? Is it not obvious that such an one having to deal with other men, was clearly without any experience of human nature; for experience would have taught him the true state of the case, that few are the good and few the evil, and that the great majority are in the interval between them.

There are few very bad or very good men (although bad arguments may be more numerous than bad men); the main point is that he who has been often deceived by either is apt to lose faith in them.

90a

What do you mean? I said.

I mean, he replied, as you might say of the very large and very small—that nothing is more uncommon than a very large or very small man; and this applies generally to all extremes, whether of great and small, or swift and slow, or fair and foul, or black and white: and whether the instances you select be men or dogs or anything else, few are the extremes, but many are in the mean between them. Did you never observe this?

Yes, I said, I have.

And do you not imagine, he said, that if there were a competition in evil, the worst would be found to be very few?

b

Yes, that is very likely, I said.

Yes, that is very likely, he replied; although in this respect arguments are unlike men—there I was led on by you to say more than I had intended; but the point of comparison was, that when a simple man who has no skill in dialectics believes an argument to be true which he afterwards imagines to be false, whether really false or not, and then another and another, he has no longer any faith left, and great

c disputers, as you know, come to think at last that they have grown to be the wisest of mankind; for they alone perceive the utter unsoundness and instability of all arguments, or indeed, of all things, which, like the currents in the Euripus,[30] are going up and down in never-ceasing ebb and flow.

That is quite true, I said.

Yes, Phaedo, he replied; and how melancholy, if

d there be such a thing as truth or certainty or possibility of knowledge—that a man should have lighted upon some argument or other which at first seemed true and then turned out to be false, and instead of blaming himself and his own want of wit, because he is annoyed, should at last be too glad to transfer the blame from himself to arguments in general: and for ever afterwards should hate and revile them, and lose truth and the knowledge of realities.

Yes, indeed, I said; that is very melancholy.

Let us, then, in the first place,

e he said, be careful of allowing or of admitting into our souls the notion that there is no health or soundness in any arguments at all. Rather say that we have not yet attained to soundness in ourselves, and that we must struggle manfully and do our best to gain health of mind—you and all other men

Socrates, who is soon to die, has too much at stake on the argument to be a fair judge. Simmias and Cebes must help him to consider the matter impartially.

having regard to the whole of your future life, and I

91a myself in the prospect of death. For at this moment I am sensible that I have not the temper of a philosopher; like the vulgar, I am only a partisan. Now, the partisan, when he is engaged in a dispute, cares nothing about the rights of the question, but is anxious only to convince his hearers of his own assertions. And the difference between him and me at the present moment is merely this—that whereas he seeks to convince his hearers that what he says is true, I am rather seeking to convince myself; to convince my hearers is a secondary matter with me. And do but see how much I gain by the argument. For if what I say is true, then I do well to be persuaded of the truth; but if there is nothing after death, still, during the short time that remains, I shall not distress my friends with lamentations, and my ignorance will not last, but will die with me, and therefore no harm will be done. This is the state of mind, Simmias and Cebes, in which I approach the argument. And I would ask you to be thinking of the truth and not of Socrates: agree with me, if I seem to you to be speaking the truth; or if not, withstand me might and main, that I may not deceive you as well as myself in my enthusiasm, and like the bee, leave my sting in you before I die.

b

c

And now let us proceed, he said. And first of all let me be sure that I have in my mind what you were saying. Simmias, if I remember rightly, has fears and misgivings whether the soul, although a fairer and diviner thing than the body, being as she is in the form of harmony, may not perish first. On the other hand, Cebes appeared to grant that the soul was more lasting than the body, but he said that no one could

Simmias and Cebes are inclined to fear that the soul may perish before the body, but they still hold to the doctrine of reminiscence.

d

know whether the soul, after having worn out many bodies, might not perish herself and leave her last body behind her; and that this is death, which is the destruction not of the body but of the soul, for in the body the work of destruction is ever going on. Are not these, Simmias and Cebes, the points which we have to consider?

e   They both agreed to this statement of them.

He proceeded: And did you deny the force of the whole preceding argument, or of a part only?

Of a part only, they replied.

And what did you think, he said, of that part of the argument in which we said that knowledge was
92a   recollection, and hence inferred that the soul must have previously existed somewhere else before she was enclosed in the body?

Cebes said that he had been wonderfully impressed by that part of the argument, and that his conviction remained absolutely unshaken. Simmias agreed, and added that he himself could hardly imagine the possibility of his ever thinking differently.

But, rejoined Socrates, you will have to think differently, my Theban friend, if you still maintain that harmony is a compound, and
b   that the soul is a harmony which is made out of strings set in the frame of the body; for you will surely never allow yourself to say that a harmony is prior to the elements which compose it.

The elements of harmony are prior to harmony, but the body is not prior to the soul.

Never, Socrates.

But do you not see that this is what you imply when you say that the soul existed before she took the form and body of man, and was made up of elements which as yet had no existence? For harmony is not like the soul, as you suppose; but first the lyre, and the strings, and the sounds exist in a state of discord, and then harmony is made last of c all, and perishes first. And how can such a notion of the soul as this agree with the other?

Not at all, replied Simmias.

And yet, he said, there surely ought to be harmony in a discourse of which harmony is the theme?

There ought, replied Simmias.

But there is no harmony, he said, in the two propositions that knowledge is recollection, and that the soul is a harmony. Which of them will you retain?

I think, he replied, that I have a much stronger faith, Socrates, in the first of the two, which has been fully demonstrated to me, than in the latter, which has not been demonstrated at all, but rests only on probable and plausible grounds; and is therefore believed by the many. I know too well that these arguments from probabilities are impostors, and unless great caution is observed in the use of them, they are apt to be deceptive—in geometry, and in other things too. But the doctrine of knowledge and recollection has been proven to me on trustworthy grounds: and the proof was that the soul must have existed before she came into the body, because to her belongs the essence of which the e very name implies existence. Having, as I am con-

Simmias d
acknowledges that his argument does not harmonise with the proposition that knowledge is recollection.

vinced, rightly accepted this conclusion, and on sufficient grounds, I must, as I suppose, cease to argue or allow others to argue that the soul is a harmony.

93a Let me put the matter, Simmias, he said, in another point of view: Do you imagine that a harmony or any other composition can be in a state other than that of the elements, out of which it is compounded?

Certainly not.

Or do or suffer anything other than they do or suffer?

He agreed.

Then a harmony does not, properly speaking, lead the parts or elements which make up the harmony, but only follows them.

He assented.

For harmony cannot possibly have any motion, or sound, or other quality which is opposed to its parts.

That would be impossible, he replied.

And does not the nature of every harmony depend upon the manner in which the elements are harmonized?

I do not understand you, he said.

b   I mean to say that a harmony *Harmony* admits of degrees, and is more of *admits of* a harmony, and more completely a *degrees, but in* harmony, when more truly and fully *the soul there* harmonized, to any extent which is *are no degrees;* possible; and less of a harmony, and less completely a harmony, when less truly and fully harmonized.

True.

But does the soul admit of degrees? or is one

soul in the very least degree more or less, or more or less completely, a soul than another?

Not in the least.

Yet surely of two souls, one is said to have intelligence and virtue, and to be good, and the other to have folly and vice, and to be an evil soul: and this is said truly?

Yes, truly.

But what will those who maintain the soul to be a harmony say of this presence of virtue and vice in the soul?—will they say that here is another harmony, and another *and therefore there cannot be a soul or harmony within a soul.* discord, and that the virtuous soul is harmonized, and herself being a harmony has another harmony within her, and that the vicious soul is inharmonical and has no harmony within her?

I cannot tell, replied Simmias; but I suppose that something of the sort would be asserted by those who say that the soul is a harmony.

And we have already admitted that no soul is more a soul than another; which is equivalent to admitting that harmony is not more or less harmony, or more or less completely a harmony?

Quite true.

And that which is not more or less a harmony is not more or less harmonized?

True.

And that which is not more or less harmonized cannot have more or less of harmony, but only an equal harmony?

Yes, an equal harmony.

Then one soul not being more or less absolutely a soul than another, is not more or less harmonized?

Exactly.

And therefore has neither more or less of discord, nor yet of harmony?

She has not.

And having neither more nor less of harmony or of discord, one soul has no more vice or virtue than another, if vice be discord and virtue harmony?

Not at all more.

94a   Or speaking more correctly, Simmias, the soul, if she is a harmony, will never have any vice; because a harmony, being absolutely a harmony, has no part in the inharmonical.

No.

And therefore a soul which is absolutely a soul has no vice?   *If the soul is a harmony, all souls must be equally good.*

How can she have, if the previous argument holds?

Then, if all souls are equally by their nature souls, all souls of all living creatures will be equally good?

I agree with you, Socrates, he said.

b   And can all this be true, think you? he said; for these are the consequences which seem to follow from the assumption that the soul is a harmony?

It cannot be true.

Once more, he said, what ruler is there of the elements of human nature other than the soul, and especially the wise soul? Do you know of any?

Indeed, I do not.

And is the soul in agreement with the affections of the body? or is she at variance with them? For example, when the body is hot and thirsty, does not the soul incline us against drinking? and when the body is hungry, against eating? And this is only one

instance out of ten thousand of the opposition of
the soul to the things of the body.   c

Very true.

But we have already acknowledged that the
soul, being a harmony, can never utter a note at
variance with the tensions and relaxations and vi-
brations and other affections of the strings out of
which she is composed; she can only follow, she
cannot lead them?

It must be so, he replied.

And yet do we not now discover   *The soul leads*
the soul to be doing the exact   *and does not*
opposite—leading the elements   *follow. She*
of which she is believed to be   *constrains and*
composed; almost always oppos-   *reprimands the*
ing and coercing them in all sorts *passions.*
of ways throughout life, sometimes more violently   d
with the pains of medicine and gymnastic; then
again more gently; now threatening, now admon-
ishing the desires, passions, fears, as if talking to a
thing which is not herself, as Homer in the Odyssey represents Odysseus doing in the words—

"He beat his breast, and thus reproached his
    heart:
Endure, my heart; far worse hast thou
    endured!"

Do you think that Homer wrote this under the idea
that the soul is a harmony capable of being led by
the affections of the body, and not rather of a nature which should lead and master them—herself
a far diviner thing than any harmony?

Yes, Socrates, I quite think so.

95a   Then, my friend, we can never be right in saying
that the soul is a harmony, for we should contradict
the divine Homer, and contradict ourselves.

True, he said.

Thus much, said Socrates, of Harmonia, your
Theban goddess, who has graciously yielded to us;
but what shall I say, Cebes, to her husband Cadmus,[31] and how shall I make peace with him?

I think that you will discover a way of propitiat-
ing him, said Cebes; I am sure that you have put the
argument with Harmonia in a manner that I could
b   never have expected. For when Simmias was men-
tioning his difficulty, I quite imagined that no answer
could be given to him, and therefore I was surprised
at finding that his argument could not sustain the
first onset of yours, and not impossibly the other,
whom you call Cadmus, may share a similar fate.

Nay, my good friend, said Socrates, let us not
boast, lest some evil eye should put to flight the
word which I am about to speak. That, however,
may be left in the hands of those above; while I
draw near in Homeric fashion, and try the mettle
c   of your words. Here lies the point:—You want to
have it proven to you that the soul is imperishable
and immortal, and the philosopher who is confident in death appears to you to have but a vain and
foolish confidence, if he believes that he will fare
better in the world below than one who has led
another sort of life, unless he can prove this: and
you say that the demonstration of the strength and
divinity of the soul, and of her existence prior to
our becoming men, does not nec-   *Recapitulation*
essarily imply her immortality.   *of the argument*
Admitting the soul to be long-lived,   *of Cebes.*

and to have known and done much in a former
state, still she is not on that account immortal; and   d
her entrance into the human form may be a sort of
disease which is the beginning of dissolution, and
may at last, after the toils of life are over, end in
that which is called death. And whether the soul
enters into the body once only or many times, does
not, as you say, make any difference in the fears of
individuals. For any man, who is not devoid of
sense, must fear, if he has no knowledge and can   e
give no account of the soul's immortality. This, or
something like this, I suspect to be your notion,
Cebes; and I designedly recur to it in order that
nothing may escape us, and that you may, if you
wish, add or subtract anything.

But, said Cebes, as far as I see at present, I have
nothing to add or subtract: I mean what you say
that I mean.

Socrates paused awhile, and seemed to be ab-
sorbed in reflection. At length he said: You are rais-   96a
ing a tremendous question, Cebes, involving the
whole nature of generation and corruption, about
which, if you like, I will give you my own experience; and if anything which I say is likely to avail
towards the solution of your difficulty you may
make use of it.

I should very much like, said Cebes, to hear
what you have to say.

Then I will tell you, said Socrates. *The speculations*
When I was young, Cebes, I had *of Socrates*
a prodigious desire to know that *about physics*
department of philosophy which *made him forget*
is called the investigation of na- *the commonest*
ture; to know the causes of things, *things.*

and why a thing is and is created or destroyed
appeared to me to be a lofty profession; and I
b   was always agitating myself with the consideration
of questions such as these:—Is the growth of animals the result of some decay which the hot and
cold principle contracts, as some have said?[32] Is the
blood the element with which we think, or the air,
or the fire? or perhaps nothing of the kind—but the
brain may be the originating power of the percep-
tions of hearing and sight and smell, and memory
and opinion may come from them, and science may
be based on memory and opinion when they have
attained fixity. And then I went on to examine the
c   corruption of them, and then to the things of heaven
and earth, and at last I concluded myself to be utterly and absolutely incapable of these enquiries, as
I will satisfactorily prove to you. For I was fascinated
by them to such a degree that my eyes grew blind
to things which I had seemed to myself, and also to
others, to know quite well; I forgot what I had before thought self-evident truths; for example, such a
d   fact as that the growth of man is the result of eating
and drinking; for when by the digestion of food flesh
is added to flesh and bone to bone, and whenever
there is an aggregation of congenial elements, the
lesser bulk becomes larger and the small man great.
Was not that a reasonable notion?

Yes, said Cebes, I think so.

Well; but let me tell you some-   *Difficulty of*
thing more. There was a time   *explaining*
when I thought that I understood   *relative notions.*
the meaning of greater and less pretty well; and
when I saw a great man standing by a little one,
I fancied that one was taller than the other by a

head; or one horse would appear to be greater than
another horse: and still more clearly did I seem to   e
perceive that ten is two more than eight, and that
two cubits are more than one, because two is the
double of one.

And what is now your notion of such matters?
said Cebes.

I should be far enough from imagining, he replied, that I knew the cause of any of them, by
heaven I should; for I cannot satisfy myself that,   97a
when one is added to one, the one to which the addition is made becomes two, or that the two units
added together make two by reason of the addition.
I cannot understand how, when separated from the
other, each of them was one and not two, and now,
when they are brought together, the mere juxtaposition or meeting of them should be the cause of
their becoming two: neither can I understand how
the division of one is the way to make two; for then   b
a different cause would produce the same
effect,—as in the former instance the addition and
juxtaposition of one to one was the cause of two, in
this the separation and subtraction of one from the
other would be the cause. Nor am I any longer satisfied that I understand the reason why one or anything else is either generated or destroyed or is at
all, but I have in my mind some confused notion of
a new method, and can never admit the other.

Then I heard some one read-   *The great*   c
ing, as he said, from a book of   *expectations*
Anaxagoras, that mind was the   *which Socrates*
disposer and cause of all,[33] and I   *had from the*
was delighted at this notion, which   *doctrine of*
appeared quite admirable, and I   *Anaxagoras, that*
                                       all was Mind.

said to myself: if mind is the disposer, mind will dispose all for the best, and put each particular in the best place; and I argued that if any one desired to find out the cause of the generation or destruc-

d tion or existence of anything, he must find out what state of being or doing or suffering was best for that thing, and therefore a man had only to consider the best for himself and others, and then he would also know the worse, since the same science comprehended both. And I rejoiced to think that I had found in Anaxagoras a teacher of the causes of

e existence such as I desired, and I imagined that he would tell me first whether the earth is flat or round; and whichever was true, he would proceed to explain the cause and the necessity of this being so, and then he would teach me the nature of the best and show that this was best; and if he said that the earth was in the centre, he would further explain that this position was the best, and I should be satisfied with the explanation given, and not

98a want any other sort of cause. And I thought that I would then go on and ask him about the sun and moon and stars, and that he would explain to me their comparative swiftness, and their returnings

b and various states, active and passive, and how all of them were for the best. For I could not imagine that when he spoke of mind as the disposer of them, he would give any other account of their being as they are, except that this was best; and I thought that when he had explained to me in detail the cause of each and the cause of all, he would go on to explain to me what was best for each and what was good for all. These hopes I would not have sold for a large sum of money, and I seized

the books and read them as fast as I could in my
eagerness to know the better and the worse.

What expectations I had *The greatness*
formed, and how grievously was *of his*
I disappointed! As I proceeded, I *disappointment.*
found my philosopher altogether forsaking mind
or any other principle of order, but having re-   c
course to air, and ether, and water, and other ec-
centricities. I might compare him to a person who
began by maintaining generally that mind is the
cause of the actions of Socrates, but who, when he
endeavoured to explain the causes of my several
actions in detail, went on to show that I sit here
because my body is made up of bones and muscles;
and the bones, as he would say, are hard and have
joints which divide them, and the muscles are elas-   d
tic, and they cover the bones, which have also a
covering or environment of flesh and skin which
contains them; and as the bones are lifted at their
joints by the contraction or relaxation of the muscles, I am able to bend my limbs, and this is why I
am sitting here in a curved posture—that is what
he would say; and he would have a similar explanation of my talking to you, which he would attribute
to sound, and air, and hearing, and he would assign
ten thousand other causes of the same sort, forgetting to mention the true cause, which is, that the
Athenians have thought fit to condemn me, and ac-   e
cordingly I have thought it better and more right
to remain here and undergo my sentence; for I am
inclined to think that these muscles and bones of   99a
mine would have gone off long ago to Megara or
Boeotia—by the dog they would, if they had been
moved only by their own idea of what was best,

and if I had not chosen the better and nobler part, instead of playing truant and running away, of enduring any punishment which the State inflicts. There is surely a strange confusion of causes and conditions in all this. It may be said, indeed, that without bones and muscles and the other parts of the body I cannot execute my purposes. But to say that I do as I do because of them, and that this is the way in which mind acts, and not from the choice of the

b best, is a very careless and idle mode of speaking. I wonder that they cannot distinguish the cause from the condition, which the many, feeling about in the dark, are always mistaking and misnaming. And thus one man makes a vortex all round and steadies the earth by the heaven; another gives

c the air as a support to the earth, which is in a sort of broad trough.[34] Any power which in arranging them as they are arranges them for the best never enters into their minds; and instead of finding any superior strength in it, they rather expect to discover another Atlas[35] of the world who is stronger and more everlasting and more containing than the good;—of the obligatory and containing power of the good they think nothing; and yet this is the principle which I would fain learn if any one would teach me. But as I have failed either to discover myself, or to learn of any one else, the nature of

d the best, I will exhibit to you, if you like, what I have found to be the second best mode of enquiring into the cause.

I should very much like to hear, he replied.

Socrates proceeded:—I thought   *The eye of the*
that as I had failed in the contem-   *soul.*
plation of true existence, I ought to be careful that

I did not lose the eye of my soul; as people may injure their bodily eye by observing and gazing on the sun during an eclipse, unless they take the precaution of only looking at the image reflected in   e the water, or in some similar medium. So in my own case, I was afraid that my soul might be blinded altogether if I looked at things with my eyes or tried to apprehend them *The abstract as* by the help of the senses. And I *plain as or as* thought that I had better have re- *plainer than the* course to the world of mind and *concrete.* seek there the truth of existence. I dare say that the simile is not perfect—for I am very far from admit-   100a ting that he who contemplates existences through the medium of thought, sees them only "through a glass darkly,"[36] any more than he who considers them in action and operation. However, this was the method which I adopted: I first assumed some principle which I judged to be the strongest, and then I affirmed as true whatever seemed to agree with this, whether relating to the cause or to anything else; and that which disagreed I regarded as untrue. But I should like to explain my meaning more clearly, as I do not think that you as yet understand me.

No indeed, replied Cebes, not very well.

There is nothing new, he said, *If the ideas have*   b in what I am about to tell you; but *an absolute* only what I have been always and *existence the* everywhere repeating in the pre- *soul is immortal.* vious discussion and on other occasions: I want to show you the nature of that cause which has occupied my thoughts. I shall have to go back to those familiar words which are in the mouth of every one, and first of all assume that there is an absolute beauty and goodness and greatness, and the like; grant me this, and I hope to be able to show you the nature of the cause, and to prove the immortality of the soul.

c   Cebes said: You may proceed at once with the proof, for I grant you this.

Well, he said, then I should like to know whether you agree with me in the next step; for I cannot help thinking, if there be anything beautiful other than absolute beauty, should there be such, that it can be beautiful only in so far as it partakes of absolute beauty—and I should say the same of everything. Do you agree in this notion of the cause?

Yes, he said, I agree.

He proceeded: I know noth-   *All things exist* ing and can understand nothing   *by participation* of any other of those wise causes   *in general ideas.*
d   which are alleged; and if a person says to me that the bloom of colour, or form, or any such thing is a source of beauty, I leave all that, which is only confusing to me, and simply and singly, and perhaps foolishly, hold and am assured in my own mind that nothing makes a thing beautiful but the presence and participation of beauty in whatever way or manner obtained; for as to the manner I am
e   uncertain, but I stoutly contend that by beauty all beautiful things become beautiful. This appears to me to be the safest answer which I can give, either to myself or to another, and to this I cling, in the persuasion that this principle will never be overthrown, and that to myself or to any one who asks the question, I may safely reply, That by beauty

beautiful things become beautiful. Do you not agree with me?

I do.

And that by greatness only great things become great and greater greater, and by smallness the less become less?

True.

Then if a person were to re- *We thus* mark that A is taller by a head *escape certain* 101a than B, and B less by a head than *contradictions* A, you would refuse to admit his *of relation.* statement, and would stoutly contend that what you mean is only that the greater is greater by, and by reason of, greatness, and the less is less only by, and by reason of, smallness; and thus you would avoid the danger of saying that the greater is greater and the less less by the measure of the head, which is the same in both, and would also avoid the monstrous absurdity of supposing that the greater man is greater by reason of the head, b which is small. You would be afraid to draw such an inference, would you not?

Indeed, I should, said Cebes, laughing.

In like manner you would be afraid to say that ten exceeded eight by, and by reason of, two; but would say by, and by reason of, number; or you would say that two cubits exceed one cubit not by a half, but by magnitude?—for there is the same liability to error in all these cases.

Very true, he said.

Again, would you not be cautious of affirming that the addition of one to one, or the division of c one, is the cause of two? And you would loudly as-severate that you know of no way in which anything comes into existence except by participation in its own proper essence, and consequently, as far as you know, the only cause of two is the participation in duality—this is the way to make two, and the participation in one is the way to make one. You would say: I will let alone puzzles of division and addition—wiser heads than mine may answer them; inexperienced as I am, and ready to start, as

d   the proverb says, at my own shadow, I cannot afford to give up the sure ground of a principle. And if any one assails you there, you would not mind him, or answer him, until you had seen whether the consequences which follow agree with one another or not, and when you are further required to give an explanation of this principle, you would go on to assume a higher principle, and a higher, until you found a resting-place in the best of the higher; but you would not confuse the principle and the consequences in your reasoning, like the

e   Eristics[37]—at least if you wanted to discover real existence. Not that this confusion signifies to them, who never care or think about the matter at all, for they have the wit to be well pleased with them-

102a selves however great may be the turmoil of their ideas. But you, if you are a philosopher, will certainly do as I say.

What you say is most true, said Simmias and Cebes, both speaking at once.

Ech.: Yes, Phaedo; and I do not wonder at their assenting. Any one who has the least sense will acknowledge the wonderful clearness of Socrates' reasoning.

Phaed.: Certainly, Echecrates; and such was the feeling of the whole company at the time.

Ech.: Yes, and equally of ourselves, who were not of the company, and are now listening to your recital. But what followed?

Phaed.: After all this had been admitted, and they had agreed that ideas exist, and that other things participate in them and derive their names from them, Socrates, if I remember rightly, said:—

b

This is your way of speaking; and yet when you say that Simmias is greater than Socrates and less than Phaedo, do you not predicate of Simmias both greatness and smallness?

There may still remain the contradiction of the same person being both greater and less, but this is only because he has greatness or smallness relatively to another person.

Yes, I do.

But still you allow that Simmias does not really exceed Socrates, as the words may seem to imply, because he is Simmias, but by reason of the size which he has; just as Simmias does not exceed Socrates because he is Simmias, any more than because Socrates is Socrates, but because he has smallness when compared with the greatness of Simmias?

c

True.

And if Phaedo exceeds him in size, this is not because Phaedo is Phaedo, but because Phaedo has greatness relatively to Simmias, who is comparatively smaller?

That is true.

And therefore Simmias is said to be great, and is also said to be small, because he is in a mean between them, exceeding the smallness of the one by his greatness, and allowing the greatness of the other to exceed his smallness. He added, laughing,

d

I am speaking like a book, but I believe that what I am saying is true.

Simmias assented.

I speak as I do because I want you to agree with me in thinking, not only that absolute greatness will never be great and also small, but that greatness in us or in the concrete will never admit the small or admit of being exceeded: instead of this, one of two things will happen, ei- *The idea of*
ther the greater will fly or retire *greatness*
before the opposite, which is the *can never be*
less, or at the approach of the less *small; and the*
has already ceased to exist; but *greatness in*
will not, if allowing or admitting of *us drives out*
smallness, be changed by that; *smallness.*
even as I, having received and admitted smallness when compared with Simmias, remain just as I was, and am the same small person. And as the idea of greatness cannot condescend ever to be or become small, in like manner the smallness in us cannot be or become great; nor can any other opposite which remains the same ever be or become its own opposite, but either passes away or perishes in the change.

That, replied Cebes, is quite my notion.

Hereupon one of the com- *Yet the greater*
pany, though I do not exactly re- *comes from the*
member which of them, said: In *less, and the*
heaven's name, is not this the di- *less from the*
rect contrary of what was admit- *greater.*
ted before—that out of the greater came the less and out of the less the greater, and that opposites were simply generated from opposites; but now this principle seems to be utterly denied.

Socrates inclined his head to the speaker and listened. I like your courage, he said, in reminding us of this. But you do not observe that there is a difference in the two cases. For then we were speaking of opposites in the concrete, and now of the essential opposite which, as is affirmed, neither in us nor in nature can ever be at variance with itself: then, my friend, we were speaking of things in which opposites are inherent and which are called after them, but now about the opposites which are inherent in them and which give their name to them; and these essential opposites will never, as we maintain, admit of generation into or out of one another. At the same time, turning to Cebes, he said: Are you at all disconcerted, Cebes, at our friend's objection?

Distinguish:— b
The things in which the opposites inhere generate into and out of one another: never the opposites themselves.

c

No, I do not feel so, said Cebes; and yet I cannot deny that I am often disturbed by objections.

Then we are agreed after all, said Socrates, that the opposite will never in any case be opposed to itself?

To that we are quite agreed, he replied.

Yet once more let me ask you to consider the question from another point of view, and see whether you agree with me:— There is a thing which you term heat, and another thing which you term cold?

Snow may be converted into water at the approach of heat, but not cold into heat.

Certainly.

But are they the same as fire and snow?

Most assuredly not.

d

Heat is a thing different from fire, and cold is not the same with snow?

Yes.

And yet you will surely admit, that when snow, as was before said, is under the influence of heat, they will not remain snow and heat; but at the advance of the heat, the snow will either retire or perish?

Very true, he replied.

And the fire too at the advance of the cold will either retire or perish; and when the fire is under the influence of the cold, they will not remain as before, fire and cold.

e   That is true, he said.

And in some cases the name of the idea is not only attached to the idea in an eternal connection, but anything else which, not being the idea, exists only in the form of the idea, may also lay claim to it. I will try to make this clearer by an example:—The odd number is always called by the name of odd?

Very true.

But is this the only thing which is called odd? Are

104a   there not other things which have their own name, and yet are called odd, because, although not the same as oddness, they are never without oddness?— that is what I mean to ask—whether numbers, such as the number three, are not of the class of odd. And there are many other examples: would you not say, for example, that three may be called by its proper

b   name, and also be called odd, which is not the same with three? and this may be said not only of three but also of five, and of every alternate number— each of them without being oddness is odd, and in the same way two and four, and the other series of

alternate numbers, has every number even, without
being evenness. Do you agree?

Of course.

Then now mark the point at
which I am aiming:—not only do
essential opposites exclude one
another, but also concrete things,
which, although not in themselves
opposed, contain opposites; these,
I say, likewise reject the idea
which is opposed to that which is *other.*

*Not only
essential
opposites,
but some
concrete things
which contain
opposites,
exclude each
other.*

contained in them, and when it approaches them   c
they either perish or withdraw. For example: Will
not the number three endure annihilation or anything sooner than be converted into an even number, while remaining three?

Very true, said Cebes.

And yet, he said, the number two is certainly not
opposed to the number three?

It is not.

Then not only do opposite ideas repel the advance of one another, but also there are other natures which repel the approach of opposites.

Very true, he said.

Suppose, he said, that we endeavour, if possible,
to determine what these are.

By all means.

Are they not, Cebes, such as
compel the things of which they
have possession, not only to take
their own form, but also the form
of some opposite?

*That is to say
the opposites
which give an
impress to other
things.*   d

What do you mean?

I mean, as I was just now saying, and as I am

sure that you know, that those things which are possessed by the number three must not only be three in number, but must also be odd.

Quite true.

And on this oddness, of which the number three
e has the impress, the opposite idea will never intrude?

No.

And this impress was given by the odd principle?

Yes.

And to the odd is opposed the even?

True.

Then the idea of the even number will never arrive at three?

No.

Then three has no part in the even?

None.

Then the triad or number three is uneven?

Very true.

To return then to my distinction of natures which are not opposed, and yet do not admit opposites—as, in the instance given, three, although not opposed to the even,
105a does not any the more admit of the even, but always brings the opposite into play on the other side; or as two does not receive the odd, or fire the cold—from these examples (and there are many more

Natures may not be opposed, and yet may not admit of opposites: e.g., three is not opposed to two, and yet does not admit of the even any more than two admits of the odd.

of them) perhaps you may be able to arrive at the general conclusion, that not only opposites will not receive opposites, but also that nothing which brings the opposite will admit the opposite of that which it brings, in that to which it is brought. And here let me recapitulate—for there is no harm in repetition. The number five will not admit the nature of the even, any more than ten, which is the double of five, will admit the nature of the odd. The double has another opposite, and is not strictly opposed to   b the odd, but nevertheless rejects the odd altogether. Nor again will parts in the ratio 3:2, nor any fraction in which there is a half, nor again in which there is a third, admit the notion of the whole, although they are not opposed to the whole: You will agree?

Yes, he said, I entirely agree and go along with you in that.

And now, he said, let us begin   *The merely* again; and do not you answer my   *verbal truth* questions in the words in which I   *may be replaced* ask them: let me have not the old   *by a higher one.* safe answer of which I spoke at first, but another equally safe, of which the truth will be inferred by you from what has been just said. I mean that if any one asks you "what that is, of which the inherence makes the body hot," you will reply not heat (this is   c what I call the safe and stupid answer), but fire, a far superior answer, which we are now in a condition to give. Or if any one asks you "why a body is diseased," you will not say from disease, but from fever; and instead of saying that oddness is the cause of odd numbers, you will say that the monad is the cause of them: and so of things in general, as I dare say that you will understand sufficiently without my adducing any further examples.

Yes, he said, I quite understand you.

Tell me, then, what is that of which the inherence will render the body alive?[38]

The soul, he replied.

d   And is this always the case?

Yes, he said, of course.

Then whatever the soul possesses, to that she comes bearing
life?

Yes, certainly.

And is there any opposite to life?

There is, he said.

And what is that?

Death.

Then the soul, as has been acknowledged, will never receive
the opposite of what she brings.

*We may now
say, not life
makes alive, but
the soul makes
alive; and the
soul has a life-
giving power
which does not
admit of death
and is therefore
immortal.*

Impossible, replied Cebes.

And now, he said, what did we just now call that
principle which repels the even?

The odd.

And that principle which repels the musical or
the just?

e   The unmusical, he said, and the unjust.

And what do we call that principle which does
not admit of death?

The immortal, he said.

And does the soul admit of death?

No.

Then the soul is immortal?

Yes, he said.

And may we say that this has been proven?

Yes, abundantly proven, Socrates, he replied.

106a   Supposing that the odd were imperishable, must
not three be imperishable?   *Illustrations.*

Of course.

And if that which is cold were imperishable,
when the warm principle came attacking the

snow, must not the snow have retired whole and unmelted—for it could never have perished, nor could it have remained and admitted the heat?

True, he said.

Again, if the uncooling or warm principle were imperishable, the fire when assailed by cold would not have perished or have been extinguished, but would have gone away unaffected?

Certainly, he said.

And the same may be said of the immortal: if b the immortal is also imperishable, the soul when attacked by death cannot perish; for the preceding argument shows that the soul will not admit of death, or ever be dead, any more than three or the odd number will admit of the even, or fire, or the heat in the fire, of the cold. Yet a person may say: "But although the odd will not become even at the approach of the even, why may not the odd perish and the even take the place of the odd?" Now to c him who makes this objection, we cannot answer that the odd principle is imperishable; for this has not been acknowledged, but if this had been acknowledged, there would have been no difficulty in contending that at the approach of the even the odd principle and the number three took their departure; and the same argument would have held good of fire and hate and any other thing.

Very true.

And the same may be said of the immortal: if the immortal is also imperishable, *The immortal* then the soul will be imperishable *is imperishable,* as well as immortal; but if not, *and therefore* d some other proof of her imperish- *the soul is* ableness will have to be given. *imperishable.*

No other proof is needed, he said; for if the immortal, being eternal, is liable to perish, then nothing is imperishable.

Yes, replied Socrates, and yet all men will agree that God, and the essential form of life, and the immortal in general, will never perish.

Yes, all men, he said—that is true; and what is more, gods, if I am not mistaken, as well as men.

e   Seeing then that the immortal is indestructible, must not the soul, if she is immortal, be also imperishable?

Most certainly.

Then when death attacks a man, the mortal portion of him may be supposed to die, but the immortal retires at the approach of death and is preserved safe and sound?

True.

Then, Cebes, beyond question, *At death the*
107a   the soul is immortal and imperish- *soul retires into*
able, and our souls will truly exist *another world.*
in another world!

I am convinced, Socrates, said Cebes, and have nothing more to object; but if my friend Simmias, or any one else, has any further objection to make, he had better speak out, and not keep silence, since I do not know to what other season he can defer the discussion, if there is anything which he wants to say or to have said.

But I have nothing more to say, replied Simmias; nor can I see any reason for doubt after what has been said. But I still feel and cannot help feel-
b   ing uncertain in my own mind, when I think of the greatness of the subject and the feebleness of man.

Yes, Simmias, replied Socrates, that is well said:

and I may add that first principles, even if they appear certain, should be carefully considered; and when they are satisfactorily ascertained, then, with a sort of hesitating confidence in human reason, you may, I think, follow the course of the argument; and if that be plain and clear, there will be no need for any further enquiry.

Very true.

But then, O my friends, he said, if the soul is really immortal, what care should be taken of her, not only in respect of the portion of time which is called life, but of eternity! And the danger of ne-

"Wherefore, seeing all these things, what manner of persons ought we to be?"

c

glecting her from this point of view does indeed appear to be awful. If death had only been the end of all, the wicked would have had a good bargain in dying, for they would have been happily quit not only of their body, but of their own evil together with their souls. But now, inasmuch as the soul is manifestly immortal, there is no release or salvation from evil except the attainment of the highest virtue and wisdom. For the soul when on her progress to the world below takes nothing with her but nurture and education; and these are said greatly to benefit or greatly to injure the departed, at the very beginning of his journey thither.

d

For after death, as they say, the genius of each individual, to whom he belonged in life, leads him to a certain place in which the dead are gathered together, whence after

The attendant genius of each brings him after death to the judgment.

judgment has been given they pass into the world below, following the guide, who is appointed to

e

conduct them from this world to the other: and
when they have there received their due and remained their time, another guide brings them back
108a   again after many revolutions of ages. Now this way
to the other world is not, as Aeschylus says in the
Telephus, a single and straight path—if that were
so no guide would be needed, for no one could miss
it; but there are many partings of the road, and
windings, as I infer from the rites and sacrifices
which are offered to the gods below in places where
three ways meet on earth. The wise and orderly
soul follows in the straight path   *The different*
and is conscious of her surround-   *destinies of pure*
ings; but the soul which desires the *and impure*
body, and which, as I was relating   *souls.*
before, has long been fluttering about the lifeless
b   frame and the world of sight, is after many struggles
and many sufferings hardly and with violence carried away by her attendant genius; and when she
arrives at the place where the other souls are gathered, if she be impure and have done impure deeds,
whether foul murders or other crimes which are
the brothers of these, and the works of brothers in
crime—from that soul every one flees and turns
away; no one will be her companion, no one her
guide, but alone she wanders in extremity of evil
until certain times are fulfilled, and when they are
c   fulfilled, she is borne irresistibly to her own fitting
habitation; as every pure and just soul which has
passed through life in the company and under the
guidance of the gods has also her own proper home.

Now the earth has divers won-   *Description*
derful regions, and is indeed in   *of the divers*
nature and extent very unlike the *regions of eath.*

notions of geographers, as I believe on the authority of one who shall be nameless.

What do you mean, Socrates? said Simmias. I   d
have myself heard many descriptions of the earth,
but I do not know, and I should very much like to
know, in which of these you put faith.

And I, Simmias, replied Socrates, if I had the art
of Glaucus would tell you; although I know not that
the art of Glaucus could prove the truth of my tale,
which I myself should never be able to prove, and
even if I could, I fear, Simmias, that my life would
come to an end before the argument was completed.
I may describe to you, however, the form and regions
of the earth according to my conception of them.   e

That, said Simmias, will be enough.

Well, then, he said, my convic-   *The earth is a*
tion is that the earth is a round   *round body kept*
body in the centre of the heavens,   *in her place by*
                                       equipoise and
and therefore has no need of air or   *the equability of*
any similar force to be a support,   *the surrounding*   109a
but is kept there and hindered .   *element.*
from falling or inclining any way
by the equability of the surrounding heaven and
by her own equipoise.[39] For that which, being in
equipoise, is in the centre of that which is equably
diffused, will not incline any way in any degree, but
will always remain in the same state and not devi-
ate. And this is my first notion.

Which is surely a correct one, said Simmias.

Also I believe that the earth is   *Mankind lives*
very vast, and that we who dwell   *only in a small*   b
in the region extending from the   *portion of*
                                       the earth at a
river Phasis to the Pillars of Hera-   *distance from*
cles[40] inhabit a small portion only *the surface.*

about the sea, like ants or frogs about a marsh, and
that there are other inhabitants of many other like
places; for everywhere on the face of the earth
there are hollows of various forms and sizes, into
which the water and the mist and the lower air col-
lect. But the true earth is pure and situated in the
c pure heaven—there are the stars also; and it is the
heaven which is commonly spoken of by us as the
ether, and of which our own earth is the sediment
gathering in the hollows beneath. But we who live
in these hollows are deceived into the notion that
we are dwelling above on the surface of the earth;
which is just as if a creature who was at the bottom
of the sea were to fancy that he was on the surface
of the water, and that the sea was the heaven
through which he saw the sun and the other stars,
d he having never come to the surface by reason of
his feebleness and sluggishness, and having never
lifted up his head and seen, nor ever heard from
one who had seen, how much purer and fairer the
world above is than his own. And such is exactly
our case: for we are dwelling in a hollow of the
earth, and fancy that we are on the surface; and the
air we call the heaven, in which we imagine that
the stars move. But the fact is, that owing to our
feebleness and sluggishness we
e are prevented from reaching the
surface of the air: for if any man
could arrive at the exterior limit,
or take the wings of a bird and
come to the top, then like a fish
who puts his head out of the water
and sees this world, he would see
a world beyond; and, if the nature

*If, like fishes who
now and then
put their heads
out of the water,
we could rise to
the top of the
atmosphere, we
should behold the
true heaven and
the true earth.*

of man could sustain the sight, he would acknowledge that this other world was the place of the true   110a
heaven and the true light and the true earth. For
our earth, and the stones, and the entire region
which surrounds us, are spoilt and corroded, as in
the sea all things are corroded by the brine, neither
is there any noble or perfect growth, but caverns
only, and sand, and an endless slough of mud; and
even the shore is not to be compared to the fairer
sights of this world. And still less is this our world
to be compared with the other. Of that upper earth   b
which is under the heaven, I can tell you a charming tale, Simmias, which is well worth hearing.

And we, Socrates, replied Simmias, shall be
charmed to listen to you.

The tale, my friend, he said, is   *The upper*
as follows:—In the first place, the   *earth is in every*
earth, when looked at from above,   *respect far*
is in appearance streaked like one   *fairer than the*
of those balls which have leather   *lower. There is*
coverings in twelve pieces, and is   *gold and purple,*
decked with various colours, of   *and pure light,*
which the colours used by paint-   *and trees and*
ers on earth are in a manner sam-   *flowers lovelier*
ples. But there the whole earth is   *far than our*
made up of them, and they are   *own, and all the*
brighter far and clearer than ours;   *stones are more*   c
there is a purple of wonderful lus-   *precious than*
                                         our precious
                                         stones.
tre, also the radiance of gold, and the white which
is in the earth is whiter than any chalk or snow. Of   d
these and other colours the earth is made up, and
they are more in number and fairer than the eye of
man has ever seen; the very hollows (of which I
was speaking) filled with air and water have a co-

lour of their own, and are seen like light gleaming amid the diversity of the other colours, so that the whole presents a single and continuous appearance of variety in unity. And in this fair region everything that grows—trees, and flowers, and fruits—are in a like degree fairer than any here; and there are hills, having stones in them in a like degree smoother, and more transparent, and fairer in colour than our highly valued emeralds and

e   sardonyxes and jaspers, and other gems, which are but minute fragments of them: for there all the stones are like our precious stones, and fairer still. The reason is, that they are pure, and not, like our precious stones, infected or corroded by the corrupt briny elements which coagulate among us, and which breed foulness and disease both in earth and stones, as well as in animals and plants. They are the jewels of the upper earth, which also shines

111a   with gold and silver and the like, and they are set in the light of day and are large and abundant and in all places, making the earth a sight to gladden the beholder's eye. And there are animals and men, some in a middle region, others dwelling about the air as we dwell about the sea; others in islands which the air flows round, near the continent; and, in a word, the air is used by them as the water

b   and the sea are by us, and the ether is to them what the air is to us. Moreover, the temperament of their seasons is such that they have no disease, and live much longer than we do, and have sight and hearing and smell, and all the

The blessed gods dwell there and hold converse with the inhabitants. Description of the interior of the earth and of the subterranean seas and rivers.

other senses, in far greater perfection, in the same
proportion that air is purer than water or the ether
than air. Also they have temples and sacred places
in which the gods really dwell, and they hear their
voices and receive their answers, and are conscious   c
of them and hold converse with them; and they see
the sun, moon, and stars as they truly are, and their
other blessedness is of a piece with this.

Such is the nature of the whole earth, and of
the things which are around the earth; and there
are divers regions in the hollows on the faces of
the globe everywhere, some of them deeper and
more extended than that which we inhabit, others
deeper but with a narrower opening than ours, and
some are shallower and also wider. All have nu-   d
merous perforations, and there are passages broad
and narrow in the interior of the earth, connect-
ing them with one another; and there flows out of
and into them, as into basins, a vast tide of water,
and huge subterranean streams of perennial rivers,
and springs hot and cold, and a great fire, and great   e
rivers of fire, and streams of liquid mud, thin or
thick (like the rivers of mud in Sicily, and the lava
streams which follow them), and the regions about
which they happen to flow are filled up with them.
And there is a swinging or seesaw in the interior of
the earth which moves all this up and down, and
is due to the following cause:—There is a chasm
which is the vastest of them all, and pierces right   112a
through the whole earth; this is that chasm which
Homer describes in the words,—

"Far off, where is the inmost depth beneath the
    earth";

and which he in other places, and many other
poets, have called Tartarus.[41] And the seesaw is
caused by the streams flowing into and out of this
b   chasm, and they each have the nature of the soil
through which they flow. And the reason why the
streams are always flowing in and out, is that the
watery element has no bed or bottom, but is swinging and surging up and down, and the surrounding
wind and air do the same; they follow the water up
and down, hither and thither, over the earth—just
as in the act of respiration the air is always in process of inhalation and exhalation,—and the wind
c   swinging with the water in and out produces fear-
ful and irresistible blasts; when the waters retire
with a rush into the lower parts of the earth, as they
are called, they flow through the earth in those regions, and fill them up like water raised by a pump,
and then when they leave those regions and rush
back hither, they again fill the hollows here, and
when these are filled, flow through subterranean
d   channels and find their way to their several places,
forming seas, and lakes, and rivers, and springs.
Thence they again enter the earth, some of them
making a long circuit into many lands, others going
to a few places and not so distant; and again fall
into Tartarus, some at a point a good deal lower
than that at which they rose, and others not much
lower, but all in some degree lower than the point
from which they came. And some burst forth again
on the opposite side, and some on the same side,
e   and some wind round the earth with one or many
folds like the coils of a serpent, and descend as far
as they can, but always return and fall into the
chasm. The rivers flowing in either direction can

descend only to the centre and no further, for opposite to the rivers is a precipice.

Now these rivers are many, and   *Oceanus,*
mighty, and diverse, and there are   *Acheron,*
four principal ones, of which the   *Pyriphlegethon,*
greatest and outermost is that   *and Styx (or*
called Oceanus,[42] which flows   *Cocytus).*
round the earth in a circle; and in the opposite direction flows Acheron, which passes under the
earth through desert places into the Acherusian   113a
lake: this is the lake to the shores of which the souls
of the many go when they are dead, and after waiting an appointed time, which is to some a longer
and to some a shorter time, they are sent back to
be born again as animals. The third river passes out
between the two, and near the place of outlet
pours into a vast region of fire, and forms a lake
larger than the Mediterranean Sea, boiling with
water and mud; and proceeding muddy and tur-   b
bid, and winding about the earth, comes, among
other places, to the extremities of the Acherusian
lake, but mingles not with the waters of the lake,
and after making many coils about the earth
plunges into Tartarus at a deeper level. This is that
Pyriphlegethon,[43] as the stream is called, which
throws up jets of fire in different parts of the earth.
The fourth river goes out on the opposite side, and
falls first of all into a wild and savage region, which
is all of a dark blue colour, like lapis lazuli; and this
is that river which is called the Stygian river,[44] and   c
falls into and forms the Lake Styx, and after falling
into the lake and receiving strange powers in the
waters, passes under the earth, winding round in
the opposite direction, and comes near the Acheru-

sian lake from the opposite side to Pyriphlegethon.
And the water of this river too mingles with no
other, but flows round in a circle and falls into Tartarus over against Pyriphlegethon; and the name of
the river, as the poets say, is Cocytus.[45]

d   Such is the nature of the other   *The judgment of*
world; and when the dead arrive   *the dead.*
at the place to which the genius of each severally
guides them, first of all, they have sentence passed
upon them, as they have lived well and piously or
not. And those who appear to have lived neither
well nor ill, go to the river Acheron, and embark-
ing in any vessels which they may find, are carried
in them to the lake, and there they dwell and are
purified of their evil deeds, and having suffered
the penalty of the wrongs which they have done to
others, they are absolved, and receive the rewards
of their good deeds, each of them according to his
e   deserts. But those who appear to be incurable by
reason of the greatness of their crimes—who have
committed many and terrible deeds of sacrilege,
murders foul and violent, or the like—such are
hurled into Tartarus which is their suitable destiny,
and they never come out. Those again who have
committed crimes, which, although great, are not
irremediable—who in a moment of anger, for example, have done some violence to a father or a
114a   mother, and have repented for the remainder of
their lives, or, who have taken the life of another
under the like extenuating circumstances—these
are plunged into Tartarus, the pains of which they
are compelled to undergo for a year, but at the end
of the year the wave casts them forth—mere ho-
micides by way of Cocytus, parricides and matri-

cides by Pyriphlegethon—and they are borne to
the Acherusian lake, and there they lift up their
voices and call upon the victims whom they have
slain or wronged, to have pity on them, and to   b
be kind to them, and let them come out into the
lake. And if they prevail, then they come forth
and cease from their troubles; but if not, they are
carried back again into Tartarus and from thence
into the rivers unceasingly, until they obtain mercy
from those whom they have wronged: for that is
the sentence inflicted upon them by their judges.
Those too who have been preeminent for holiness
of life are released from this earthly prison, and go
to their pure home which is above, and dwell in   c
the purer earth; and of these, such as have duly purified themselves with philosophy live henceforth
altogether without the body, in mansions fairer still
which may not be described, and of which the time
would fail me to tell.

Wherefore, Simmias, seeing all these things,
what ought not we to do that we may obtain virtue
and wisdom in this life? Fair is the prize, and the
hope great!

A man of sense ought not to   *These*   d
say, nor will I be very confident,   *descriptions*
that the description which I have   *are not true to*
given of the soul and her mansions   *the letter, but*
is exactly true. But I do say that,   *something like*
inasmuch as the soul is shown to   *them is true.*
be immortal, he may venture to think, not improp-
erly or unworthily, that something of the kind is
true. The venture is a glorious one, and he ought to
comfort himself with words like these, which is the
reason why I lengthen out the tale. Wherefore, I   e

say, let a man be of good cheer about his soul, who having cast away the pleasures and ornaments of the body as alien to him and working harm rather than good, has sought after the pleasures of knowledge; and has arrayed the soul, not in some foreign attire, but in her own proper jewels, temperance, and justice, and courage, and nobility, and truth—in these adorned she is ready to go on her journey to the world below, when her hour comes. You, Simmias and Cebes, and all other men, will depart at some time or other. Me already, as a tragic poet would say, the voice of fate calls. Soon I must drink the poison; and I think that I had better repair to the bath first, in order that the women may not have the trouble of washing my body after I am dead.

When he had done speaking, Crito said: And have you any commands for us, Socrates—anything to say about your children, or any other matter in which we can serve you?

Nothing particular, Crito, he replied: only, as I have always told you, take care of yourselves; that is a service which you may be ever rendering to me and mine and to all of us, whether you promise to do so or not. But if you have no thought for yourselves, and care not to walk according to the rule which I have prescribed for you, not now for the first time, however much you may profess or promise at the moment, it will be of no avail.

We will do our best, said Crito: And in what way shall we bury you?

In any way that you like; but you must get hold of me, and take care that I do not run away from you. Then he turned to us, and added with a

smile:—I cannot make Crito believe that I am the
same Socrates who has been talking and conduct-
ing the argument; he fancies that I   *The dead body*
am the other Socrates whom he   *which remains*
will soon see, a dead body—and   *is not the true*   d
he asks, How shall he bury me?   *Socrates.*
And though I have spoken many words in the endeavour to show that when I have drunk the poison
I shall leave you and go to the joys of the blessed,—
these words of mine, with which I was comforting
you and myself, have had, as I perceive, no effect
upon Crito. And therefore I want you to be surety
for me to him now, as at the trial he was surety to
the judges for me: but let the promise be of another sort; for he was surety for me to the judges
that I would remain, and you must be my surety to
him that I shall not remain, but go away and de-   e
part; and then he will suffer less at my death, and
not be grieved when he sees my body being burned
or buried. I would not have him sorrow at my hard
lot, or say at the burial, Thus we lay out Socrates,
or, Thus we follow him to the grave or bury him;
for false words are not only evil in themselves, but
they inflict the soul with evil. Be of good cheer
then, my dear Crito, and say that you are burying
my body only, and do with that whatever is usual,   116a
and what you think best.

When he had spoken these words, he arose and
went into a chamber to bathe; Crito followed him
and told us to wait. So we remained behind, talking
and thinking of the subject of discourse, and also of
the greatness of our sorrow; he was like a father of
whom we were being bereaved, and we were about
to pass the rest of our lives as orphans. When he

had taken the bath his children were brought to
b   him (he had two young sons and   *He takes leave of*
an elder one); and the women of   *his family.*
his family also came, and he talked to them and
gave them a few directions in the presence of
Crito; then he dismissed them and returned to us.

Now the hour of sunset was near, for a good deal
of time had passed while he was within. When he
came out, he sat down with us again after his bath,
c   but not much was said. Soon the jailer, who was the
servant of the Eleven, entered and stood by him,
saying:—To you, Socrates, whom   *The humanity of*
I know to be the noblest and gen-   *the jailer.*
tlest and best of all who ever came to this place, I
will not impute the angry feeling of other men,
who rage and swear at me, when, in obedience to
the authorities, I bid them drink the poison—
indeed, I am sure that you will not be angry with
me; for others, as you are aware, and not I, are to
d   blame. And so fare you well, and try to bear lightly
what must needs be—you know my errand. Then
bursting into tears he turned away and went out.

Socrates looked at him and said: I return your
good wishes, and will do as you bid. Then turning to
us, he said, How charming the man is: since I have
been in prison he has always been coming to see me,
and at times he would talk to me, and was as good to
me as could be, and now see how generously he sorrows on my account. We must do as he says, Crito;
and therefore let the cup be brought, if the poison is
prepared: if not, let the attendant prepare some.

e   Yet, said Crito, the sun is still   *Crito would*
upon the hilltops, and I know   *detain Socrates*
that many a one has taken the   *a little while.*

draught late, and after the announcement has been made to him, he has eaten and drunk, and enjoyed the society of his beloved; do not hurry—there is time enough.

Socrates said: Yes, Crito, and they of whom you speak are right in so acting, for they think that they will be gainers by the delay; *Socrates thinks that there is nothing to be gained by delay.* but I am right in not following their example, for I do not think that I should gain anything by drinking the poison a little later; I should only be ridiculous in my own eyes for sparing and saving a life which is already forfeit. Please then to do as I say, and not to refuse me.

117a

Crito made a sign to the servant, who was standing by; and he *The poison is brought.* went out, and having been absent for some time, returned with the jailer carrying the cup of poison. Socrates said: You, my good friend, who are experienced in these matters, shall give me directions how I am to proceed. The man answered: You have only to walk about until your legs are heavy, and then to lie down, and the poison will act. At the same time he handed the cup to Socrates, who in the easiest and *He drinks the poison.* gentlest manner, without the least fear or change of colour or feature, looking at the man with all his eyes, Echecrates, as his manner was, took the cup and said: What do you say about making a libation out of this cup to any god? May I, or not? The man answered: We only prepare, Socrates, just so much as we deem enough. I understand, he said: but I may and must ask the gods to prosper my journey from this to the other world—even so—and so be

b

c

it according to my prayer. Then raising the cup to his lips, quite readily and cheerfully he drank off the poison. And hitherto most of us had been able to control our sorrow; but now when we saw him drinking, and saw too that he had finished the draught, we could no longer forbear, and in spite of myself my *The company of friends are unable to control themselves.*
own tears were flowing fast; so that I covered my face and wept, not for him, but at the thought of my own calamity in having to part from such a

d friend. Nor was I the first; for Crito, when he found himself unable to restrain his tears, had got up, and I followed; and at that moment, Apollodorus, who had been weeping all the time, broke out in a loud and passionate cry which made cowards of us all. *Says Socrates, "A man should die in peace."*
Socrates alone retained his calmness: What is this strange outcry? he said. I sent away the women mainly in order that they might not misbehave in

e this way, for I have been told that a man should die in peace. Be quiet then, and have patience. When we heard his words we were ashamed, and refrained our tears; and he walked about until, as he said, his legs began to fail, and then he lay on his back, according to directions, and the man who gave him the poison now and then looked at his

118a feet and legs; and after a while he pressed his foot hard, and asked him if he could feel; and he said, No; and then his leg, and so upwards and upwards, and showed us that he was cold and stiff. And he felt them himself, and said: When the poison reaches the heart, that will be the end. He was beginning to grow cold about the groin, when he uncovered his face, for he had covered himself up, and said—they were his last words—he said: Crito, I owe a cock to Asclepius;[46] will you remember to pay the debt? The debt shall be *The debt to* paid, said Crito; is there anything *Asclepius.* else? There was no answer to this question; but in a minute or two a movement was heard, and the attendants uncovered him; his eyes were set, and Crito closed his eyes and mouth.

Such was the end, Echecrates, of our friend; concerning whom I may truly say, that of all men of his time whom I have known, he was the wisest and justest and best.

Symposium

Persons of the Dialogue

APOLLODORUS, *who repeats to his companion the Dialogue*
which he had heard from Aristodemus, and had already once
narrated to Glaucon, PHAEDRUS, PAUSANIAS, ERYXIMACHUS,
ARISTOPHANES, AGATHON, SOCRATES, ALCIBIADES,
A TROOP OF REVELLERS

Scene

THE HOUSE OF AGATHON

Apollodorus: Concerning the things about which you ask to be informed I believe that I am not ill-prepared with an answer. For the day before yesterday I was coming from my own home at Phalerum to the city, and one of my acquaintance, who had caught sight of me from behind, calling out playfully in the distance, said: Apollodorus, O thou Phalerian[1] man, halt! So I did as I was bid; and then he said, I was looking for you, Apollodorus, only just now, that I might ask you *The speeches delivered at the banquet of Agathon.* about the speeches in praise of love, which were delivered by Socrates, Alcibiades, and others, at Agathon's supper. Phoenix, the son of Philip, told another person who told me of them; his narrative was very indistinct, but he said that you knew, and I wish that you would give me an account of them. Who, if not you, should be the reporter of the words of your friend? And first tell me, he said, were you present at this meeting?

Your informant, Glaucon, I said, must have been very indistinct indeed, if you imagine that the occasion was recent; or that I could have been of the party.

Why, yes, he replied, I thought so.

Impossible: I said. Are you ignorant that for many years Agathon has not resided at Athens; and not three have elapsed since I became acquainted with Socrates, and have made it my daily business to know all that he says and does? There was a time when I was running about the world, fancying myself to be well employed, but I was really a

172a

b

c

173a

most wretched being, no better than you are now. I thought that I ought to do anything rather than be a philosopher.

Well, he said, jesting apart, tell me when the meeting occurred.

In our boyhood, I replied, when Agathon won the prize with his first tragedy, on the day after that on which he and his chorus offered the sacrifice of victory.

The banquet took place many years ago when Agathon won his first prize. The speeches had been preserved by Aristodemus.

Then it must have been a long while ago, he said; and who told you—did Socrates?

b   No, indeed, I replied, but the same person who told Phoenix;—he was a little fellow, who never wore any shoes, Aristodemus, of the deme of Cydathenaeum. He had been at Agathon's feast; and I think that in those days there was no one who was a more devoted admirer of Socrates. Moreover, I have asked Socrates about the truth of some parts of his narrative, and he confirmed them. Then, said Glaucon, let us have the tale over again; is not the road to Athens just made for c   conversation? And so we walked, and talked of the discourses on love: and therefore, as I said at first, I am not ill-prepared to comply with your request, and will have another rehearsal of them if you like. For to speak or to hear others speak of philosophy always gives me the greatest pleasure, to say nothing of the profit. But when I hear another strain, especially that of you rich men and traders, d   such conversation displeases me; and I pity you who are my companions, because you think that you are doing something when in reality you are doing nothing. And I dare say that you pity me in return, whom you regard as an unhappy creature, and very probably you are right. But I certainly know of you what you only think of me—there is the difference.

Companion: I see, Apollodorus, that you are just the same—always speaking evil of yourself, and of others; and I do believe that you pity all mankind, with the exception of Socrates, yourself first of all, true in this to your old name, which, however deserved, I know not how you acquired, of Apollodorus the madman; for you are always raging against yourself and everybody but Socrates.

Apoll.: Yes, friend, and the reason why I am said   e to be mad, and out of my wits, is just because I have these notions of myself and you; no other evidence is required.

Com.: No more of that, Apollodorus; but let me renew my request that you would repeat the conversation.

Apoll.: Well, the tale of love was on this wise:—   174a But perhaps I had better begin at the beginning, and endeavour to give you the exact words of Aristodemus:

He said that he met Socrates fresh from the bath- and sand-alled; and as the sight of the sandals was unusual, he asked him whither he was going that he had been converted into such a beau:—

Aristodemus the narrator had gone to the banquet on the invitation of Socrates.

To a banquet at Agathon's, he replied, whose invitation to his sacrifice of victory I refused yesterday, fearing a crowd, but promising that I would

b come to-day instead; and so I have put on my fin-
ery, because he is such a fine man. What say you to
going with me unasked?

I will do as you bid me, I replied.

Follow then, he said, and let us demolish the
proverb:—

"To the feasts of inferior men the good unbidden
    go";

instead of which our proverb will run:—

"To the feasts of the good the good[2] unbidden
    go";

and this alteration may be sup-   *Homer violates*
ported by the authority of Homer   *his own rule.*
himself, who not only demolishes but literally out-
rages the proverb. For, after picturing Agamemnon
c as the most valiant of men, he makes Menelaus,
who is but a faint-hearted warrior, come unbidden
to the banquet of Agamemnon, who is feasting and
offering sacrifices, not the better to the worse, but
the worse to the better.

I rather fear, Socrates, said Aristodemus, lest
this may still be my case; and that, like Menelaus
in Homer, I shall be the inferior person, who

"To the feasts of the wise unbidden goes."

d But I shall say that I was bidden of you, and then
you will have to make an excuse.

"Two going together,"

he replied, in Homeric fashion, one or other of them may invent an excuse by the way.

This was the style of their conversation as they went along. Socrates dropped behind in a fit of abstraction, and desired Aristodemus, who was waiting, to go on before him. When he reached the   e house of Agathon he found the doors wide open, and a comical thing happened. A servant coming out met him, and led him at once into the banqueting-hall in which the guests were reclining, for the banquet was about to begin. Welcome, Aristodemus, said Agathon, as soon as he appeared—you are just in time to sup with us; if you come on any other matter put it off, and make one of us, as I was looking for you yesterday and meant to *Aristodemus is welcome on his own account, but where is his inseparable companion?* have asked you, if I could have found you. But what have you done with Socrates?

I turned round, but Socrates was nowhere to be seen; and I had to explain that he had been with me a moment before, and that I came by his invitation to the supper.

You were quite right in coming, said Agathon; but where is he himself?

He was behind me just now, as I entered, he   175a said, and I cannot think what has become of him.

Go and look for him, boy, said Agathon, and bring him in; and do you, Aristodemus, meanwhile take the place by Eryximachus.

The servant then assisted him to wash, and he lay down, and presently another servant came in and reported that our friend Socrates had retired into the portico of the neighbouring house. "There he is fixed," said he, "and when I call to him he will not stir."

How strange, said Agathon; then you must call him again, and keep calling him.

b   Let him alone, said my informant; he has a way of stopping anywhere and losing himself without any reason. I believe that he will soon appear; do not therefore disturb him.

Well, if you think so, I will leave   *The courtesy of* him, said Agathon. And then,   *Agathon.* turning to the servants, he added, "Let us have supper without waiting for him. Serve up whatever you please, for there is no one to give you orders; hitherto I have never left you to yourselves. But on this occasion imagine that you are our hosts, and c   that I and the company are your guests; treat us well, and then we shall commend you." After this, supper was served, but still no Socrates; and during the meal Agathon several times expressed a wish to send for him, but Aristodemus objected; and at last when the feast was about half over—for the fit, as usual, was not of long duration—Socrates entered. Agathon, who was reclin-   *At length* ing alone at the end of the table,   *Socrates enters;* begged that he would take the   *the compliments* place next to him; that "I may   *which pass* touch you," he said, "and have the   *between him* d   benefit of that wise thought which   *and Agathon.* came into your mind in the portico, and is now in your possession; for I am certain that you would not have come away until you had found what you sought."

How I wish, said Socrates, taking his place as he was desired, that wisdom could be infused by

touch, out of the fuller into the emptier man, as
water runs through wool out of a fuller cup into an   e
emptier one; if that were so, how greatly should I
value the privilege of reclining at your side! For
you would have filled me full with a stream of wisdom plenteous and fair; whereas my own is of a
very mean and questionable sort, no better than a
dream. But yours is bright and full of promise, and
was manifested forth in all the splendour of youth
the day before yesterday, in the presence of more
than thirty thousand Hellenes.

You are mocking, Socrates, said Agathon, and
ere long you and I will have to determine who
bears off the palm of wisdom—of this Dionysus[3]
shall be the judge; but at present you are better
occupied with supper.

Socrates took his place on the couch, and   176a
supped with the rest; and then libations were offered, and after a hymn had been sung to the god,
and there had been the usual ceremonies, they
were about to commence drinking, when Pausanias said, And now, my friends, how can we drink
with least injury to ourselves? I can assure you that
I feel severely the effect of yesterday's potations,
and must have time to recover; and I suspect that
most of you are in the same pre-   *The good advice*
dicament, for you were of the   *of Pausanias.*
party yesterday. Consider then: How can the drink-   b
ing be made easiest?

I entirely agree, said Aristoph-   *Men who drank*
anes, that we should, by all means,   *hard yesterday*
avoid hard drinking, for I was my-   *should avoid*
self one of those who were yester-   *drinking today.*
day drowned in drink.

I think that you are right, said Eryximachus, the son of Acumenus; but I should still like to hear one other person speak: Is Agathon able to drink hard?

I am not equal to it, said Agathon.

c   Then, said Eryximachus, the weak heads like myself, Aristodemus, Phaedrus, and others who never can drink, are fortunate in finding that the stronger ones are not in a drinking mood. (I do not include Socrates, who is able either to drink or to abstain, and will not mind, whichever we do.) Well, as of none of the company seem disposed to drink much, I may be forgiven for saying, as a physician, that drinking deep is a bad practice, which I never

d   follow, if I can help, and certainly do not recommend to another, least of all to any one who still feels the effects of yesterday's carouse.

I always do what you advise, and especially what you prescribe as a physician, rejoined Phaedrus the Myrrhinusian, and the rest of the company, if they are wise, will do the same.

e   It was agreed that drinking was not to be the order of the day, but that they were all to drink only so much as they pleased.

Then, said Eryximachus, as you are all agreed that drinking is to be voluntary, and that there is to be no compulsion, I move, in the next place, that the flute-girl, who has just made her appearance, be told to go away and play to herself, or, if she likes, to the women who are within. To-day let us

177a   have conversation instead; and, if you will allow me, I will tell you what sort of conversation. This proposal having been accepted, Eryximachus proceeded as follows:—

I will begin, he said, after the manner of Mela-
nippe in Euripides,

"Not mine the word"

which I am about to speak, but *Eryximachus*
that of Phaedrus. For often he *descants upon*
says to me in an indignant tone:— *the neglect of*
"What a strange thing it is, Eryxi- *the poets to*
machus, that, whereas other gods *hymn Love's*
have poems and hymns made in *praises.*
their honour, the great and glorious god, Love,   b
has no encomiast[4] among all the poets who are so
many. There are the worthy Sophists too—the excellent Prodicus, for example—who have descanted
in prose on the virtues of Heracles and other heroes; and, what is still more extraordinary, I have
met with a philosophical work in which the utility
of salt has been made the theme of an eloquent
discourse; and many other like things have had   c
a like honour bestowed upon them. And only to
think that there should have been an eager interest
created about them, and yet that to this day no one
has ever dared worthily to hymn Love's praises! So
entirely has this great deity been neglected." Now
in this Phaedrus seems to me to be quite right, and
therefore I want to offer him a contribution; also I
think that at the present moment we who are here
assembled cannot do better than honour the god   d
Love. If you agree with me, there will be no lack
of conversation; for I mean to propose that each
of us in turn, going from left to right, shall make a
speech in honour of Love. Let him give us the best
which he can; and Phaedrus, because he is sitting

first on the left hand, and because he is the father
of the thought, shall begin.

No one will vote against you, Eryximachus, said
Socrates. How can I oppose your motion, who profess to understand nothing but   *It is agreed*
matters of love? Nor, I presume,   *to make a*
will Agathon and Pausanias; and   *succession of*
there can be no doubt of Aristoph- *speeches in his*
anes, whose whole concern is with   *honour.*
Dionysus and Aphrodite;[5] nor will any one disagree of those whom I see around me. The proposal, as I am aware, may seem rather hard upon
us whose place is last; but we shall be contented if
we hear some good speeches first. Let Phaedrus
begin the praise of Love, and good luck to him. All
178a   the company expressed their assent, and desired
him to do as Socrates bade him.

Aristodemus did not recollect all that was said,
nor do I recollect all that he related to me; but I
will tell you what I thought most worthy of remembrance, and what the chief speakers said.

Phaedrus began by affirming that Love is a
mighty god, and wonderful among gods and men,
b   but especially wonderful in his birth. For he is the
eldest of the gods, which is an honour to him; and
a proof of his claim to this honour is, that of his
parents there is no memorial; neither poet nor
prose-writer has ever affirmed that he had any. As
Hesiod says:—

"First Chaos came, and then broad-bosomed
    Earth,
The everlasting seat of all that is,
And Love."

In other words, after Chaos, the Earth and Love, these two, came into being. Also Parmenides sings of Generation:

"First in the train of gods, he fashioned Love."

And Acusilaus[6] agrees with Hesiod. Thus numerous are the witnesses who acknowledge Love to be the eldest of the gods. And not only is he the eldest, he is also the source of the greatest benefits to us. For I know not any greater blessing to a young man who is beginning life than a virtuous lover,

Love is the eldest of the gods, and the source of the greatest good. For an honourable love is the best incentive to virtue.   c

or to the lover than a beloved youth. For the principle which ought to be the guide of men who would nobly live—that principle, I say, neither kindred, nor honour, nor wealth, nor any other motive is able to implant so well as love. Of what am I speaking? Of the sense of honour and dishonour, d without which neither States nor individuals ever do any good or great work. And I say that a lover who is detected in doing any dishonourable act, or submitting through cowardice when any dishonour is done to him by another, will be more pained at being detected by his beloved than at being seen by his father, or by his companions, or by any one else. The beloved too, when he is found in any disgraceful situation, has the same feeling about his e lover. And if there were only some way of contriving that a state or an army should be made up of lovers and their loves, they would be the very best governors of their own city, abstaining from all dis-

179a honour, and emulating one another in honour; and when fighting at each other's side, although a mere handful, they would overcome the world. For what lover would not choose rather to be seen by all mankind than by his beloved, either when abandoning his post or throwing away his arms? He would be ready to die a thousand deaths rather than endure this. Or who would desert his beloved or fail him in the hour of danger? The veriest coward would become an inspired hero, equal to the

b bravest, at such a time; Love would inspire him. That courage which, as Homer says, the god breathes into the souls of some heroes, Love of his own nature infuses into the lover.

Love will make men dare to die for their beloved—love alone; and women as well as men. Of this, Alcestis, the daughter of Pelias, is a monument to all Hel-

c las; for she was willing to lay down her life on behalf of her husband,

Love has made men and women dare to die for their beloved. The examples of Alcestis and Achilles.

when no one else would, although he had a father and mother; but the tenderness of her love so far exceeded theirs, that she made them seem to be strangers in blood to their own son, and in name only related to him; and so noble did this action of hers appear to the gods, as well as to men, that among the many who have done virtuously she is one of the very few to whom, in admiration of her noble action, they have granted the privilege of returning alive to earth; such exceeding honour is

d paid by the gods to the devotion and virtue of love. But Orpheus,[7] the son of Oeagrus, the harper, they sent empty away, and presented to him an appari-

tion only of her whom he sought, but herself they
would not give up, because he showed no spirit; he
was only a harp-player, and did not dare like Alcestis to die for love, but was contriving how he
might enter Hades alive; moreover, they afterwards
caused him to suffer death at the hands of women,
as the punishment of his cowardliness. Very dif-   e
ferent was the reward of the true love of Achilles
towards his lover Patroclus—his lover and not his
love (the notion that Patroclus was the beloved one
is a foolish error into which Aeschylus has fallen,
for Achilles was surely the fairer of the two, fairer
also than all the other heroes; and, as Homer in-   180a
forms us, he was still beardless, and younger far).
And greatly as the gods honour the virtue of love,
still the return of love on the part of the beloved to
the lover is more admired and valued and rewarded
by them, for the lover is more divine; because he
is inspired by God. Now Achilles was quite aware,
for he had been told by his mother, that he might
avoid death and return home, and live to a good
old age, if he abstained from slaying Hector. Nevertheless he gave his life to revenge his friend, and   b
dared to die, not only in his defence, but after he
was dead. Wherefore the gods honoured him even
above Alcestis, and sent him to the Islands of the
Blest. These are my reasons for affirming that Love
is the eldest and noblest and mightiest of the gods,
and the chiefest author and giver of virtue in life,
and of happiness after death.

   This, or something like this, was the speech of   c
Phaedrus; and some other speeches followed which
Aristodemus did not remember; the next which he
repeated was that of Pausanias. Phaedrus, he said,

the argument has not been set before us, I think,
quite in the right form;—we should not be called
upon to praise Love in such an indiscriminate manner. If there were only one Love, then what you
said would be well enough; but since there are
more Loves than one, you should have begun by
determining which of them was to be the theme of
our praises. I will amend this defect; and first of all
I will tell you which Love is deserving of praise, and
then try to hymn the praiseworthy one in a manner
worthy of him. For we all know that Love is inseparable from Aphrodite, and if there were only one
Aphrodite there would be only one Love; but as
there are two goddesses there must be two Loves.
And am I not right in asserting that there are two
goddesses? The elder one, having *The spiritual*
no mother, who is called the heav- *and the*
enly Aphrodite—she is the daugh- *common love*
ter of Uranus; the younger, who is *derived from*
the daughter of Zeus and Dione— *the heavenly*
her we call common;[8] and the *and the earthly*
Love who is her fellow-worker is *Aphrodite.*
rightly named common, as the other love is called
heavenly. All the gods ought to have praise given to
them, but not without distinction of their natures;
and therefore I must try to distinguish the characters of the two Loves. Now actions vary according
to the manner of their performance. Take, for example, that which we are now doing, drinking, singing and talking—these actions are not in themselves
either good or evil, but they turn out in this or that
way according to the mode of performing them;
and when well done they are good, and when
wrongly done they are evil; and in like manner not

every love, but only that which has a noble purpose, is noble and worthy of praise. The Love who is the offspring of the common Aphrodite is essentially common, and has no discrimination, being such as the meaner sort of men feel, and is apt to be of women as well as of youths, and is of the body rather than of the soul—the most foolish beings are the objects of this love which desires only to gain an end, but never thinks of accomplishing the end nobly, and therefore does good and evil quite indiscriminately. The goddess who is his mother is far younger than the other, and she was born of the union of the male and female, and partakes of both. But the offspring of the heavenly Aphrodite is derived from a mother in whose birth *The higher* c
the female has no part,—she is *love is of the* from the male only; this is that love *male, which* which is of youths,[9] and the god- *may be a divine* dess being older, there is nothing *inspiration,* of wantonness in her. Those who *and which may* are inspired by this love turn to the *also be grossly abused.*

male, and delight in him who is the more valiant and intelligent nature; any one may recognise the pure enthusiasts in the very character of their attachments. For they love not boys, but intelligent d
beings whose reason is beginning to be developed, much about the time at which their beards begin to grow. And in choosing young men to be their companions, they mean to be faithful to them, and pass their whole life in company with them, not to take them in their inexperience, and deceive them, and play the fool with them, or run away from one to another of them. But the love of young boys should be forbidden by law, because their future is uncer-

tain; they may turn out good or bad, either in body
or soul, and much noble enthusiasm may be thrown
e　　away upon them; in this matter the good are a law
to themselves, and the coarser sort of lovers ought
to be restrained by force, as we restrain or attempt
to restrain them from fixing their affections on
182a　　women of free birth. These are the persons who
bring a reproach on love; and some have been led
to deny the lawfulness of such attachments because
they see the impropriety and evil of them; for surely
b　　nothing that is decorously and lawfully done can
justly be censured. Now here and in Lacedaemon
the rules about love are perplex-　　*The feeling*
ing, but in most cities they are　　*about male loves*
simple and easily intelligible; in　　*differs in the*
Elis and Boeotia, and in countries　　*different states*
　　of Hellas.
having no gifts of eloquence, they
are very straightforward; the law is simply in favour
of these connexions, and no one, whether young or
old, has anything to say to their discredit; the reason being, as I suppose, that they are men of few
words in those parts, and therefore the lovers do
not like the trouble of pleading their suit. In Ionia
and other places, and generally in countries which
are subject to the barbarians, the custom is held to
be dishonourable; lovers of youths share the evil repute in which philosophy and gymnastic are held,
c　　because they are inimical to tyranny; for the interests of rulers require that their subjects should be
poor in spirit; and that there should be no strong
bond of friendship or society among them, which
love, above all other motives, is likely to inspire, as
our Athenian tyrants learned by experience; for the
d　　love of Aristogeiton and the constancy of Harmo-

dius[10] had a strength which undid their power. And, therefore, the ill-repute into which these attachments have fallen is to be ascribed to the evil condition of those who make them to be ill-reputed; that is to say, to the self-seeking of the governors and the cowardice of the governed; on the other hand, the indiscriminate honour which is given to them in some countries is attributable to the laziness of those who hold this opinion of them. In our own country a far better principle prevails, but, as I was saying, the explanation of it is rather perplexing. For, observe that open loves are held to be more honourable than secret ones, and that the love of the noblest and highest, even if their persons are less beautiful than others, is especially honourable. Consider, too, how great is the encouragement which all the world gives to the lover; neither is he supposed to be doing anything dishonourable; but if he succeeds he is praised, and if *Custom allows* he fails he is blamed. And in the *the lover to do* pursuit of his love the custom of *strange things.*   e mankind allows him to do many strange things,   183a which philosophy would bitterly censure if they were done from any motive of interest, or wish for office or power. He may pray, and entreat, and supplicate, and swear, and lie on a mat at the door, and endure a slavery worse than that of any slave—in any other case friends and enemies would be equally ready to prevent him, but now there is no friend who will be ashamed of him and admonish   b him, and no enemy will charge him with meanness or flattery; the actions of a lover have a grace which ennobles them; and custom has decided that they are highly commendable and that there no loss of character in them; and, what is strangest of all, he only may swear and forswear himself (so men say), and the gods will forgive his transgression, for there is no such thing as a lover's oath. Such is the

c entire liberty which gods and men have allowed the lover, according to the custom which prevails in our part of the world. From this point of view a man fairly argues that in Athens to love and to be loved is held to be a very honourable thing. But when parents forbid their sons to talk with their lovers, and place them under a tutor's care, who is appointed to see to these things, and their companions and equals cast in their teeth anything of

d the sort which they may observe, and their elders refuse to silence the reprovers and do not rebuke them—any one who reflects on all this will, on the contrary, think that we hold these practices to be most disgraceful. But, as I was saying at first, the truth as I imagine is, that whether such practices are honourable or whether they are dishonourable is not a simple question; they are honourable to him who follows them honourably, dishonourable to him who follows them dishonourably. There is dishonour in yielding to the evil, or in an evil manner; but there is honour in yielding to the good, or in an honourable manner. Evil is the vulgar lover who loves the body rather than the soul, inas-much as he is not even stable, be-

e cause he loves a thing which is in itself unstable, and therefore when the bloom of youth which he was desiring is over, he takes wing and flies away, in spite of all

The true love is the love of the soul, which has no regard to beauty or money or power, and which when tested by time is found to be enduring.

his words and promises; whereas the love of the
noble disposition is lifelong, for it becomes one
with the everlasting. The custom of our country
would have both of them proven well and truly,   184a
and would have us yield to the one sort of lover and
avoid the other, and therefore encourages some to
pursue, and others to fly; testing both the lover and
beloved in contests and trials, until they show to
which of the two classes they respectively belong.
And this is the reason why, in the first place, a hasty
attachment is held to be dishonourable, because
time is the true test of this as of most other things;
and secondly there is a dishonour in being overcome by the love of money, or of wealth, or of political power, whether a man is frightened into
surrender by the loss of them, or, having experi-   b
enced the benefits of money and political corruption, is unable to rise above the seductions of them.
For none of these things are of a permanent or
lasting nature; not to mention that no generous
friendship ever sprang from them. There remains,
then, only one way of honourable attachment
which custom allows in the beloved, and this is the
way of virtue; for as we admitted that any service   c
which the lover does to him is not to be accounted
flattery or a dishonour to himself, so the beloved
has one way only of voluntary service which is not
dishonourable, and this is virtuous service.

For we have a custom, and according to our custom any one who does service to another under the
idea that he will be improved by him either in wisdom, or in some other particular of virtue—such a
voluntary service, I say, is not to be regarded as a
dishonour, and is not open to the charge of flattery.

d　　And these two customs, one the
love of youth, and the other the
practice of philosophy and virtue
in general, ought to meet in one,
and then the beloved may honourably indulge the lover. For
when the lover and beloved come

*Love is fellow-
service; and the
love of youth
and the practice
of philosophy
should meet in
one.*

together, having each of them a law, and the lover
thinks that he is right in doing any service which he
can to his gracious loving one; and the other that
he is right in showing any kindness which he can to
him who is making him wise and good; the one ca-
e　　pable of communicating wisdom and virtue, the
other seeking to acquire them with a view to education and wisdom; when the two laws of love are
fulfilled and meet in one—then, and then only,
may the beloved yield with honour to the lover.
Nor when love is of this disinterested sort is there
any disgrace in being deceived, but in every other
case there is equal disgrace in being or not being
185a　deceived. For he who is gracious to his lover under
the impression that he is rich, and is disappointed
of his gains because he turns out to be poor, is dis-
graced all the same: for he has done his best to
show that he would give himself up to any one's
"uses base"[11] for the sake of money; but this is not
honourable. And on the same principle, he who
gives himself to a lover because he is a good man,
and in the hope that he will be improved by his
company, shows himself to be virtuous, even
b　　though the object of his affection turn out to be a
villain, and to have no virtue; and if he is deceived
he has committed a noble error. For he has proved
that for his part he will do anything for anybody

with a view to virtue and improvement, than which there can be nothing nobler. Thus noble in every case is the acceptance of another for the sake of virtue. This is that love which is the love of the heavenly goddess, and is heavenly, and of great price to individuals and cities, making the lover and the beloved alike eager in the work of their own improvement. But all other loves are the off- c spring of the other, who is the common goddess. To you, Phaedrus, I offer this my contribution in praise of love, which is as good as I could make extempore.

Pausanias came to a pause— *Aristophanes* this is the balanced way in which *has the* I have been taught by the wise to *hiccough, and* speak; and Aristodemus said that *Eryximachus* the turn of Aristophanes was next, *speaks in his* but either he had eaten too much, *turn.* or from some other cause he had the hiccough, and was obliged to change turns with Eryximachus the physician, who was reclining on the couch d below him. Eryximachus, he said, you ought either to stop my hiccough, or to speak in my turn until I have left off.

I will do both, said Eryximachus: I will speak in your turn, and do you speak in mine; and while I am speaking let me recommend you to hold your breath, and if after you have done so for some time the hiccough is no better, then gargle with a little water; and if it still continues, tickle your nose with something and sneeze; and if you sneeze once or e twice, even the most violent hiccough is sure to go. I will do as you prescribe, said Aristophanes, and now get on.

Eryximachus spoke as follows: *Medicine is the*
Seeing that Pausanias made a fair *knowledge of*
the loves and
186a beginning, and but a lame ending, *desires of the*
I must endeavour to supply his de- *body, which are*
ficiency. I think that he has rightly *twofold.*
distinguished two kinds of love.
But my art further informs me that the double love
is not merely an affection of the soul of man towards the fair, or towards anything, but is to be
found in the bodies of all animals and in produc-
tions of the earth, and I may say in all that is; such
is the conclusion which I seem to have gathered
b from my own art of medicine, whence I learn how
great and wonderful and universal is the deity of
love, whose empire extends over all things, divine
as well as human. And from medicine I will begin
that I may do honour to my art. There are in the
human body these two kinds of love, which are
confessedly different and unlike, and being unlike,
they have loves and desires which are unlike; and
the desire of the healthy is one, and the desire of
the diseased is another; and as Pausanias was just
now saying that to indulge good men is honour-
c able, and bad men dishonourable:—so too in the
body the good and healthy elements are to be indulged, and the bad elements and the elements of
disease are not to be indulged, but discouraged.
And this is what the physician has to do, and in this
the art of medicine consists: for medicine may be
regarded generally as the knowledge of the loves
and desires of the body, and how to satisfy them or
not; and the best physician is he who is able to sep-
d arate fair love from foul, or to convert one into the
other; and he who knows how to eradicate and how

to implant love, whichever is required, and can
reconcile the most hostile elements in the constitution and make them loving friends, is a skilful
practitioner. Now the most hostile are the most opposite, such as hot and cold, bitter and sweet, moist
and dry, and the like. And my an-   *Harmony is the*
cestor, Asclepius,[12] knowing how   *reconciliation,*   e
to implant friendship and accord   *not of opposite*
in these elements, was the creator   *elements, but of*
of our art, as our friends the poets   *elements which*
here tell us, and I believe them;   *disagreed once,*
and not only medicine in every   *and are now*
                                         harmonized.
branch, but the arts of gymnastic and husbandry
are under his dominion. Any one who pays the   187a
least attention to the subject will also perceive that
in music there is the same reconciliation of opposites; and I suppose that this must have been the
meaning of Heracleitus,[13] although his words are
not accurate; for he says that The One is united by
disunion, like the harmony of the bow and the lyre.
Now there is an absurdity in saying that harmony is
discord or is composed of elements which are still
in a state of discord. But what he probably meant
was, that harmony is composed of differing notes
of higher or lower pitch which disagreed once, but
are now reconciled by the art of music; for if the   b
higher and lower notes still disagreed, there could
be no harmony,—clearly not. For harmony is a
symphony, and symphony is an agreement; but an
agreement of disagreements while they disagree
there cannot be; you cannot harmonize that which   c
disagrees. In like manner rhythm is compounded
of elements short and long, once differing and now
in accord; which accordance, as in the former in-

stance, medicine, so in all these other cases, music implants, making love and unison to grow up among them; and thus music, too, is concerned with the principles of love in their application to harmony and rhythm. Again, in the essential nature of harmony and rhythm there is no difficulty in discerning love which has not yet become dou-

d   ble. But when you want to use them in actual life, either in the composition of songs or in the correct performance of airs or meters composed already, which latter is called education, then the difficulty begins, and the good artist is needed. Then the old tale has to be repeated of fair and heavenly love— the love of Urania[14] the fair and heavenly muse, and of the duty of accepting the temperate, and those who are as yet intemperate only that they may become temperate, and of preserving their

e   love; and again, of the vulgar Polyhymnia,[15] who must be used with circumspection that the pleasure be enjoyed, but may not generate licentiousness; just as in my own art it is a great matter so to regulate the desires of the epicure that he may gratify his tastes without the attendant evil of disease. Whence I infer that in music, in medicine, in all other things human as well as divine, both loves ought to be noted as far as may be, for they are

188a   both present.

The course of the seasons is also full of both these principles; and when, as I was saying, the elements of hot and cold, moist and dry, attain the harmonious love of one another and blend in temperance and harmony, they bring to men, animals, and plants health and plenty, and do them no harm; whereas the wanton love, getting the upper hand

and affecting the seasons of the year, is very de-
structive and injurious, being the source of pesti-
lence, and bringing many other *The harmony*   b
kinds of diseases on animals and *of the true and*
plants; for hoarfrost and hail and *false love may*
blight spring from the excesses *be discerned*
and disorders of these elements of *animals, in the*
love, which to know in relation to *seasons, in the*
the revolutions of the heavenly *whole province*
bodies and the seasons of the year *of divination.*
is termed astronomy. Furthermore, all sacrifices
and the whole province of divination, which is the
art of communion between gods and men—these,   c
I say, are concerned only with the preservation of
the good and the cure of the evil love. For all manner of impiety is likely to ensue if, instead of accepting and honouring and reverencing the
harmonious love in all his actions, a man honours
the other love, whether in his feelings towards
gods or parents, towards the living or the dead.
Wherefore the business of divination is to see to
these loves and to heal them, and divination is the
peacemaker of gods and men, working by a knowl-   d
edge of the religious or irreligious tendencies
which exist in human loves. Such is the great and
mighty, or rather omnipotent force of love in general. And the love, more especially, which is concerned with the good, and which is perfected in
company with temperance and justice, whether
among gods or men, has the greatest power, and is
the source of all our happiness and harmony, and
makes us friends with the gods who are above us,
and with one another. I dare say that I too have
omitted several things which might be said in

e　praise of Love, but this was not intentional, and
you, Aristophanes, may now supply the omission
or take some other line of commendation; for I
perceive that you are rid of the hiccough.

189a　　　Yes, said Aristophanes, who followed, the hiccough is gone; not, however, until I applied the
sneezing; and I wonder whether the harmony of
the body has a love of such noises and ticklings, for
I no sooner applied the sneezing than I was cured.

Eryximachus said: Beware, friend Aristophanes,
although you are going to speak, you are making fun
b　of me; and I shall have to watch and see whether
I cannot have a laugh at your expense, when you
might speak in peace.

You are quite right, said Aristophanes, laughing. I
will unsay my words; but do you please not to watch
me, as I fear that in the speech which I am about to
make, instead of others laughing with me, which is
to the manner born of our muse and would be all
the better, I shall only be laughed at by them.

Do you expect to shoot your bolt and escape,
Aristophanes? Well, perhaps if you are very careful
and bear in mind that you will be called to account,
c　I may be induced to let you off.

Aristophanes professed to open another vein of
discourse; he had a mind to praise Love in another
way, unlike that either of Pausanias or Eryximachus. Mankind, he said, judging by their neglect of
him, have never, as I think, at all understood the
power of Love. For if they had understood him
they would surely have built noble temples and al-
tars, and offered solemn sacrifices in his honour;
but this is not done, and most certainly ought to be
d　done: since of all the gods he is the best friend of

men, the helper and the healer of the ills which are
the great impediment to the happiness of the race.
I will try to describe his power to *The original*
you, and you shall teach the rest of *human nature*
the world what I am teaching you. *unlike the*
In the first place, let me treat of *present. The*
three sexes;
the nature of man and what has *their form and*
happened to it; for the original *origin.*
human nature was not like the
present, but different. The sexes were not two as
they are now, but originally three in number; there   e
was man, woman, and the union of the two, having
a name corresponding to this double nature, which
had once a real existence, but is now lost, and the
word "Androgynous"[16] is only preserved as a term
of reproach. In the second place, the primeval man
was round, his back and sides forming a circle; and
he had four hands and four feet, one head with two
faces, looking opposite ways, set on a round neck   190a
and precisely alike; also four ears, two privy members, and the remainder to correspond. He could
walk upright as men now do, backwards or for-
wards as he pleased, and he could also roll over and
over at a great pace, turning on his four hands and
four feet, eight in all, like tumblers going over and
over with their legs in the air; this was when he   b
wanted to run fast. Now, the sexes were three, and
such as I have described them; because the sun,
moon, and earth are three; and the man was originally the child of the sun, the woman of the earth,
and the man-woman of the moon, which is made
up of sun and earth, and they were all round and
moved round and round like their *Their rebellious*
parents. Terrible was their might *spirit.*

and strength, and the thoughts of their hearts were great, and they made an attack upon the gods; of them is told the tale of Otys and Ephi-

c altes who, as Homer says, dared to scale heaven, and would have laid hands upon the gods. Doubt reigned in the celestial councils. Should they kill them and annihilate the race with thunderbolts, as they had done the giants, then there would be an end of the sacrifices and worship which men offered to them; but, on the other hand, the gods could not suffer their insolence to be unrestrained. At last, after a good deal of reflection, Zeus discovered a way. He said: *Various* "Methinks I have a plan which *operations are* will humble their pride and im- *performed on* prove their manners; men shall *them by the* continue to exist, but I will cut *command of* them in two and then they will be *Zeus.*

d diminished in strength and increased in numbers; this will have the advantage of making them more profitable to us. They shall walk upright on two legs, and if they continue insolent and will not be quiet, I will split them again and they shall hop about on a single leg." He spoke and cut men in two, like a sorb-apple which is halved for pickling,

e or as you might divide an egg with a hair; and as he cut them one after another, he bade Apollo give the face and the half of the neck a turn in order that the man might contemplate the section of himself: he would thus learn a lesson of humility. Apollo was also bidden to heal their wounds and compose their forms. So he gave a turn to the face and pulled the skin from the sides all over that which in our language is called the belly, like

the purses which draw in, and he made one mouth
at the centre, which he fastened in a knot (the
same which is called the navel); he also moulded
the breast and took out most of the wrinkles,
much as a shoemaker might smooth leather upon   191a
a last; he left a few, however, in the region of the
belly and navel, as a memorial of the primeval
state. After the division the two parts of man,
each desiring his other half, came together, and
throwing their arms about one another, entwined
in mutual embraces, longing to grow into one;
they were on the point of dying from hunger and   b
self-neglect, because they did not like to do anything apart; and when one of the *The two halves*
halves died and the other sur- *wander about*
vived, the survivor sought an- *longing after*
other mate, man or woman, as we *one another.*
call them,—being the sections of entire men or
women,—and clung to that. They were being destroyed, when Zeus in pity of them invented a
new plan: he turned the parts of generation round
to the front, for this had not been always their
position, and they sowed the seed no longer as
hitherto like grasshoppers in the ground, but in   c
one another; and after the transposition the male
generated in the female in order that by mutual embraces of man and woman they might
breed, and the race might continue; or if man
came to man they might be satisfied, and rest, and
go their ways to the business of life: so ancient is
the desire of one another which is implanted in
us, reuniting our original nature, making one of
two, and healing the state of man. Each of us   d
when separated, having one side only, like a flat

fish, is but the indenture of a man, and he is always looking for his other half. *The characters of men and women depend upon the nature from which they were originally severed.* Men who are a section of that double nature which was once called Androgynous are lovers of women; adulterers are generally of this breed, and also adulterous women who lust after men: the women who are a section of the woman do not care for men, but have female attachments; the female companions are of this sort. But they who are a section of the male, follow the male, and while they are young, being slices of the original man, they hang about men and embrace them, and they are themselves the best of boys and youths, because they have the most manly nature. Some indeed assert that they are shameless, but this is not true; for they do not act thus from any want of shame, but because they are valiant and manly, and have a manly countenance, and they embrace that which is like them. And these when they grow up become our statesmen, and these only, which is a great proof of the truth of what I am saying. When they reach manhood they are lovers of youth, and are not naturally inclined to marry or beget children,—if at all, they do so only in obedience to the law; but they are satisfied if they may be allowed to live with one another unwedded; and such a nature is prone to love and ready to return love, always embracing that which is akin to him. *The strong presentiment which lovers have of they know not what.* And when one of them meets with his other half, the actual half of himself, whether he be a lover of youth or a lover

of another sort, the pair are lost in an amazement
of love and friendship and intimacy, and one will
not be out of the other's sight, as I may say, even for
a moment: these are the people who pass their
whole lives together; yet they could not explain
what they desire of one another. For the intense
yearning which each of them has towards the other
does not appear to be the desire of lover's intercourse, but of something else which the soul of either evidently desires and cannot tell, and of which
she has only a dark and doubtful presentiment.   d
Suppose Hephaestus,[17] with his instruments, to
come to the pair who are lying side by side and to
say to them, "What do you people want of one another?" they would be unable to explain. And suppose further, that when he saw their perplexity he
said: "Do you desire to be wholly one; always day
and night to be in one another's company? for if
this is what you desire, I am ready to melt you into
one and let you grow together, so that being two
you shall become one, and while you live a com-   e
mon life as if you were a single man, and after your
death in the world below still be one departed soul
instead of two—I ask whether this is what you lov-
ingly desire, and whether you are satisfied to attain
this?"—there is not a man of them who when he
heard the proposal would deny or would not acknowledge that this meeting and melting into one
another, thus becoming one instead of two, was the
very expression of his ancient need. And the reason is that human nature was originally one and we
were a whole, and the desire and pursuit of the   193a
whole is called love. There was a time, I say, when
we were one, but now because of the wickedness

of mankind God has dispersed us, as the Arcadians
were dispersed into villages by the *Worse may*
Lacedaemonians.[18] And if we are *yet befall men*
not obedient to the gods, there is a *unless they*
danger that we shall be split up *worship the gods: they may*
again and go about in *basso-* *be not halved*
rilievo,[19] like the profile figures *only, but*
having only half a nose which are *quartered.*
sculptured on monuments, and that we shall be like
tallies. Wherefore let us exhort all men to piety, that

b we may avoid evil, and obtain the good, of which
Love is to us the lord and minister; and let no one
oppose him—he is the enemy of the gods who op-
poses him. For if we are friends of the God and at
peace with him we shall find our own true loves,
which rarely happens in this world at present. I am
serious, and therefore I must beg Eryximachus not
to make fun or to find any allusion in what I am saying to Pausanias and Agathon, who, as I suspect, are

c both of the manly nature, and belong to the class
which I have been describing. But my words have a
wider application—they include men and women
everywhere; and I believe that if our loves were
perfectly accomplished, and each one returning to
his primeval nature had his original true love, then
our race would be happy. And if this would be best
of all, the best in the next degree and under present
circumstances must be the nearest approach to
such an union; and that will be the attainment of a
congenial love. Wherefore, if we would praise him
who has given to us the benefit, we must praise the

d god Love, who is our greatest benefactor, both
leading us in this life back to our own nature, and
giving us high hopes for the future, for he promises

that if we are pious, he will restore us to our original
state, and heal us and make us happy and blessed.
This, Eryximachus, is my discourse of love, which,
although different from yours, I must beg you to
leave unassailed by the shafts of your ridicule, in
order that each may have his turn; *Aristophanes*   e
each, or rather either, for Agathon *deprecates*
and Socrates are the only ones left. *ridicule.*

Indeed, I am not going to attack you, said Eryximachus, for I thought your speech charming, and
did I not know that Agathon and Socrates are masters in the art of love, I should be really afraid that
they would have nothing to say, after the world of
things which have been said already. But, for all
that, I am not without hopes.

Socrates said: You played your part well, Eryxi-   194a
machus; but if you were as I am now, or rather as
I shall be when Agathon has spoken, you would,
indeed, be in a great strait.

You want to cast a spell over me, Socrates, said
Agathon, in the hope that I may be disconcerted at
the expectation raised among the audience that I
shall speak well.

I should be strangely forgetful, Agathon, replied   b
Socrates, of the courage and magnanimity which
you showed when your own compositions were
about to be exhibited, and you came upon the
stage with the actors and faced the vast theatre altogether undismayed, if I thought that your nerves
could be fluttered at a small party of friends.

Do you think, Socrates, said Agathon, that my
head is so full of the theatre as not to know how
much more formidable to a man of sense a few
good judges are than many fools?

c   Nay, replied Socrates, I should be very wrong in attributing to you, Agathon, that or any other want of refinement. And I am quite aware that if you happened to meet with any whom you thought wise, you would care for their opinion much more than for that of the many. But then we, having been a part of the foolish many in the theatre, cannot be regarded as the select wise; though I know that if you chanced to be in the presence, not of one of ourselves, but of some really wise man, you would be ashamed of disgracing yourself before him—would you not?

Yes, said Agathon.

But before the many you would not be ashamed, if you thought that you were doing something disgraceful in their presence?

d   Here Phaedrus interrupted them, saying: Do not answer him, *Socrates is not allowed to talk.* my dear Agathon; for if he can only get a partner with whom he can talk, especially a good-looking one, he will no longer care about the completion of our plan. Now, I love to hear him talk; but just at present I must not forget the encomium on Love which I ought to receive from him and from every one. When you and he have paid your tribute to the god, then you may talk.

e   Very good, Phaedrus, said Agathon; I see no reason why I should not proceed with my speech, as I shall have many other opportunities of conversing with Socrates. Let me say first how I ought to speak, and then speak:—

The previous speakers, instead of praising the god Love, or unfolding his nature, appear to have con-
195a   gratulated mankind on the benefits which he confers

upon them. But I would rather praise the god first, and then speak of his gifts; this is always the right way of praising everything. May I say without impiety or offence, that of all the blessed gods he is the most blessed because he is the fairest and best? And he is the fairest: for, in the first place, he is the youngest, and of his youth he is himself the witness, fleeing out of the way of age, who is swift enough, swifter truly than most of us like:—Love

The god Love should be praised on his own account, and not for the benefits which he confers upon mankind.

b

hates him and will not come near him; but youth and love live and move together—like to like, as the proverb says. Many things were said by Phaedrus about Love in which I agree with him; but I cannot agree that he is older than Iapetus and Cronos:[20]—not so; I maintain him to be the youngest of the gods, and youthful ever. The ancient doings among the gods of which Hesiod and Parmenides spoke, if the tradition of them be true, were done of Necessity and not of Love; had Love been in those days, there would have been no chaining or mutilation of the gods, or other violence, but peace and sweetness, as there is now in heaven, since the rule of Love began. Love is young and also tender; he ought to have a poet like

c

Love is not old, but young and tender;

Homer to describe his tenderness, as Homer says of Ate,[21] that she is a goddess and tender:—

d

"Her feet are tender, for she set her steps,
Not on the ground but on the heads of men":

herein is an excellent proof of her tenderness,—that she walks not upon the hard but upon the soft.

e   Let us adduce a similar proof of the tenderness of
Love; for he walks not upon the earth, nor yet upon
the skulls of men, which are not so very soft, but in
the hearts and souls of both gods and men, which
are of all things the softest: in them he walks and
dwells and makes his home. Not in every soul without exception, for where there is hardness he departs, where there is softness there he dwells; and
nestling always with his feet and in all manner of
ways in the softest of soft places, how can he be

196a   other than the softest of all things? Of a truth he is
the tenderest as well as the youngest, and also he is
of flexile form; for if he were hard and without flex-
ure he could not enfold all things,   *soft;*
or wind his way into and out of every soul of man
undiscovered. And a proof of his flexibility and
symmetry of form is his grace, which is universally
admitted to be in an especial manner the attribute
of Love; ungrace and love are always at war with
one another. The fairness of his complexion is revealed by his habitation among   *fair;*

b   the flowers; for he dwells not amid bloomless or
fading beauties, whether of body or soul or aught
else, but in the place of flowers and scents, there
he sits and abides. Concerning the beauty of the
god I have said enough; and yet there remains
much more which I might say. Of his virtue I have
now to speak: his greatest glory is that he can neither do nor suffer wrong to or from any god or any
man; for he suffers not by force if   *just;*

c   he suffers; force comes not near him, neither when
he acts does he act by force. For all men in all
things serve him of their own free will, and where
there is voluntary agreement, there, as the laws

which are the lords of the city say, is justice. And
not only is he just but exceedingly *temperate;*
temperate, for Temperance is the acknowledged
ruler of the pleasures and desires, and no pleasure
ever masters Love; he is their master and they are
his servants; and if he conquers them he must be   d
temperate indeed. As to courage, even the God of
War is no match for him; he is the   *courageous;*
captive and Love is the lord, for love, the love of
Aphrodite, masters him, as the tale runs; and the
master is stronger than the servant. And if he conquers the bravest of all others, he must be himself
the bravest. Of his courage and justice and temperance I have spoken, but I have yet to speak of his
wisdom; and according to the *wise;*
measure of my ability I must try to do my best. In   e
the first place he is a poet (and here, like Eryximachus, I magnify my art), and he is   *a poet too, and*
also the source of poesy in others, which he could
not be if he were not himself a poet. And at the
touch of him every one becomes a   *a maker of*
poet even though he had no music   *poets;*
in him before; this also is a proof
that Love is a good poet and accomplished in all the
fine arts; for no one can give to another that which
he has not himself, or teach that of which he has no
knowledge. Who will deny that the creation of the
animals is his doing? Are they not   *an artist, and*   197a
all the works of his wisdom, born   *creator of order;*
and begotten of him? And as to the artists, do we
not know that he only of them whom love inspires
has the light of fame?—he whom Love touches not
walks in darkness. The arts of medicine and archery
and divination were discovered by Apollo, under

the guidance of love and desire; so that he too is a
b   disciple of Love. Also the melody of the Muses, the
metallurgy of Hephaestus, the weaving of Athene,
the empire of Zeus over gods and men, are all due
to Love, who was the inventor of them. And so
Love set in order the empire of the gods—the love
of beauty, as is evident, for with deformity Love has
no concern. In the days of old, as I began by saying,
dreadful deeds were done among the gods, for they
were ruled by Necessity; but now since the birth of
Love, and from the Love of the beautiful, has
c   sprung every good in heaven and earth. Therefore,
Phaedrus, I say of Love that he is the fairest and
best in himself, and the cause of what is fairest and
best in all other things. And there comes into my
mind a line of poetry in which he is   *a peacemaker;*
said to be the god who

> "Gives peace on earth and calms the stormy
>   deep,
> Who stills the winds and bids the sufferer sleep."[22]

d   This is he who empties men of disaffection and fills
them with affection, who makes them to meet together at banquets such as these: in sacrifices,
feasts, dances, he is our lord—who sends courtesy
and sends away discourtesy, who gives kindness
ever and never gives unkindness; the friend of the
good, the wonder of the wise, the amazement of
the gods; desired by those who have no part in him,
and precious to those who have the better part in
him; parent of delicacy, luxury, desire, fondness,
softness, grace; regardful of the good, regardless of
the evil: in every word, work, wish,   *a savior;*

fear—saviour, pilot, comrade, helper; glory of gods
and men, leader best and brightest: in whose foot-   e
steps let every man follow, sweetly singing in his
honour and joining in that sweet *best and*
strain with which love charms the *brightest.*
souls of gods and men. Such is the speech, Phaedrus, half-playful, yet having a certain measure of
seriousness, which, according to my ability, I dedi-
cate to the god.

When Agathon had done speaking, Aristodemus   198a
said that there was a general cheer; the young man
was thought to have spoken in a manner worthy of
himself, and of the god. And Socrates, looking at
Eryximachus, said: Tell me, son of Acumenus, was
there not reason in my fears? and was I not a true
prophet when I said that Agathon would make a
wonderful oration, and that I should be in a strait?

The part of the prophecy which concerns Agathon, replied Eryximachus, appears to me to be
true; but not the other part—that you will be in a
strait.

Why, my dear friend, said   *Socrates tries to*   b
Socrates, must not I or any one be   *excuse himself*
in a strait who has to speak after he   *from speaking*
has heard such a rich and varied   *on the ground*
that he never
discourse? I am especially struck   *understood the*
with the beauty of the conclud-   *nature of the*
ing words—who could listen to   *compact. They*
them without amazement? When   *have attributed*
to Love an
I reflected on the immeasurable   *imaginary*
inferiority of my own powers, I   *greatness and*
was ready to run away for shame,   *goodness; but he*
if there had been a possibility of   *can only praise*
escape. For I was reminded of   *truly.*   c

Gorgias, and at the end of his speech I fancied that
Agathon was shaking at me the Gorginian or Gorgonian[23] head of the great master of rhetoric, which
was simply to turn me and my speech into stone,
as Homer says, and strike me dumb. And then I
d   perceived how foolish I had been in consenting to
take my turn with you in praising love, and saying
that I too was a master of the art, when I really had
no conception how anything ought to be praised.
For in my simplicity I imagined that the topics of
praise should be true, and that this being presup-
posed, out of the true the speaker was to choose
the best and set them forth in the best manner. And
I felt quite proud, thinking that I knew the nature
e   of true praise, and should speak well. Whereas I
now see that the intention was to attribute to Love
every species of greatness and glory, whether really belonging to him or not, without regard to truth
or falsehood—that was no matter; for the original
proposal seems to have been not that each of you
should really praise Love, but only that you should
appear to praise him. And so you attribute to Love
every imaginable form of praise which can be gath-
199a   ered anywhere; and you say that "he is all this," and
"the cause of all that," making him appear the fairest and best of all to those who know him not, for
you cannot not impose upon those who know him.
And a noble and solemn hymn of praise have you
rehearsed. But as I misunderstood the nature of
the praise when I said that I would take my turn, I
must beg to be absolved from the promise which I
made in ignorance, and which (as Euripides would
say) was a promise of the lips and not of the mind.
Farewell then to such a strain: for I do not praise

in that way; no, indeed, I cannot. But if you like
to hear the truth about love, I am ready to speak   b
in my own manner, though I will not make myself
ridiculous by entering into any rivalry with you. Say
then, Phaedrus, whether you would like to have the
truth about love, spoken in any words and in any
order which may happen to come into my mind at
the time. Will that be agreeable to you?

Aristodemus said that Phaedrus and the company bid him speak in any manner which he
thought best. Then, he added, let me have your
permission first to ask Agathon a few more questions, in order that I may take his admissions as the
premisses of my discourse.

I grant the permission, said Phaedrus: put your   c
questions. Socrates then proceeded as follows:—

In the magnificent oration   *Love is of*
which you have just uttered, I   *something*
think that you were right, my dear   *and desires*
Agathon, in proposing to speak of   *something*
the nature of Love first and after-   *which he does*
wards of his works—that is a way   *not possess in*
of beginning which I very much   *himself.*
approve. And as you have spoken so eloquently of
his nature, may I ask you further, Whether love is   d
the love of something or of nothing? And here I
must explain myself: I do not want you to say that
love is the love of a father or the love of a mother—
that would be ridiculous; but to answer as you
would, if I asked is a father a father of something?
to which you would find no difficulty in replying, of
a son or daughter: and the answer would be right.

Very true, said Agathon.

And you would say the same of a mother?

He assented.

e	Yet let me ask you one more question in order to illustrate my meaning: Is not a brother to be regarded essentially as a brother of something?

Certainly, he replied.

That is, of a brother or sister?

Yes, he said.

And now, said Socrates, I will ask about Love:—Is Love of something or of nothing?

Of something, surely, he replied.

200a	Keep in mind what this is, and tell me what I want to know—whether Love desires that of which love is.

Yes; surely.

And does he possess, or does he not possess, that which he loves and desires?

Probably not, I should say.

Nay, replied Socrates, I would have you consider whether "necessarily" is not rather the word. The inference that he who desires something is in want of some-

Love, therefore, is not good or great, but desires to be good or great.

b	thing, and that he who desires nothing is in want of nothing, is in my judgment, Agathon, absolutely and necessarily true. What do you think?

I agree with you, said Agathon.

Very good. Would he who is great, desire to be great, or he who is strong, desire to be strong?

That would be inconsistent with our previous admissions.

True. For he who is anything cannot want to be that which he is?

Very true.

And yet, added Socrates, if a

A seeming exception; of course we admit that a man may desire the continuance or increase of that which he has.

man being strong desired to be strong, or being
swift desired to be swift, or being healthy desired
to be healthy, in that case he might be thought to
desire something which he already has or is. I give   c
the example in order that we may avoid misconception. For the possessors of these qualities, Agathon, must be supposed to have their respective
advantages at the time, whether they choose or
not; and who can desire that which he has? Therefore, when a person says, I am well and wish to be
well, or I am rich and wish to be rich, and I desire
simply to have what I have—to him we shall reply:
"You, my friend, having wealth and health and   d
strength, want to have the continuance of them;
for at this moment, whether you choose or no, you
have them. And when you say, I desire that which I
have and nothing else, is not your meaning that you
want to have what you now have in the future?" He
must agree with us—must he not?

He must, replied Agathon.

Then, said Socrates, he desires that what he has
at present may be preserved to him in the future,
which is equivalent to saying that he desires something which is non-existent to him, and which as
yet he has not got?

Very true, he said.   e

Then he and every one who desires, desires that
which he has not already, and which is future and
not present, and which he has not, and is not, and
of which he is in want;—these are the sort of things
which love and desire seek?

Very true, he said.

Then now, said Socrates, let us   *Recapitulation*
recapitulate the argument. First,   *of the argument.*

is not love of something, and of something too which is wanting to a man?

201a   Yes, he replied.

Remember further what you said in your speech, or if you do not remember I will remind you: you said that the love of the beautiful set in order the empire of the gods, for that of deformed things there is no love—did you not say something of that kind?

Yes, said Agathon.

Yes, my friend, and the remark was a just one. And if this is true, Love is the love of beauty and not of deformity?

He assented.

b   And the admission has been already made that Love is of something which a man wants and has not?

True, he said.

Then Love wants and has not beauty?

Certainly, he replied.

And would you call that beauti-   *The conclusion* ful which wants and does not pos-   *is, that love is* sess beauty?   *not beautiful* *but is of the* Certainly not.   *beautiful,* Then would you still say that   *and that the* love is beautiful?   *beautiful is the* Agathon replied: I fear that I   *good.* did not understand what I was saying.

c   You made a very good speech, Agathon, replied Socrates; but there is yet one small question which I would fain ask:—Is not the good also the beautiful?

Yes.

Then in wanting the beautiful, love wants also the good?

I cannot refute you, Socrates, said Agathon:— Let us assume that what you say is true.

Say rather, beloved Agathon, that you cannot refute the truth; for Socrates is easily refuted.

The argument was communicated to Socrates by Diotima.

And now, taking my leave of you, I will rehearse a tale of love which I heard from Diotima of Mantineia,[24] a woman wise in this and in many other kinds of knowledge, who in the days of old, when the Athenians offered sacrifice before the coming of the plague, delayed the disease ten years. She was my instructress in the art of love, and I shall repeat to you what she said to me, beginning with the admissions made by Agathon, which are nearly if not quite the same which I made to the wise woman when she questioned me: I think that this will be the easiest way, and I shall take both parts myself as well as I can. As you, Agathon, suggested, I must speak first of the being and nature of Love, and then of his works. First I said to her in nearly the same words which he used to me, that Love was a mighty god, and likewise fair; and she proved to me as I proved to him that, by my own showing, Love was neither fair nor good.

Love is not to be esteemed foul and evil because he is not fair and good:

"What do you mean, Diotima," I said, "is love then evil and foul?" "Hush," she cried; "must that be foul which is not fair?" "Certainly," I said. "And is that which is not wise, ignorant? Do you not see that there is a mean between wisdom and ignorance?" "And what may that be?" I said. "Right opinion," she replied; "which, as you know, being incapable of giving a reason, is not knowledge (for how can knowledge be devoid of reason? nor again, ignorance, for neither can ignorance attain the truth), but is clearly something which is a mean between ignorance and wisdom." "Quite

b   true," I replied. "Do not then insist," she said, "that what is not fair is of necessity foul, or what is not good evil; or infer that because Love is not fair and good he is therefore foul and evil; for he is in a mean between them." "Well," I said, "Love is

c   surely admitted by all to be a great god." "By those who know or by those who do not know?" "By all." "And how, Socrates," she said with a smile, "can Love be acknowledged to be a great god by those who say that he is not a god at all?" "And who are they?" I said. "You and I are two of them," she replied. "How can that be?" I said. "It is quite intelligible," she replied; "for you yourself would acknowledge that the gods are happy and fair—of course you would—would you *but, on the other* dare to say that any god was not?" *hand, he is not* "Certainly not," I replied. "And *a god who does* you mean by the happy, those who *not possess the* are the possessors of things good *good and the*

d   or fair?" "Yes." "And you admitted *fair.* that Love, because he was in want, desires good and fair things of which he is in want?" "Yes, I did." "But how can he be a god who has no portion in what is either good or fair?" "Impossible." "Then you see that you also deny the divinity of Love."

"What then is Love?" I asked. *He is a great* "Is he mortal?" "No." "What *spirit who* then?" "As in the former instance, *mediates between* he is neither mortal nor immor- *gods and men;*

tal, but in a mean between the two." "What is he,
Diotima?" "He is a great spirit (δαιμων), and like
all spirits he is intermediate between the divine   e
and the mortal." "And what," I said, "is his
power?" "He interprets," she replied, "between
gods and men, conveying and taking across to the
gods the prayers and sacrifices of men, and to
men the commands and replies of the gods; he is
the mediator who spans the chasm which divides
them, and therefore in him all is bound together,
and through him the arts of the prophet and the   203a
priest, their sacrifices and mysteries and charms,
and all prophecy and incantation, find their way.
For God mingles not with man; but through Love
all the intercourse and converse of God with man,
whether awake or asleep, is carried on. The wisdom which understands this is spiritual; all other
wisdom, such as that of arts and handicrafts, is
mean and vulgar. Now these spirits or intermediate powers are many and diverse, and one of them   b
is Love." "And who," I said, "was his father, and
who his mother?" "The tale," she said, "will take
time; nevertheless I will tell you.   *the son of Plenty*
On the birthday of Aphrodite   *and Poverty;*
there was a feast of the gods, at which the god
Poros, or Plenty, who is the son of Metis, or Dis-
cretion, was one of the guests. When the feast was
over, Penia, or Poverty, as the manner is on such
occasions, came about the doors to beg. Now
Plenty, who was the worse for nectar (there was
no wine in those days), went into the garden of
Zeus and fell into a heavy sleep; and Poverty considering her own straitened circumstances, plot-   c
ted to have a child by him, and accordingly she lay

down at his side and conceived Love, who partly because he is naturally a lover of the beautiful, and because Aphrodite is herself beautiful, and also because he was born on her birthday, is her follower and attendant. And as his parentage is, so also are his fortunes. In the first place he is always poor, and anything but tender and fair, as the many imagine him; and he is *a shoeless, houseless, ill-favoured vagabond, who is always conspiring against the fair and good;*

d   rough and squalid, and has no shoes, nor a house to dwell in; on the bare earth exposed he lies under the open heaven, in the streets, or at the doors of houses, taking his rest; and like his mother he is always in distress. Like his father too, whom he also partly resembles, he is always plotting against the fair and good; he is bold, enterprising, strong, a mighty hunter, always weaving some intrigue or other, keen in the pursuit of wisdom, fertile in resources; a philosopher at all

e   times, terrible as an enchanter, sorcerer, sophist. He is by nature neither mortal nor immortal, but alive and flourishing at one moment when he is in plenty, and dead at another moment, and again alive by reason of his father's nature. But that which is always flowing in is always flowing out, and so he is never in want and never in wealth; and, further, he is in a mean between ignorance and knowledge: The truth of the *not wise, but a* matter is this: No god is a philos- *lover of wisdom.* opher or seeker after wisdom, for he is wise already; nor does any man who is wise seek after wisdom. Neither do the ignorant seek after wisdom. For herein is the evil of ignorance, that he

who is neither good nor wise is nevertheless satis- 204a
fied with himself: he has no desire for that of
which he feels no want." "But who, then, Diotima," I said, "are the lovers of wisdom, if they
are neither the wise nor the foolish?" "A child   b
may answer that question," she replied; "they are
those who are in a mean between the two; Love is
one of them. For wisdom is a most beautiful
thing, and Love is of the beautiful; and therefore
Love is also a philosopher, or lover of wisdom,
and being a lover of wisdom is in a mean between
the wise and the ignorant. And of this too his
birth is the cause; for his father is wealthy and
wise, and his mother poor and foolish. Such, my
dear Socrates, is the nature of the spirit Love.   c
The error in your conception of him was very
natural, and as I imagine from what you say, has
arisen out of a confusion of love and the beloved,
which made you think that love was all beautiful.
For the beloved is the truly beautiful, and deli-
cate, and perfect, and blessed; but the principle
of love is of another nature, and is such as I have
described."

I said: "O thou stranger woman, *Love is of the*
thou sayest well, but, assuming *beautiful, but in*   d
Love to be such as you say, what is *what?*
the use of him to men?" "That, Socrates," she replied, "I will attempt to unfold: of his nature and
birth I have already spoken; and you acknowledge
that love is of the beautiful. But some one will say:
Of the beautiful in what, Socrates and Diotima?—or
rather let me put the question more clearly, and
ask: When a man loves the beautiful, what does he
desire?" I answered her, "That the beautiful may be

his." "Still," she said, "the answer suggests a further question: What is given by   *Of the*
the possession of beauty?" "To   *possession of*
what you have asked," I replied, "I   *the beautiful,*
have no answer ready." "Then,"   *which is also the*
she said, "let me put the word   *possession of the*
e   'good' in the place of the beauti-   *good, which is*
ful, and repeat the question once   *happiness.*
more: If he who loves loves the good, what is it
then that he loves?" "The possession of the good,"
I said. "And what does he gain who possesses the
good?" "Happiness," I replied; "there is less difficulty in answering that question." "Yes," she said,
"the happy are made happy by the acquisition of
205a   good things. Nor is there any need to ask why a
man desires happiness; the answer is already final."
"You are right," I said. "And is this wish and this
desire common to all? and do all men always desire
their own good, or only some men?—what say
you?" "All men," I replied; "the desire is common
to all." "Why, then," she rejoined, "are not all men,
b   Socrates, said to love, but only some of them?
whereas you say that all men are always loving the
same things." "I myself wonder," I said, "why this
is." "There is nothing to wonder   *Yet love is not*
at," she replied; "the reason is that   *commonly used*
one part of love is separated off   *in this general*
and receives the name of the   *sense.*
whole, but the other parts have other names."
"Give an illustration," I said. She answered me as
follows: "There is poetry, which, as you know, is
d   complex and manifold. All creation or passage of
non-being into being is poetry or making, and the
processes of all art are creative; and the masters of

arts are all poets or makers." "Very true." "Still,"
she said, "you know that they are not called poets,
but have other names; only that portion of the art
which is separated off from the rest, and is concerned with music and meter, is termed poetry,
and they who possess poetry in this sense of the
word are called poets." "Very true," I said. "And
the same holds of love. For you may say generally
that all desire of good and happiness is only the
great and subtle power of love; but they who are
drawn towards him by any other path, whether the
path of money-making or gymnastic or philosophy, are not called lovers—the name of the whole
is appropriated to those whose affection takes one
form only—they alone are said to love, or to be lovers." "I dare say," I replied, "that you are right."
"Yes," she added, "and you hear people say that
lovers are seeking for their other half; but I say that
they are seeking neither for the half of themselves,
nor for the whole, unless the half or the whole be   e
also a good. And they will cut off their own hands
and feet and cast them away, if they are evil; for
they love not what is their own, unless perchance
there be some one who calls what belongs to him
the good, and what belongs to another the evil. For   206a
there is nothing which men love but the good. Is
there anything?" "Certainly, I should say, that there
is nothing." "Then," she said, "the simple truth is,
that men love the good." "Yes," I said. "To which
must be added that they love the possession of the
good?" "Yes, that must be added." "And not only
the possession, but the everlasting possession of
the good?" "That must be added too." "Then love,"
she said, "may be described generally as the love of

the everlasting possession of the good?" "That is
most true."

b   "Then if this be the nature of   *Love is birth, is*
love, can you tell me further," she   *creation; is the*
said, "what is the manner of the   *divine power of*
pursuit? What are they doing who   *conception or*
show all this eagerness and heat   *parturition;*
which is called love? and what is the object which
they have in view? Answer me." "Nay, Diotima," I
replied, "if I had known, I should not have wondered at your wisdom, neither should I have come
to learn from you about this very matter." "Well,"
she said, "I will teach you:—The object which they
have in view is birth in beauty, whether of body or

c   soul." "I do not understand you," I said; "the oracle
requires an explanation." "I will make my meaning
clearer," she replied. "I mean to say, that all men
are bringing to the birth in their bodies and in their
souls. There is a certain age at which human nature is desirous of procreation—procreation which
must be in beauty and not in deformity; and this
procreation is the union of man and woman, and is
a divine thing; for conception and generation are

d   an immortal principle in the mortal creature, and
in the inharmonious they can never be. But the deformed is always inharmonious with the divine,
and the beautiful harmonious. Beauty, then, is the
destiny or goddess of parturition[25] who presides at
birth, and therefore, when approaching beauty,
the conceiving power is propitious, and diffusive,
and benign, and begets and bears fruit: at the sight
of ugliness she frowns and contracts and has a
sense of pain, and turns away, and shrivels up, and
not without a pang refrains from conception. And

this is the reason why, when the hour of conception arrives, and the teeming nature is full, there is such a flutter and ecstasy about beauty whose approach is the alleviation of the pain of tra- *is not the love* vail. For love, Socrates, is not, as *of the beautiful* e you imagine, the love of the beau- *only, but of* tiful only." "What then?" "The *birth in beauty.* love of generation and of birth in beauty." "Yes," I said. "Yes, indeed," she replied. "But why of generation?" "Because to the mortal creature, generation is a sort of eternity and immortality," she replied; "and if, as has been already admitted, love is of the everlasting possession of the good, all men will necessarily desire immortality together with 207a good: Wherefore love is of immortality."

All this she taught me at various times when she spoke of love. And I remember her once saying to me, "What is the cause, Socrates, of love, and the attendant desire? See you not how all animals, birds, as well as beasts, in their desire of procre- ation, are in agony when they take *Whence arises* the infection of love, which begins *the great power* with the desire of union; whereto *of love in men* is added the care of offspring, on *and animals?* b whose behalf the weakest are ready to battle against the strongest even to the uttermost, and to die for them, and will let themselves be tormented with hunger or suffer anything in order to maintain their young? Man may be supposed to act thus from reason; but why should animals have these passionate feelings? Can you tell me why?" Again I c replied that I did not know. She said to me: "And do you expect ever to become a master in the art of love, if you do not know this?" "But I have told you

already, Diotima, that my ignorance is the reason why I come to you; for I am conscious that I want a teacher; tell me then the cause of this and of the other mysteries of love." "Marvel not," she said, "if you believe that love is of the immortal, as we have several times acknowledged; for here again, and on
d the same principle too, the mortal nature is seeking as far as is possible to be everlasting and immortal: and this is only to be attained by generation, because generation always leaves behind a new existence in the place of the old. Nay, even in the life of the same individual there is succession and not absolute unity: a man is called the same, and yet in the short interval which elapses between youth and age, and in which every animal is said to have life and identity, he is undergoing a perpetual process of loss and
e reparation—hair, flesh, bones, blood, and the whole body are always changing. Which is true not only of the body, but also of the soul, whose habits, tempers, opinions, desires, pleasures, pains,

The mortal nature is always changing and generating, body and soul alike; the sciences come and go, and are preserved by recollection; and all human things, unlike the divine, are made immortal by a law of succession.

fears, never remain the same in any one of us, but are always coming and going; and equally true of knowledge, and what is still more surprising to us
208a mortals, not only do the sciences in general spring up and decay, so that in respect of them we are never the same; but each of them individually experiences a like change. For what is implied in the word 'recollection,' but the departure of knowledge, which is ever being forgotten, and is renewed

and preserved by recollection, and appears to be the same although in reality new, according to that law of succession by which all mortal things are preserved, not absolutely the same, but by substitution, the old worn-out mortality leaving another new and similar existence behind— unlike the divine, which is always the same and not another? And in this way, Socrates, the mortal body, or mortal anything, partakes of immortality; but the immortal in another way. Marvel not then at the love which all men have of their offspring; for that universal love and interest is for the sake of immortality."

b

I was astonished at her words, and said: "Is this really true, O thou wise Diotima?" And she answered with all the authority of an accomplished Sophist: "Of that, Socrates, you may be assured;— think only of the ambition of men, and you will wonder at the senselessness of their ways, unless you consider how they are stirred by the love of an immortality of fame. They are ready to run all risks greater far than they would have run for their children, and to spend money and undergo any sort of toil, and even to die, for the sake of leaving behind them a name which shall be eternal. Do you imagine that Alcestis would have died to save Admetus, or Achilles to avenge Patroclus, or your own Codrus in order to preserve the kingdom for his sons, if they had not imagined that the memory of their virtues, which still survives among us, would be immortal? Nay," she said, "I am persuaded that all men do all things, and the

c

The struggles and sufferings of human life are all of them animated by the desire of immortality.

d

e better they are the more they do them, in hope of the glorious fame of immortal virtue; for they desire the immortal.

"Those who are pregnant in the body only, betake themselves to women and beget children—this is the character of their love; their offspring, as they hope, will preserve their memory and giving them the blessedness and immortality which they desire in the future. 209a But souls which are pregnant— for there certainly are men who are more creative in their souls

The creations of the soul,— conceptions of wisdom and virtue, the works of poets and legislators,—are fairer far than any mortal children.

than in their bodies—conceive that which is proper for the soul to conceive or contain. And what are these conceptions?—wisdom and virtue in general. And such creators are poets and all artists who are deserving of the name inventor. But the greatest and fairest sort of wisdom by far is that which is concerned with the ordering of states and families, and which is called temperance and justice. And he who in youth has the seed of these implanted in b him and is himself inspired, when he comes to maturity desires to beget and generate. He wanders about seeking beauty that he may beget offspring— for in deformity he will beget nothing—and naturally embraces the beautiful rather than the deformed body; above all, when he finds a fair and noble and well-nurtured soul, he embraces the two in one person, and to such an one he is full of c speech about virtue and the nature and pursuits of a good man; and he tries to educate him; and at the touch of the beautiful which is ever present to his

memory, even when absent, he brings forth that which he had conceived long before, and in company with him tends that which he brings forth; and they are married by a far nearer tie and have a closer friendship than those who beget mortal children, for the children who are their common offspring are fairer and more immortal. Who, when he thinks of Homer and Hesiod and other great poets, would not rather have their children than ordinary   d
human ones? Who would not emulate them in the creation of children such as theirs, which have preserved their memory and given them everlasting glory? Or who would not have such children as Lycurgus[26] left behind him to be the saviours, not only of Lacedaemon, but of Hellas, as one may say? There is Solon,[27] too, who is the revered father of Athenian laws; and many others there are in many other places, both among Hellenes and barbarians, who have given to the world many noble works, and   e
have been the parents of virtue of every kind; and many temples have been raised in their honour for the sake of children such as theirs; which were never raised in honour of any one, for the sake of his mortal children.

"These are the lesser mysteries of love, into which even you, Socrates, may enter; to the greater and more hidden ones which are the crown of these, and to which, if you pursue them in a right spirit, they will lead, I know not whether you will be able to attain. But I will do my utmost to inform you, and do you follow if you can.

He who would be truly initiated should pass from the concrete to the abstract, from the individual to the universal, from the universal to the universe of truth and beauty.   210a

For he who would proceed aright in this matter
should begin in youth to visit beautiful forms; and
first, if he be guided by his instructor aright, to love
one such form only—out of that he should create

b   fair thoughts; and soon he will of himself perceive
that the beauty of one form is akin to the beauty
of another; and then if beauty of form in general is
his pursuit, how foolish would he be not to recognize that the beauty in every form is one and the
same! And when he perceives this he will abate his
violent love of the one, which he will despise and
deem a small thing, and will become a lover of all
beautiful forms; in the next stage he will consider
that the beauty of the mind is more honourable
than the beauty of the outward form. So that if a
virtuous soul have but a little comeliness, he will

c   be content to love and tend him, and will search
out and bring to the birth thoughts which may improve the young, until he is compelled to contemplate and see the beauty of institutions and laws,
and to understand that the beauty of them all is of
one family, and that personal beauty is a trifle; and

d   after laws and institutions he will go on to the sciences, that he may see their beauty, being not like a
servant in love with the beauty of one youth or man
or institution, himself a slave mean and narrow-
minded, but drawing towards and contemplating
the vast sea of beauty, he will create many fair and
noble thoughts and notions in boundless love of

e   wisdom; until on that shore he grows and waxes
strong, and at last the vision is revealed to him of
a single science, which is the science of beauty everywhere. To this I will proceed; please to give me
your very best attention:

"He who has been instructed *He should view* thus far in the things of love, and *beauty, not* who has learned to see the beauti- *relatively, but absolutely; and* ful in due order and succession, *he should pass* when he comes towards the end *by stepping-* will suddenly perceive a nature of *stones from* wondrous beauty (and this, *earth to heaven.* Socrates, is the final cause of all our former toils)—a nature which in the first place is everlast-   211a ing, not growing and decaying, or waxing and waning; secondly, not fair in one point of view and foul in another, or at one time or in one relation or at one place fair, at another time or in another relation or at another place foul, as if fair to some and foul to others, or in the likeness of a face or hands or any other part of the bodily frame, or in any form of speech or knowledge, or existing in any other being, as, for example, in an animal, or in heaven, or in earth, or in any other place but beauty   b absolute, separate, simple, and everlasting, which without diminution and without increase, or any change, is imparted to the ever-growing and perishing beauties of all other things. He who from these ascending under the influence of true love, begins to perceive that beauty, is not far from the end. And the true order of going, or being led by another, to the things of love, is to begin from the   c beauties of earth and mount upwards for the sake of that other beauty, using these as steps only, and from one going on to two, and from two to all fair forms, and from fair forms to fair practices, and from fair practices to fair notions, until from fair notions he arrives at the notion of absolute beauty, and at last knows what the essence of beauty is.

d   This, my dear Socrates," said the stranger of Mantineia, "is that life above all others which man
should live, in the contemplation of beauty absolute; a beauty which if you once beheld, you would
see not to be after the measure of gold, and garments, and fair boys and youths, whose presence
now entrances you; and you and many an one
would be content to live seeing them only and conversing with them without meat or drink, if that
were possible—you only want to look at them and
to be with them. But what if man had eyes to see

e   the true beauty—the divine beauty, I mean, pure
and clear and unalloyed, not clogged with the pol-
lutions of mortality and all the colours and vanities
of human life—thither looking, and holding con-

212a verse with the true beauty simple and divine? Remember how in that communion only, beholding
beauty with the eye of the mind, he will be enabled
to bring forth, not images of beauty, but realities
(for he has hold not of an image but of a reality),
and bringing forth and nourishing true virtue to
become the friend of God and be immortal, if mortal man may. Would that be an ignoble life?"

b   Such, Phaedrus—and I speak not only to you,
but to all of you—were the words of Diotima, and I
am persuaded of their truth. And being persuaded
of them, I try to persuade others, that in the attainment of this end human nature will not easily find
a helper better than love. And therefore, also, I say
that every man ought to honour him as I myself honour him, and walk in his ways, and exhort others to
do the same, and praise the power and spirit of love
according to the measure of my ability now and ever.

c   The words which I have spoken, you, Phaedrus,

may call an encomium of love, or anything else
which you please.

When Socrates had done speaking, the company applauded, and Aristophanes was beginning
to say something in answer to the allusion which
Socrates had made to his own speech, when suddenly there was a great knocking at the door of the
house, as of revellers, and the sound of a flute-girl   d
was heard. Agathon told the atten-   *Alcibiades is led*
dants to go and see who were the   *in drunk and*
intruders. "If they are friends of   *bearing a crown*
ours," he said, "invite them in, but   *which he places*
                                         on the head of
if not, say that the drinking is   *Agathon.*
over." A little while afterwards
they heard the voice of Alcibiades resounding in
the court; he was in a great state of intoxication,
and kept roaring and shouting "Where is Agathon?
Lead me to Agathon," and at length, supported by
the flute-girl and some of his attendants, he found
his way to them. "Hail, friends," he said, appearing   e
at the door crowned with a massive garland of ivy
and violets, his head flowing with ribands.[28] "Will
you have a very drunken man as a companion of
your revels? Or shall I crown Agathon, which was
my intention in coming, and go away? For I was
unable to come yesterday, and therefore I am here
to-day, carrying on my head these ribands, that taking them from my own head, I may crown the head
of this fairest and wisest of men, as I may be allowed to call him. Will you laugh at me because I
am drunk? Yet I know very well that I am speaking   213a
the truth, although you may laugh. But first tell
me; if I come in shall we have the understanding of
which I spoke? Will you drink with me or not?"

The company were vociferous in begging that
he would take his place among them, and Agathon
specially invited him. Thereupon he was led in by
the people who were with him; and as he was being
led, intending to crown Agathon, he took the ribands from his own head and held them in front of
his eyes; he was thus prevented   *Alcibiades takes*
from seeing Socrates, who made   *the vacant*
way for him, and Alcibiades took   *place between*
b the vacant place between Agathon *Agathon and*
and Socrates, and in taking the   *Socrates.*
place he embraced Agathon and crowned him.
Take off his sandals, said Agathon, and let him
make a third on the same couch.

By all means; but who makes the third partner
in our revels? said Alcibiades, turning round and
starting up as he caught sight of Socrates. By Heracles, he said, what is this? here is   *He insinuates*
c Socrates always lying in wait for   *that Agathon is*
me, and always, as his way is, com-   *the beloved of*
ing out at all sorts of unsuspected   *Socrates.*
places: and now, what have you to say for yourself,
and why are you lying here, where I perceive that
you have contrived to find a place, not by a joker or
lover of jokes, like Aristophanes, but by the fairest
of the company?

Socrates turned to Agathon and   *He begins to*
d said: I must ask you to protect me,   *be violent, and*
Agathon; for the passion of this   *Socrates claims*
man has grown quite a serious   *the protection of*
matter to me. Since I became his   *Agathon.*
admirer I have never been allowed to speak to any
other fair one, or so much as to look at them. If I
do, he goes wild with envy and jealousy, and not

only abuses me but can hardly keep his hands off me, and at this moment he may do me some harm. Please to see to this, and either reconcile me to him, or, if he attempts violence, protect me, as I am in bodily fear of his mad and passionate attempts.

There can never be reconciliation between you and me, said Alcibiades; but for the present I will defer your chastisement. And I must beg you, Agathon, to give me back some of the ribands that I may crown the marvellous head of this universal despot—I would not have him complain of me for crowning you, and neglecting him, who in conversation is the conqueror of all mankind; and this not only once, as you were the day before yesterday, but always. Whereupon, taking some of the ribands, he crowned Socrates, and again reclined.

He crowns Socrates as well as Agathon.

e

Then he said: You seem, my friends, to be sober, which is a thing not to be endured; you must drink—for that was the agreement under which I was admitted—and I elect myself master of the feast until you are well drunk. Let us have a large goblet, Agathon, or rather, he said, addressing the attendant, bring me that wine-cooler. The wine-cooler which had caught his eye was a vessel holding more than two quarts—this he filled and emptied, and bade the attendant fill it again for Socrates. Observe, my friends, said Alcibiades, that this ingenious trick of mine will have no effect on Socrates, for he can drink any quantity of wine and not be at all nearer being drunk. Socrates drank the cup which the attendant filled for him.

A new spirit passes over the dream.

214a

Socrates' powers of drinking.

Eryximachus said: What is this, Alcibiades?
b Are we to have neither conversation nor singing
over our cups; but simply to drink as if we were
thirsty?

Alcibiades replied: Hail, worthy son of a most
wise and worthy sire!

The same to you, said Eryximachus; but what
shall we do?

That I leave to you, said Alcibiades.

"The wise physician skilled our wounds to heal"[29]

shall prescribe and we will obey. What do you want?

Well, said Eryximachus, before you appeared
we had passed a resolution that each one of us in
c turn should make a speech in praise of love, and as
good a one as he could: the turn was passed round
from left to right; and as all of us have spoken, and
you have not spoken but have well drunken, you
ought to speak, and then impose upon Socrates
any task which you please, and he on his right-hand
neighbour, and so on.

That is good, Eryximachus, said Alcibiades; and
yet the comparison of a drunken man's speech
with those of sober men is hardly fair; and I should
like to know, sweet friend, whether you really believe what Socrates was just now saying; for I can
assure you that the very reverse is the fact, and
d that if I praise any one but himself in his presence, whether God or man, he will hardly keep his
hands off me.

For shame, said Socrates.

Hold your tongue, said Alcibiades, for by Posei-

don, there is no one else whom I will praise when
you are of the company.

Well, then, said Eryximachus, if you like, praise
Socrates.

What do you think, Eryximachus? said Alcibi-   e
ades: shall I attack him and inflict the punishment
before you all?

What are you about? said Socrates; are you
going to raise a laugh at my expense? Is that the
meaning of your praise?

I am going to speak the truth, if you will permit
me.

I not only permit, but exhort you to speak the
truth.

Then I will begin at once, said Alcibiades, and if
I say anything which is not true, you may interrupt
me if you will, and say "That is a lie," though my
intention is to speak the truth. But you must not
wonder if I speak anyhow as things come into my
mind; for the fluent and orderly enumeration of
all your singularities is not a task which is easy to a
man in my condition.

And now, my boys, I shall praise Socrates in a   215a
figure which will appear to him to be a caricature,
and yet I speak, not to make fun of him, but only
for the truth's sake. I say, that he is exactly like the
busts of Silenus,³⁰ which are set up in the statuaries' shops, holding pipes and flutes in their mouths;   b
and they are made to open in the middle, and have
images of gods inside them. I say also that he is like
Marsyas the satyr. You yourself will not deny,
Socrates, that your face is like that of a satyr. Aye,
and there is a resemblance in other points too. For

example, you are a bully, as I can prove by witnesses, if you will not confess. And are you not a flute-player? That you are, and a performer far more wonderful than Marsyas. He indeed with instruments used to charm the souls of men by the power of his breath, c and the players of his music do so still: for the melodies of Olympus are derived from Marsyas who taught them, and these, whether they are played by a great master or by a miserable flute-girl, have a power which no others have; they alone possess the soul and reveal the wants of those who have need of gods and mysteries, because they are divine. But you produce the same effect with your words only, and do not require the flute:

Socrates is like the busts of Silenus, which conceal within them images of gods; like Marsyas too, for his face is that of a Satyr, and his words, even when half-uttered or imperfectly repeated, exercise a greater charm over men than the melodies which Marsyas taught to Olympus.

that is the difference between you and him. When we hear any other speaker, even a very good one, he produces absolutely no effect upon us, or not d much, whereas the mere fragments of you and your words, even at second-hand, and however imperfectly repeated, amaze and possess the souls of every man, woman, and child who comes within hearing of them. And if I were not afraid that you would think me hopelessly drunk, I would have sworn as well as spoken to the influence which they have always had and still have over me. For my e heart leaps within me more than that of any Corybantian[31] reveller, and my eyes rain tears when I hear them. And I observe that many others are af-

fected in the same manner. I have heard Pericles
and other great orators, and I   *Greater than*
thought that they spoke well, but I *Pericles, and the*
never had any similar feeling; my   *true and only*
soul was not stirred by them, nor   *orator.*
was I angry at the thought of my own slavish state.
But this Marsyas has often brought me to such a
pass, that I have felt as if I could hardly endure the
life which I am leading (this, Socrates, you will   216a
admit); and I am conscious that if I did not shut my
ears against him, and fly as from the voice of the
siren, my fate would be like that of others,—he
would transfix me, and I should grow old sitting at
his feet. For he makes me confess that I ought not
to live as I do, neglecting the wants of my own soul,
and busying myself with the concerns of the Athenians; therefore I hold my ears   *He would*   b
and tear myself away from him.   *have reformed*
And he is the only person who   *Alcibiades*
                                     himself if
ever made me ashamed, which   *the love of*
you might think not to be in my   *popularity in*
nature, and there is no one else   *him had not*
who does the same. For I know   *been too strong.*
that I cannot answer him or say that I ought not to
do as he bids, but when I leave his presence the
love of popularity gets the better of me. And therefore I run away and fly from him, and when I see
him I am ashamed of what I have confessed to him.
Many a time have I wished that he were dead, and
yet I know that I should be much more sorry than   c
glad, if he were to die: so that I am at my wit's end.

    And this is what I and many   *His love of the*
others have suffered from the   *fair.*
flute-playing of this satyr. Yet hear me once more

while I show you how exact the image is, and how
marvellous his power. For let me tell you; none of
you know him; but I will reveal him to you; having
d begun, I must go on. See you how fond he is of the
fair? He is always with them and is always being
smitten by them, and then again he knows nothing
and is ignorant of all things—such is the appearance which he puts on. Is he not like a Silenus in
this? To be sure he is: his outer mask is the carved
head of the Silenus; but, O my companions in
e drink, when he is opened, what temperance there
is residing within! Know you that beauty and
wealth and honour, at which the many wonder, are
of no account with him, and are utterly despised by
him: he regards not at all the persons who are
gifted with them; mankind are nothing to him; all
his life is spent in mocking and *His outer form*
flouting at them. But when I *only is like the*
opened him, and looked within at *outward form of*
217a his serious purpose, I saw in him *Silenus; within*
divine and golden images of such *are images of*
fascinating beauty that I was *fascinating*
ready to do in a moment whatever *beauty.*
Socrates commanded: they may have escaped the
observation of others, but I saw them. Now I fancied that he was seriously enamoured of my beauty,
and I thought that I should therefore have a grand
opportunity of hearing him tell what he knew, for I
had a wonderful opinion of the attractions of my
youth. In the prosecution of this design, when I
b next went to him, I sent away the attendant who
usually accompanied me (I will confess the whole
truth, and beg you to listen; and if I speak falsely,
do you, Socrates, expose the falsehood). Well, he

and I were alone together, and I thought that when there was nobody with us, I should hear him speak the language which lovers use to their loves when they are by themselves, and I was delighted. Nothing of the sort; he conversed as usual, and spent the day with me and then went away. Afterwards I challenged him to the palaestra;[32] and he wrestled and closed with me several times when there was no one present; I fancied that I might succeed in this manner. Not a bit; I made no way with him. Lastly, as I had failed hitherto, I thought that I must take stronger measures and attack him boldly, and, as I had begun, not give him up, but see how matters stood between him and me. So I invited him to sup with me, just as if he were a fair youth, and I a designing lover. He was not easily persuaded to come; he did, however, after a while accept the invitation, and when he came the first time, he wanted to go away at once as soon as supper was over, and I had not the face to detain him. The second time, still in pursuance of my design, after we had supped, I went on conversing far into the night, and when he wanted to go away, I pretended that the hour was late and that he had much better remain. So he lay down on the couch next to me, the same on which he had supped, and there was no one but ourselves sleeping in the apartment. All this may be told without shame to any one. But what follows I could hardly tell you if I were sober. Yet as the proverb says, "In vino veritas,"[33] whether with boys, or without them; and therefore I must speak. Nor, again, should I be justified in concealing the lofty actions of Socrates when I come to praise him. Moreover, I have felt

c

d

e

the serpent's sting; and he who has suffered, as
218a they say, is willing to tell his fellow-sufferers only,
as they alone will be likely to understand him, and
will not be extreme in judging of the sayings or doings which have been wrung from his agony. For I
have been bitten by a more than viper's tooth; I
have known in my soul, or in my heart, or in some
other part, that worst of pangs, more violent in in-
genuous youth than any serpent's tooth, the pang
of philosophy, which will make a man say or do
anything. And you whom I see around me, Phaedrus and Agathon and Eryximachus and Pausa-
b   nias and Aristodemus and Aristophanes, all of you,
and I need not say Socrates himself, have had experience of the same madness and passion in your
longing after wisdom. Therefore listen and excuse
my doings then and my sayings now. But let the
attendants and other profane and unmannered
persons close up the doors of their ears.

c   When the lamp was put out *The behaviour*
and the servants had gone away, I *of Socrates, and*
thought that I must be plain with *his rejection of*
him and have no more ambigu- *the advances of*
ity. So I gave him a shake, and I *Alcibiades.*
said: "Socrates, are you asleep?" "No," he said. "Do
you know what I am meditating?" "What are you
meditating?" he said. "I think," I replied, "that of
all the lovers whom I have ever had you are the
only one who is worthy of me, and you appear to
be too modest to speak. Now I feel that I should
be a fool to refuse you this or any other favour,
d   and therefore I come to lay at your feet all that
I have and all that my friends have, in the hope
that you will assist me in the way of virtue, which

I desire above all things, and in which I believe
that you can help me better than any one else.
And I should certainly have more reason to be
ashamed of what wise men would say if I were to
refuse a favour to such as you, than of what the
world, who are mostly fools, would say of me if I
granted it." To these words he replied in the ironical manner which is so characteristic of him:—"O
Alcibiades, my friend, you have indeed an elevated
aim if what you say is true, and if there really is in
me any power by which you may become better;　e
truly you must see in me some rare beauty of a
kind infinitely higher than any which I see in you.
And therefore, if you mean to share with me and to
exchange beauty for beauty, you will have greatly
the advantage of me; you will gain true beauty in
return for appearance—like Diomede, gold in
exchange for brass. But look again, sweet friend,　219a
and see whether you are not deceived in me. The
mind begins to grow critical when the bodily eye
fails, and it will be a long time before you get old."
Hearing this, I said: "I have told you my purpose,
which is quite serious, and do you consider what
you think best for you and me." "That is good," he　b
said; "at some other time then we will consider and
act as seems best about this and about other matters." Whereupon, I fancied that he was smitten,
and that the words which I had uttered like arrows
had wounded him, and so without waiting to hear
more I got up, and throwing my coat about him
crept under his threadbare cloak, as the time of
year was winter, and there I lay during the whole
night having this wonderful monster in my arms.　c
This again, Socrates, will not be denied by you.

And yet, notwithstanding all, he was so superior to
my solicitations, so contemptuous and derisive and
disdainful of my beauty—which really, as I fancied,
had some attractions—hear, O judges; for judges
you shall be of the haughty virtue of Socrates—
nothing more happened, but in the morning when
d   I awoke (let all the gods and goddesses be my witnesses) I arose as from the couch of a father or an
elder brother.

What do you suppose must have been my feelings, after this rejection, at the thought of my own
dishonour? And yet I could not help wondering at
his natural temperance and self-restraint and man-
liness. I never imagined that I could have met with
a man such as he is in wisdom and endurance. And
therefore I could not be angry with him or re-
nounce his company, any more than I could hope
e   to win him. For I well knew that if Ajax could not
be wounded by steel, much less he by money; and
my only chance of captivating him by my personal
attractions had failed. So I was at my wit's end; no
one was ever more hopelessly en-   *The wonderful*
slaved by another. All this hap-   *endurance*
pened before he and I went on the   *of Socrates*
expedition to Potidaea; there we   *when he and*
                                     Alcibiades
messed together, and I had the   *served together*
opportunity of observing his ex-   *at Potidaea.*
traordinary power of sustaining
fatigue. His endurance was simply marvellous
when, being cut off from our supplies, we were
220a compelled to go without food—on such occasions,
which often happen in time of war, he was superior
not only to me but to everybody; there was no one
to be compared to him. Yet at a festival he was the

only person who had any real powers of enjoyment;
though not willing to drink, he could if compelled
beat us all at that,—wonderful to relate! no human
being had ever seen Socrates drunk; and his powers, if I am not mistaken, will be tested before long.   b
His fortitude in enduring cold was also surprising.
There was a severe frost, for the winter in that region is really tremendous, and everybody else either remained indoors, or if they went out had on
an amazing quantity of clothes, and were well shod,
and had their feet swathed in felt and fleeces: in the
midst of this, Socrates with his bare feet on the ice
and in his ordinary dress marched better than the
other soldiers who had shoes, and they looked dag-
gers at him because he seemed to despise them.

I have told you one tale, and now I must tell you
another, which is worth hearing,   c

"Of the doings and sufferings of the enduring
    man"[34]

while he was on the expedition.   *The long fits of*
One morning he was thinking   *abstraction to*
about something which he could   *which he was*
                                   subject.
not resolve; he would not give it
up, but continued thinking from early dawn until
noon—there he stood fixed in thought; and at noon
attention was drawn to him, and the rumour ran
through the wondering crowd that Socrates had
been standing and thinking about something ever
since the break of day. At last, in the evening after
supper, some Ionians out of curiosity (I should explain that this was not in winter but in summer),   d
brought out their mats and slept in the open air

that they might watch him and see whether he
would stand all night. There he stood until the following morning; and with the return of light he offered up a prayer to the sun, and went his way. I
will also tell, if you please—and *How he saved*
indeed I am bound to tell—of his *the life of*
courage in battle; for who but he *Alcibiades, and*
saved my life? Now this was the *ought to have*
engagement in which I received *received the*
the prize of valour: for I was *prize of valour*
e   wounded and he would not leave *conferred on*
me, but he rescued me and my *Alcibiades on*
arms; and he ought to have re- *account of his*
ceived the prize of valour which *rank.*

the generals wanted to confer on me partly on account of my rank, and I told them so (this, again,
Socrates will not impeach or deny), but he was
more eager than the generals that I and not he
221a should have the prize. There was another occasion
on which his behaviour was very remarkable—in
the flight of the army after the battle of Delium,
when he served among the heavy-armed,—I had a
better opportunity of seeing him than at Potidaea,
for I was myself on horseback, and therefore comparatively out of danger. He and Laches were re-
treating, for the troops were in flight, and I met
them and told them not to be discouraged, and
promised to remain with them; and there you
b   might see him, Aristophanes, as you describe, just
as he is in the streets of Athens, stalking like a peli-
can, and rolling his eyes, calmly contemplating enemies as well as friends, and making very intelligible
to anybody, even from a distance, that whoever attacked him would be likely to meet with a stout

resistance; and in this way he and his companion
escaped—for this is the sort of man who is never
touched in war; those only are pursued who are
running away headlong. I particularly observed
how superior he was to Laches in presence of mind.
Many are the marvels which I *His coolness*   c
might narrate in praise of Socrates; *in battle;*
most of his ways might perhaps be *his absolute*
paralleled in another man, but his *unlikeness to*   d
absolute unlikeness to any human *any other man.*
being that is or ever has been is perfectly astonish-
ing. You may imagine Brasidas and others to have
been like Achilles; or you may imagine Nestor and
Antenor to have been like Pericles; and the same
may be said of other famous men, but of this strange
being you will never be able to find any likeness,
however remote, either among men who now are
or who ever have been—other than that which I
have already suggested of Silenus and the satyrs;
and they represent in a figure not only himself, but
his words. For, although I forgot to mention this to   e
you before, his words are like the images of Silenus
which open; they are ridiculous when you first hear
them; he clothes himself in language that is like the
skin of the wanton satyr—for his talk is of pack-
asses and smiths and cobblers and curriers, and he
is always repeating the same things in the same
words, so that any ignorant or inex- *He is the satyr*
perienced person might feel dis- *without and the*
posed to laugh at him; but he who *god within.*   222a
opens the bust and sees what is within will find that
they are the only words which have a meaning in
them, and also of the most divine, abounding in fair
images of virtue, and of the widest comprehension,

or rather extending to the whole duty of a good and
honourable man.

This, friends, is my praise of Socrates. I have
b added my blame of him for his ill-treatment of
me; and he has ill-treated not only me, but Charmides the son of Glaucon, and Euthydemus the
son of Diocles, and many others in the same
way—beginning as their lover he has ended by
making them pay their addresses to him. Wherefore I say to you, Agathon, "Be not deceived by
him; learn from me and take warning, and do not
be a fool and learn by experience, as the proverb
says."

c   When Alcibiades had finished, there was a laugh
at his outspokenness; for he seemed to be still in
love with Socrates. You are sober, Alcibiades, said
Socrates, or you would never have *The purport*
gone so far about to hide the pur- *of Alcibiades'*
pose of your satyr's praises, for all *speech,*
this long story is only an ingenious *according to*
circumlocution, of which the *Socrates, was*
point comes in by the way at the *only to get up a*
end; you want to get up a quarrel *quarrel between*
between me and Agathon, and *him and*
                                      Agathon.
your notion is that I ought to love you and nobody
d else, and that you and you only ought to love Agathon. But the plot of this Satyric or Silenic drama
has been detected, and you must not allow him,
Agathon, to set us at variance.

I believe you are right, said *Agathon changes*
e Agathon, and I am disposed to *his place that he*
think that his intention in placing *may be nearer*
himself between you and me was *Socrates and not*
only to divide us; but he shall gain *so near Alcibiades.*

nothing by that move; for I will go and lie on the couch next to you.

Yes, yes, replied Socrates, by all means come here and lie on the couch below me.

Alas, said Alcibiades, how I am fooled by this man; he is determined to get the better of me at every turn. I do beseech you, allow Agathon to lie between us.

Certainly not, said Socrates; as you praised me, and I in turn ought to praise my neighbour on the right, he will be out of order in praising me again when he ought rather to be praised by me, and I must entreat you to consent to this, and not be jealous, for I have a great desire to praise the youth.   223a

Hurrah! cried Agathon, I will rise instantly, that I may be praised by Socrates.

The usual way, said Alcibiades; where Socrates is, no one else has any chance with the fair; and now how readily has he invented a specious reason for attracting Agathon to himself.

Agathon arose in order that he might take his place on the couch by Socrates, when suddenly a band of revellers entered, and spoiled the order of the banquet. Some one who was going out having left the door open, they had found their way in, and made themselves at home; great confusion ensued, and every one was compelled to drink large quantities of wine. Aristodemus said that Eryximachus, Phaedrus, and others went away—he himself fell asleep, and as the nights were long took a good rest: he was awakened towards daybreak by a crowing of cocks, and

Another band of revellers enters, and the company drink largely, the wiser part withdrawing.   b

c

when he awoke, the others were either asleep, or
had gone away; there remained only Socrates,
Aristophanes, and Agathon, who were drinking out
of a large goblet which they passed round, and
Socrates was discoursing to them. Aristodemus
was only half awake, and he did   *On the*
not hear the beginning of the dis- *following*
course; the chief thing which he   *morning*
d remembered was Socrates com-   *Socrates is still*
pelling the other two to acknowl-   *awake, and is*
edge that the genius of comedy   *maintaining*
was the same with that of tragedy, *the thesis that*
and that the true artist in tragedy *the genius of*
was an artist in comedy also. To   *comedy is the*
this they were constrained to as-   *same as that of*
                                     tragedy.
sent, being drowsy, and not quite following the argument. And first of all Aristophanes dropped off,
then, when the day was already dawning, Agathon.
e Socrates, having laid them to sleep, rose to depart;
Aristodemus, as his manner was, following him. At
the Lyceum he took a bath, and passed the day as
usual. In the evening he retired to rest at his own
home.

NOTES

Euthyphro

1. **Lyceum:** A public gymnasium and meeting place in Athens.
2. **Archon:** Archons were magistrates who oversaw legal cases related to religious offenses in Plato's time.
3. **Meletus:** One of the accusers of Socrates, who charged him with impiety, or offenses against the gods.
4. **deme:** In ancient Greece, a township or subdivision of the region of Attica, near Athens.
5. **neologian:** One who creates new words or teaches new interpretations of scripture.
6. **Athene:** Athena, goddess of wisdom, practical skills, and warfare.
7. **Panathenaea:** The most important festival celebrated in Athens, in honor of the goddess Athena, the city's patroness.
8. **Hephaestus:** Greek god of metals and fire, also known as Vulcan in Roman mythology.

9. **Here:** Hera, wife of Zeus and queen of the gods of Olympus.

10. **loved:** Plato makes a subtle distinction here between something that is pious because it is loved by the gods and something that is loved by the gods because it is pious.

11. **Daedalus:** A mythical artisan who constructed the labyrinth on Crete to contain the part-man, part-bull Minotaur. Daedalus also built wings so he and his son, Icarus, could fly out of prison.

12. **Tantalus:** According to mythology, Tantalus was an ancient ruler who acquired great wealth and was punished for his exceptional cruelty in the deepest part of the underworld.

13. **Stasinus:** A legendary ancient poet who wrote epic verse about the Trojan War.

14. **ministration:** Serving or assisting, particularly in a religious context.

15. **Proteus:** An ancient sea god who would answer only to someone who was able to capture him. He is known for changing his shape in order to avoid capture.

Apology

1. **agora:** The market, a favorite meeting place of citizens.

2. **Anytus:** Anytus, a politician, along with Meletus, a poet, and Lycon, a skilled speaker and master of rhetoric, were Socrates' accusers and served as prosecutors at his trial.

3. **Aristophanes:** Aristophanes, a famous comic poet, included a caricature of Socrates in his play *The Clouds*.

4. **Elis:** Like Gorgias, mentioned in *Meno,* Prodicus and Hippias were sophists, or professional instructors of the youth of Athens.

5. **Parian:** A poet and teacher of Plato's time, from the island of Paros.

6. **minae:** The mina (plural minae) was the Greek currency of the period.

7. **Delphi:** Apollo, the god of the sun, revealed truth as the Oracle of Delphi, speaking through a priestess.

8. **Pythian prophetess:** The priestess of Apollo at Delphi.

9. **labours:** Hercules was required to perform twelve labors, or feats so difficult that they were considered impossible.

10. **dithyrambic:** Poets who composed passionate hymns and dances in honor of Dionysus, the god of wine and fertility.

11. **Clazomenian:** Anaxagoras, a pre-Socratic philosopher from the city of Clazomenae, taught that the sun and moon were made of rock, like the earth.

12. **theatre:** Aristophanes caricatured Anaxagoras in his plays, while Euripides and other dramatists treated his ideas seriously.

13. **drachma:** A coin, worth one-hundredth of a mina.

14. **me:** Socrates says that the charges of corruption and impiety are false allegations used to cover up the true political motivations behind his arrest.

15. **Thetis:** A sea nymph and mother of Greek hero Achilles, who killed Trojan prince Hector in Homer's *Iliad*.

16. **Delium:** Socrates served in the Athenian army during the Peloponnesian War and fought in these three places.

17. **gadfly:** A person who challenges authority and power,

like a fly that irritates and stings a horse (which in this case is the Athenian government).

18. **divers:** Many, different.

19. **Prytanes:** Socrates was a member of the Prytany, or governing council, a representative body for the region around Athens. While serving on this committee, Socrates opposed the Athenian government's group trial of several generals who failed to rescue their sailors from drowning in the battle of Arginusae.

20. **the Thirty:** The Oligarchy of the Thirty, a pro-Spartan ruling elite, were appointed to govern Athens after its defeat by Sparta (another Greek city-state and arch rival of Athens) in 404 BCE and were known for arbitrary policies and cruelty toward political opponents.

21. **cross-examining:** Socrates here refers to his usual method of questioning people about their beliefs in order to challenge their assumptions and reveal their ignorance.

22. **court:** Socrates lists the names of his friends and pupils who are in attendance at his trial. Plato himself is mentioned, as is Crito, who appears in *Crito* and *Phaedo*.

23. **votes:** Less than one-fifth of the jurors casting votes in the case.

24. **Prytaneum:** A public assembly hall where important citizens, war heroes, and winners at the Olympic games were celebrated.

25. **Eleven:** Athenian police organization that supervised the court sentencing procedures.

Crito

1. **Delos:** Every year Athens sent a sacred ship to the island of Delos, bearing an offering to the shrine of Apollo. Executions could not take place during a holy season, so Socrates must wait to die until the ship returns.
2. *shalt thou go*: From Homer's *Iliad*. Phthia is a far-away region in southern Greece.
3. **Theban:** One of Socrates' students, from Thebes. Along with Cebes, Simmias is one of the characters in the dialogue *Phaedo*.
4. **Isthmus:** The Isthmus of Corinth, which separated Athens and Sparta. The Isthmus is the site of the Isthmian games, held in honor of Poseidon, god of the sea.
5. **Lacedaemon:** Sparta, a city-state and rival of Athens.
6. **Hellenic:** Greek.

Meno

1. **Thessalians:** Meno is a resident of Thessaly, a region of Greece north of Athens.
2. **Hellenes:** Residents of Hellas (Greece).
3. **Gorgias' doing:** Gorgias was one of the sophists, or private instructors who taught theoretical and practical knowledge to the youth of Athens before Sophocles and Plato defined philosophy as a discipline.
4. **Aleuadae:** One of the most ancient noble families of Thessaly, who claimed descent from the mythical king Aleuas, who in turn was said to be a descendant of Hercules. The family lived at the city of Larisa.

5. **'quale':** Here *quid* means "what something is" and *quale* refers to the properties or characteristics of that object (Latin).

6. **figures:** By "figures," Socrates here refers to shapes and geometrical figures. His distinction between "a figure" and "figure" is to show that circles are figures, but not all figures are circles, since there are many kinds of figures.

7. **'simile in multis':** What these many figures have in common, or the shared features that allow us to define what a "figure" is (Latin).

8. **eristic:** Arguing for the sake of arguing, rather than for finding the truth.

9. **dialectician's vein:** Someone who practices dialectic, or Socrates' method of one-on-one questions and answers to reveal the truth.

10. **effluences of existence:** Here Plato suggests that all things that exist send out properties or effluences that can be perceived by the senses as they pass through passages in the body. He gives the example of color, which is perceived by the sense of sight through the eyes.

11. **mysteries:** Ancient cultlike religions, often in worship of particular deities like Dionysus, that required rites of initiation.

12. **poet:** Probably a reference to Homer.

13. **torpifies:** Paralyzes or silences one's opponent.

14. *ages:* This quotation is from the poet Pindar (c. 522–443 BCE), relating the myth of Persephone, the goddess of the underworld, where souls reside after death.

15. **recollection:** By "recollection" Plato refers to the process of recalling knowledge that is somehow inborn in us. He suggests that this knowledge

is present in the soul at birth, and that we access this knowledge through recollection, not through reason. The theory that knowledge is recollection later helps Plato prove the immortality of the soul in *Phaedo*.

16. **ignorance:** Socrates here proposes that recognition of one's ignorance is the first step toward learning the truth, a central goal of his method of dialectic.

17. **Anytus:** Anytus is one of the men who later accused Socrates of corruption, as described in *Apology*.

18. **Polycrates:** An ancient king of the Greek island of Samos, who, according to legend, threw away his riches in order to avoid a fateful reversal of fortune.

19. **Heracles:** Also known as Hercules.

20. **Pheidias:** The famous Athenian sculptor who created the art that decorates the Parthenon, in Athens.

21. **diviner:** Someone who can tell the future or who possesses a supernatural ability to reveal hidden knowledge.

22. **Thucydides:** Thucydides (c. 460–395 BCE) was the most famous Greek historian of Plato's time, and author of the history of the Peloponnesian War.

23. **Theognis:** An ancient Greek poet who lived in the sixth century BCE. The quoted verses that follow are his.

24. **wrong:** Here Plato makes a distinction between two kinds of knowledge: one that is knowledge of facts and the other, which is opinion about those facts.

25. **Tiresias:** In Greek mythology, a blind prophet who could see the future. He also is a character in Euripides' play *The Bacchae*.

Phaedo

1. **Phliasian:** Phaedo is from Phlius, a city near Sparta.
2. **deme:** A township or subdivision of the region of Attica, near Athens.
3. **Eleven:** The Athenian police, in charge of carrying out the sentencing of criminals.
4. **Xanthippe:** Socrates' wife.
5. **music:** Music here literally refers to the domain of all the classical muses, which can include the arts and humanities as we define them today.
6. **Philolaus:** A philosopher from Thebes and a follower of the pre-Socratic philosopher and mathematician Pythagoras.
7. **Boeotian:** The rural dialect spoken in Boeotia, a province northwest of Athens, where the city of Thebes is located.
8. **mind alone:** Socrates claims that the mind searches for truth, while the body and its physical pleasures are deceptive distractions that prevent the soul from finding truth.
9. **mysteries:** Secret rites of worship open only to the initiated.
10. **thyrsus-bearers:** A thyrsus was a wand wrapped in garlands of leaves, carried during religious processions.
11. **poets:** A reference to Aristophanes, who caricatured Socrates in his play *The Clouds*.
12. **the world below:** The underworld, where souls reside after death.
13. **Endymion:** In Greek mythology, a beautiful youth who sleeps forever in a cave.
14. **Anaxagoras:** The original chaos of the universe, from which Mind created order, according to Anaxagoras.

15. **recollection:** As in *Meno,* here Plato says that knowledge is the recollection of information understood by the soul in a past existence.

16. **diagram:** A reference to *Meno,* in which Socrates uses a diagram to demonstrate recollection in an uneducated slave boy.

17. **process:** Socrates' method of questions and answers in search of the truth.

18. **Hellas:** Greece.

19. **changeable:** The region of the changeable is the seen world in which men live, as opposed to the more permanent realm of the unseen, which is the spiritual plane of existence.

20. **Hades:** The underworld, and also the name of the Greek god of the underworld.

21. **thraldom:** Servitude or bondage.

22. **Penelope's web:** Something never finished. In Homer's *Odyssey,* Penelope agreed to choose one of her suitors after she had finished weaving a shroud. In order to delay her decision, she took apart every night what she had woven during the day.

23. **lyre:** A stringed musical instrument, similar to a small harp, often used to accompany performances and recitals of poetry.

24. **admixture:** Combined together in the correct proportions.

25. **deliquesces:** Melts away.

26. **severed:** Cutting the hair as a sign of mourning.

27. **Argives:** The inhabitants of Argos, who swore to keep their hair short until they had recovered territory lost in war to Sparta.

28. **Iolaus:** Hercules' chariot driver and close companion.

29. **misologists:** Haters of reasoning.

30. **Euripus:** A narrow strait between mainland Greece and nearby islands, known for its strong tides.

31. **Cadmus:** The legendary first king of Thebes, who invented the Greek alphabet.

32. **said:** Socrates is asking whether heat and cold combine in some process, like fermentation, to cause growth in animals.

33. **all:** Anaxagoras wrote that the mind was the cause of order in the universe, disposing or placing everything in its proper place.

34. **trough:** Various theories that explain how the earth is supported by the heavens.

35. **Atlas:** An ancient Titan, or elder god of Greek mythology, who held the universe on his shoulders. Also a mountain range in North Africa.

36. **darkly:** Here, the translator has chosen a phrase from the Bible (1 Corinthians 13:12) to express Plato's idea of the difficulty of seeing something clearly. Corinthians is a book of the New Testament, which was not written until centuries after the death of Plato, so the translator is simply using the phrase in an effort to represent one of Plato's ideas in language the reader might understand easily.

37. **Eristics:** A school of philosophy emphasizing the art of disputing and arguing.

38. **alive:** What thing, being in the body, makes it alive?

39. **equipoise:** Balanced, in a state of equilibrium.

40. **Heracles:** The Phasis river in the east (the modern-day Rioni in Georgia, near Russia) and the Pillars of Hercules in the west (the rocky lands on both sides of the Strait of Gibraltar at the western end of the Mediterranean Sea) marked the limits of the civilized world.

41. **Tartarus:** A dark pit used as a dungeon in the mythological underworld.

42. **Oceanus:** In mythology, a world-ocean or great river surrounding the world.

43. **Pyriphlegethon:** A river of fire in the underworld.

44. **Stygian river:** The River Styx demarks the boundary between the earth and the underworld.

45. **Cocytus:** The four great rivers Pyriphlegethon, Styx, Acheron, and Cocytus all come together at the center of the underworld.

46. **Asclepius:** God of healing and medicine.

Symposium

1. **Phalerian:** A play on words, meaning from Phalerum, home of Apollodorus, and also "bald-headed."

2. *the good*: In Greek, *agathon* translates as "the good." Agathon is also the name of the host of the banquet.

3. **Dionysus:** The god of wine and celebration, known in Roman mythology as Bacchus.

4. **encomiast:** Someone who delivers a speech of praise.

5. **Aphrodite:** Greek goddess of love.

6. **Acusilaus:** A historian from Argos, whose work is now lost.

7. **Orpheus:** According to myth, Orpheus, a gifted musician, descended to Hades to rescue his wife, Eurydice. He fails.

8. **common:** There are different myths about the birth of the goddess of love, Aphrodite. In one, she is the daughter of Uranus, the elder god of heaven and Zeus's grandfather. In another version, she is the daughter of Zeus and Dione, a minor goddess. The first Aphrodite is the "heavenly" Aphrodite, and the second is the "common."

9. **youth:** Plato refers to the tradition of love between two men, which served spiritual and intellectual purposes as well as physical. The love between men and women was related to the physical needs of procreation (associated with the common Aphrodite, born of a father and a mother). The love between men was associated with the heavenly Aphrodite and served to educate the younger man in philosophy, morality, and other intellectual pursuits.

10. **Harmodius:** Aristogeiton and Harmodius, two great friends, sacrificed their own lives in a rebellion that helped bring democracy to Athens.

11. **"uses base":** Base or lowly purposes.

12. **Asclepius:** The god of medicine, and therefore the ancestor of Eryximachus, who is a physician.

13. **Heracleitus:** Heracleitus (c. 535–c. 475 BCE), was a poet and philosopher of the previous century who proposed that the universe was in a constant state of flux, or change.

14. **Urania:** Muse of astronomy.

15. **Polyhymnia:** Muse of songs and hymns.

16. **"Androgynous":** Aristophanes refers to a literal meaning of this word, or a creature that is both man and woman.

17. **Hephaestus:** Greek god of fire and metals.

18. **Lacedaemonians:** Spartans.

19. *basso-rilievo:* Bas-relief, or relief sculpture, in which a picture carved from a slab of stone has the appearance of two dimensions and is only visible from one side.

20. **Cronos:** In Greek mythology, Iapetus and Cronos were Titans, and the first two inhabitants of the earth.

21. **Ate:** Goddess of destruction.

22. *sleep*: From Homer's *Odyssey*, and possibly also from one of Agathon's own dramas.

23. **Gorgonian:** A play on Gorgias's name and the Gorgon Medusa's head, which turned those who looked upon it into stone.

24. **Diotima of Mantineia:** Diotima's name suggests she was a priestess, although whether she really existed or is an invention of Socrates (and Plato) is not known.

25. **parturition:** Childbirth.

26. **Lycurgus:** The lawgiver of Sparta.

27. **Solon:** The lawgiver of Athens, whom Plato claimed as an ancestor.

28. **ribands:** Decorative ribbons.

29. *heal*: From Homer's *Iliad*.

30. **Silenus:** The leader of the satyrs, mythological creatures half human and half beast.

31. **Corybantian:** Priests of the nature goddess Cybele, known for their wild dancing.

32. **palaestra:** Training school for athletes.

33. **veritas:** "In wine there is truth" (Latin).

34. *man*: From Homer's *Odyssey*.

INTERPRETIVE NOTES

The Plot

The *Dialogues of Plato* follow a structure similar to drama, reenacting conversations among two or more characters that lead the speakers to make important discoveries about themselves and their beliefs. Socrates is the main character in each, and many of the dialogues are named for his interlocutor, or partner, in conversation.

Euthyphro

The subject of virtue, discussed in *Meno*, is closely related to the ideas of holiness and justice, which are the topics of discussion in *Euthyphro*. Socrates meets Euthyphro outside the office that investigates religious offenses. Surprised to see his friend there, Socrates mentions the corruption charges that Meletus has filed against him and asks Euthyphro what he is doing in such a place. Euthyphro replies that he has just denounced his own father for murder. In the conversation that follows,

Socrates questions the confident Euthyphro about holiness and piety, and their relationship to justice. Aware he is losing the debate, the frustrated Euthyphro leaves Socrates before the conversation can be concluded.

Apology

This dialogue dramatizes the trial of Socrates on charges of sacrilege and corrupting the youth of Athens, brought against him by the poet Meletus, the politician Anytus, and the orator Lycon. Socrates addresses his defense to the court, and then cross-examines Meletus on the substance of these charges. Responding to Socrates' questions, Meletus cannot even define what constitutes sacrilege and corruption. It is clear that the charges are false allegations used to cover up his political persecution of Socrates. When Socrates is found guilty of the charges, his ironic response actually invites his own death sentence. He says he cannot confess to a crime he has not committed and prefers to sacrifice his own life defending this principle.

Crito

Awaiting his execution, Socrates is visited in prison by his friend Crito, who proposes an escape plan. Socrates refuses, believing escape to be an admission of guilt, and he also doesn't want to involve his friends in criminal activity. Socrates then begins a dialogue with an imagined personification of Athenian Law, revealing that doing wrong will not undo another wrong, and explaining that he owes respect and loyalty to a system that had nurtured and protected him throughout his life.

Meno

Meno is a clear, straightforward example of the Platonic dialogue, showing the Socratic method of dialectic as Socrates questions an expert to reveal exactly how much he does and does not know. Meno asks Socrates if virtue can be taught or if it is a natural gift. Socrates responds that he does not even know what virtue is and then questions Meno on the subject. Frustrated, the proud Meno accuses Socrates of doubting himself and making others doubt. Socrates agrees that he often is confused, but at least he admits it. Unlike Meno, Socrates' wisdom lies in the fact that he knows what he does not know.

Phaedo

One of Plato's most dramatic and complex dialogues, *Phaedo* is set in Socrates' prison cell on the day of his execution. Phaedo describes to his friend Echecrates the events he witnessed, including a discussion Socrates had with his pupils about death and the immortality of the human soul. Socrates argued that the world humans can perceive is based on false appearances, and that men should seek wisdom and virtue in their lives in order to attain a more permanent, divine reward. Socrates maintains that the soul is immortal, and this prepares him for death.

Symposium

The masterpiece of Plato's dialogues about Socrates, *Symposium* is a celebration of love, set at a banquet hosted by Agathon in honor of his winning first prize in a dramatic competition. Agathon's guests take turns discussing love from different perspectives. Phaedrus does not have much to say, the physician Eryximachus describes love in terms of medicine, the dramatist Aristophanes relates an entertaining, symbolic myth about the dual nature of humans and why they seek themselves in each other, Agathon uses flowery rhetoric to sing love's praises, and Socrates, calling on knowledge he says he gained from the priestess Diotima, argues that love is not a god, but a spirit that mediates between gods and men. His solemn speech is interrupted by the arrival of the drunken Alcibiades, which ends the dialogue on a note of festive humor.

Characters

Socrates. The protagonist of the dialogues, Socrates was Plato's teacher and greatest influence. Socrates believes he is wise because he knows the limits of his own knowledge and, through his method of dialectic, questions the certainty of others, ultimately revealing their ignorance as well. Socrates himself does not attempt to preach the truth but rather causes others to question themselves through his method of questions and answers. Socrates says in *Meno* that he is better off knowing his own ignorance because it helps him discover the truth. It is interesting to see Socrates here not only as a historical person, but also as a literary character created by Plato to express his own philosophical views.

Euthyphro. Like Meno, Euthyphro is confident in what he knows about piety and justice. Euthyphro is convinced he is doing the right thing in prosecuting his own father for murder until Socrates causes him to question his own thinking on the matter. Stubborn to the end, and perhaps more than a bit embarrassed by his own ignorance, Euthyphro abandons Socrates before the dialogue is over.

Meletus, Anytus, and Lycon. These three men are the accusers of Socrates. Meletus, a poet, is a character in *Apology*, and Anytus, a politician, makes a brief appearance in *Meno*. Socrates' accusers likely wished to punish him for his political associations, but in the turmoil of the aftermath of the Peloponnesian War, political revenge was outlawed. Instead, Meletus, Anytus, and Lycon charged Socrates with the more ambiguous charges of impiety and corrupting the youth of Athens, concepts Meletus is unable to define precisely for Socrates in *Apology*.

Crito. A trusted friend of Socrates, Crito visits him in prison and proposes a plan for escape. He is Socrates' interlocutor in *Crito* and also is present at Socrates' execution, described in *Phaedo*.

Meno. In the dialogue that bears his name, Meno is a proud man, confident that he knows much about the world, and unwilling to accept criticism. Through his questioning, Socrates reveals that Meno is actually misinformed about the topics he claims to know best, including the nature of human virtue.

Phaedo. Phaedo narrates the scene of Socrates' death for his friend, Echecrates, recounting the dialogue Socrates had with his friends about death and immortality. Phaedo concludes that of all the men of his time, Socrates "was the wisest and justest and best."

Apollodorus. The narrator of *Symposium*, Apollodorus relates the speeches given at Agathon's banquet, which he heard from Aristodemus, one of Socrates' pupils. By having the story told by Apollodorus, the dinner takes on an almost legendary quality. Apollodorus is also one of the friends who witness Socrates' execution in *Phaedo*.

Agathon. Known for his exceptional beauty, Agathon is the host of the banquet in *Symposium*. His flowery speech on love is considered to be excessive by Socrates, who follows Agathon's speech with his own, more solemn treatment of the subject.

Aristophanes. A great comic poet, Aristophanes presented a satirical portrayal of Socrates in his play *The Clouds*. He remains friends with Socrates and delivers one of the most poetic speeches in *Symposium*, relating an entertaining myth that explains the origins of love and human attraction.

Alcibiades. The famous general who led the Athenian fleet during the Peloponnesian War and a good friend of Socrates. In *Symposium*, Alcibiades is portrayed as a drunken soldier who interrupts Socrates' serious speech on love in order to tempt Agathon's guests with wine.

Diotima. A legendary priestess whom Socrates credits in *Symposium* with teaching him what he knows about love. It is interesting that Socrates' views on love are attributed to a woman, and his speech introduces a feminine perspective to the discussion among the male guests at the banquet.

Major Themes

Plato's Theory of Forms

The foundation of Plato's thought rests in part on his division of the universe into two parts: the world of appearances, which contains the objects we humans can perceive, and the realm of ideal forms, which exist on a more abstract plane, almost like mathematical concepts. For Plato, the sensible world is a world of individual realities, false and always changing, whereas the world of ideal forms is constant, stable, and eternal. For every particular object we can sense or perceive (such as a tree, for example) there exists a universal form ("treeness," or the ideal qualities of being a tree) on the eternal plane. Thus, an individual tree is only the temporary manifestation on this earth of an ideal form that lives independently and eternally in a higher level of reality. Plato discusses this concept in detail in *Phaedo*, but it serves as the foundation for many of the other ideas he explores in his dialogues, like the immortality of the soul and his theory that knowledge is recollection of ideas already possessed (as expressed in *Meno* and *Phaedo*). The theory of forms also relates to Plato's famous metaphor of the cave (in his other masterpiece, *The Republic*), which shows that what we see in the world is merely a shadow of reality, just as a person sitting in a dark cave sees the flickering shadows on the wall caused by the light of a fire behind him without seeing the real objects that cast the shadows.

Platonic Love

Plato's opinions on love, as expressed in *Symposium*, also derive from his dual view of the material world and ideal forms. As Diotima teaches Socrates, the physical beauty of a beloved is only the material incarnation of the ideal form of beauty, which exists eternally in its own abstract world. In this view, physical love is considered inferior to a more spiritual kind of love found in the contemplation of the ideal form of beauty. According to Plato, physical attraction causes us to be drawn to someone's beauty, but this beauty inspires us to love absolute beauty as an ideal, which he equates with God, or the ultimate good. Thus, the noblest purpose of love is spiritual, rather than physical, lifting us up from our earthly passions and leading us to search for the absolute beauty of divine goodness. True spiritual love of this sort can exist between men and women, or between members of the same gender, as the goal is not physical satisfaction but contemplation of the ultimate good.

The Search for Truth

By setting his philosophy in the form of dialogues, Plato avoids long-winded speeches by conveying his opinions through different characters who debate important issues from a variety of perspectives. In some cases, the questions raised by Socrates and his friends are left unresolved or unanswered. The use of dialogue helps Plato emphasize that the search for truth is a process, and that the way one looks for truth is just as important as whatever truth he or she finally discovers. Plato's dialogues vividly illustrate how truth can be discovered through questioning ourselves, thinking critically, and challenging assumptions that are presented as self-evident facts.

Who IS Socrates?

Socrates as an historical figure remains largely unknown. The only evidence of his existence is found in Plato's dialogues and the written work of a few other students of Socrates. Therefore, it is unclear whether the Socrates who appears in Plato's dialogues is a faithful representation of the historical person or a fictional character created by Plato as a mouthpiece for his own philosophical views. The earlier dialogues, like the trilogy of *Apology*, *Crito*, and *Phaedo*, describe important events in Socrates' life, such as his trial and execution. It is likely that the opinions Socrates expresses in these dialogues do correspond to what the historical Socrates believed. Other dialogues, like *Symposium*, may be completely fictional creations that Plato used to express his own views in an entertaining way. In any case, Plato's dialogues are not intended to be accurate, historical documents. By using the dialogue form, Plato is able to re-create and dramatize Socrates' dialectic method of using questions to reveal flawed arguments and cause his interlocutor to doubt his own knowledge. This, for Socrates, was the key to true wisdom. In some ways, Plato does the greatest service to the historical Socrates by expressing his philosophy through the lively and interactive form of the dialogue.

CRITICAL EXCERPTS

Biographical Studies

Diogenes Laertius. *The Lives and Opinions of Eminent Philosophers*. Translated by C. D. Yonge. (London: George Bell and Sons, 1901).

Diogenes, who lived in the second century CE, is considered to be one of the earliest biographers of ancient philosophers, including Plato. His account is sometimes colorful and inventive, and he tries to provide insight into the philosopher's personal life and opinions. Diogenes relates one fanciful story in which he contrasts Plato's physical size with the smallness of his voice:

And he learnt gymnastic exercises under the wrestler Ariston of Argos. And it was by him that he had the name of Plato given to him instead of his original name, on account of his robust figure. . . . But he had a very weak voice, they say; and the same fact is stated by Timotheus the Athenian, in his book on Lives. And it is said that Socrates in a dream saw a cygnet on his knees, who immediately put forth feathers, and flew up on high, uttering a sweet note, and that the next day Plato came to him, and that he pronounced him the bird which he had seen.

Taylor, Alfred Edward. *Plato*. (London: Archibald Constable and Company, 1908).

Taylor takes a critical approach to Plato's biography, emphasizing the incompleteness and unreliability of available information, and questioning assumptions about Plato in previous autobiographies. Here, Taylor discusses how Plato's birth and family are lost in legends of divine ancestors.

Plato, the son of Ariston and Perictione, was born either in Athens or, according to another account, in Aegina, in the year 427 B.C. On the mother's side . . . the family [goes] back through Dropides, a relative of the great lawgiver Solon, to a divine first ancestor, the god Poseidon. On his father's side, too, his origin was no less illustrious, since Ariston was a descendant of Codrus, the last king of Athens, who was himself sprung up from Poseidon. Even this origin, however, was not thought exalted enough for the philosopher by his admirers, and Plato's own nephew, Speusippus, is cited as an authority for the belief that the real father of Perictione's son was the god Apollo.

Marcuse, Ludwig. *Plato and Dionysius: A Double Biography*. (New York: Alfred A. Knopf, 1947).

Marcuse reconstructs the philosopher's life through a careful reading of Plato's letters (not all of which were written by him) and his dialogues, filling in the blanks with speculation about what Plato might have been thinking and experiencing at important moments in his life. In this passage, Marcuse describes Plato's state of mind after the execution of his teacher, Socrates.

The more a man's past dominates him at the expense of his present, the less hold upon him the future can assert. What Plato had lost was his own future; what he had gained was the life of dead Socrates. What, actually, were the ideas that had taken possession of this young man? A teacher is more than his teachings. A proposition is true or it is false; one's real loyalty is not to it, but to the persons who were its incarnation. Plato's adherence was not to this or that dogma, but to Socrates himself; and Socrates' last hours had become part of his very being.

Early Interpretations of Plato

Aristotle. *Metaphysics*. Translated by W. D. Ross. (Oxford: Clarendon, 1924).

Aristotle (384–322 BCE) was Plato's best-known student and also one of his first critics. Aristotle derived much of his philosophy from his teacher but disagreed with him on several important matters. Notably, he questioned Plato's theory of forms, described in the *Phaedo*, and challenged Plato's belief that ideal forms exist on some abstract level beyond the material world we can sense.

Some do not think there is anything substantial besides sensible things, but others think there are eternal substances which are more in number and more real. . . . Plato posited two kinds of substance—the Forms and objects of mathematics—as well as a third kind, the substance of sensible bodies. . . . Regarding these matters, then, we must inquire which of the common statements are right and which are not right, and what substances there are, and whether there are or are not any besides sensible substances, and how sensible substances exist, and whether there is a substance capable of separate existence (and if so why and how).

St. Augustine. *Confessions and Enchiridion*. Translated by Albert C. Outler. (Dallas: Southern Methodist University, 1955).

St. Augustine (354–430 CE) saw Plato's ideas perfected in Christianity and tried to reconcile Platonism with the teachings of the early Christian church. In his *Confessions,* he describes a spiritual journey of discovery that leads him to search for truth both in Christian scripture and in the teachings of Plato. Speaking directly to God, Augustine gives thanks for finding books by the followers of Plato and emphasizes what they have in common with Christian beliefs.

Thou didst procure for me, through one inflated with the most monstrous pride, certain books of the Platonists, translated from Greek into Latin. And therein I found, not indeed in the same words, but to the selfsame effect, enforced by many and various reasons that "in the beginning was the Word, and the Word was with God, and the Word was God. The same was in the beginning with God. All things were made by him; and without him was not anything made that was made" . . . . So I began, and I found that whatever truth I had read [in the Platonists] was here combined with the exaltation of thy grace.

Ficino, Marsilio. *Complete Works of Plato (Platonis Opera Omnia).* (Florence, 1491). Quoted by James Hankins. *Plato in the Italian Renaissance.* (New York: E. J. Brill, 1990).

Marsilio Ficino (1433–1499 CE) is one of the most influential philosophers of the Italian Renaissance. He was one of the first to translate Plato's dialogues into Latin, founded a new version of Plato's Academy in Florence, and found ways to bring Platonic thought and Christianity together in his writings. He drew parallels between the *Symposium* and the Last Supper, praised Plato for his pursuit of spiritual love, and even called him a "doctor of souls," who used his philosophy to cure diseases of the human spirit. Ficino believed that Plato addressed nearly every human concern in his dialogues.

Our Plato, with his wonderful charity towards the human race, left nothing untried in his disputations which might seem in any way to conduce to human salvation.

Critical Interpretations: Nineteenth Century to Mid-Twentieth Century

Nietzsche, Friedrich. *Twilight of the Idols/The Anti-Christ.* Trans. R. J. Hollingdale. (London: Penguin, 1999). [Originally published in 1889.]

Nietzsche believed that the ancient Greeks possessed a tragic sense of life and understood the limits of reason, which Plato undermines in his dialogues through the figure of Socrates. Nietzsche considers Socrates a martyr who committed suicide, killing himself for the sake of reason, since he went willingly to his death and provoked his own execution.

Socrates wanted to die—it was not Athens, it was he who handed himself the poison cup, who compelled Athens to hand him the poison cup . . . "Socrates is no physician," he said softly to himself: "death alone is a physician here."

Jowett, Benjamin. *Dialogues of Plato*. (Oxford: Clarendon, 1871).

In the nineteenth century, an interest in Greek architecture, mythology, literature, and philosophy swept through Europe. Jowett translated Plato's dialogues and proposed that his works should become the philosophical basis of an Oxford education. Jowett argued that Plato's sense of duty and self-sacrifice was relevant to his own time.

[My aim] has been to represent Plato as the father of Idealism, who is not to be measured by the standard of utilitarianism or any other modern philosophical system. He is the poet or maker of ideas, satisfying the wants of his own age, providing the instruments of thought for future generations. He is no dreamer, but a great philosophical genius struggling with the unequal conditions of light and knowledge under which he is living. He may be illustrated by the writings of moderns, but he must be interpreted by his own, and by his place in the history of philosophy. . . . His truth may not be our truth, and nevertheless may have an extraordinary value and interest for us.

Russell, Bertrand. *A History of Western Philosophy*. (New York: Simon & Schuster, 1945).

A controversial British philosopher, historian, and social activist, Russell won the 1950 Nobel Prize for Literature. Russell rejected the idealist philosophy of Plato praised by Jowett and became one of the founders of analytic philosophy, which emphasizes the role of logic in philosophical thought. In his insistence on using a scientific method in the search for truth, Russell finds fault with Plato's position that reality is created by the mind and ideas, and attacks the style of thinking used by his character Socrates.

The Platonic Socrates was a pattern to subsequent philosophers for many ages. What are we to think of him ethically? His merits are obvious. . . . He has, however, some very grave defects. He is dishonest and sophistical in argument, and in his private thinking he uses intellect to prove conclusions that are to him agreeable, rather than in a disinterested search for knowledge. There is something smug and unctuous about him, which reminds one of a bad type of cleric. His courage in the face of death would have been more remarkable if he had not believed that he was going to enjoy eternal bliss in the company of the gods. Unlike some of his predecessors, he was not scientific in his thinking, but was determined to prove the universe agreeable to his ethical standards.

Crombie, I. M. *An Examination of Plato's Doctrines.* (London: Routledge, 1962).

Crombie sees in Socrates a faithful representation of the historical man as Plato knew him. Unlike Russell, he finds in Socrates the ideal embodiment of how philosophy should be undertaken: through questioning life and its assumptions.

Why did Plato write so much about Socrates? We can find a plausible answer to this question if we consider the character of the Platonic Socrates. He is both a unique human person and also a representative of a certain intellectual attitude.... It follows that as a human being the Platonic Socrates is Plato's picture of the real man. His courage, his pertinacity, his romantic but platonic associations with young men, his tiresomeness, his saintliness, his magnetism, his untidiness, his head for strong drink—all these must be characteristics which Plato believed Socrates to have possessed.... But a further reason why he wrote about him ... was that he judged Socrates, as he was in reality and as he was in Plato's pages, to represent the spirit in which philosophy ought to be done and the attitude to life out of which a zeal of it arises—that "the life whose principles are not challenged is not worth living" as the Platonic Socrates is made to say.

Guthrie, W. K. C. *A History of Greek Philosophy*. 4 vols. Volume IV. (Cambridge: Cambridge University Press, 1975).

Guthrie followed the "developmentalist" interpretation of Plato, an important way of understanding the philosopher since the nineteenth century. This view maintains that Plato developed his philosophy over time, and that his dialogues are sometimes inconsistent with one another, representing different stages in the process.

It would seem natural that a philosopher's thought should display a logical order of development. He will obtain certain results first, and later build on them in working towards solutions of other problems, and he must tackle certain questions before he is ready to face others. He may also change his mind. To trace this development may be easy in a philosopher who writes, as most philosophers do, systematic treatises. It is more difficult to find in Plato's dialogues, a unique form of literature not to be compared with modern philosophical dialogues.

Recent Critical Interpretations

Kahn, Charles C. *Plato and the Socratic Dialogue: The Philosophical Use of a Literary Form.* (Cambridge: Cambridge University Press, 1996).

Kahn emphasizes the importance of the Socratic dialogue as a literary form that represents a fictional Socrates, not the historical figure. He departs from the developmentalist interpretation, defended by scholars like Guthrie, and instead supports the "unitarian" position, an opposing understanding of Plato that finds a consistent expression of his philosophy in the dialogues.

Plato . . . is a thinker with a unified world view consistent throughout his life. That is to say, he belongs rather with philosophers like Descartes or Hume, whose philosophical position remains essentially unchanged once their thought attains maturity, than with philosophers like Kant and Wittgenstein, whose conception of philosophy undergoes radical change. Thus I firmly dissent from the standard view of Plato as an author who defends fundamentally different philosophies at different stages of his career. . . . What we can trace in these dialogues is not the development of Plato's thought, but the gradual unfolding of a literary plan for presenting his philosophical views to the general public.

Nussbaum, Martha C. *The Fragility of Goodness*. (Cambridge: Cambridge University Press, 1986).

According to Nussbaum, the Greek philosophers describe the good life as vulnerable to luck, accidents, and unforeseen reversals of fortune affecting all people and those they love. She maintains that Plato's account of love in *Symposium* reflects this idea of human fragility and inspires us to search for a more stable beauty, as advised by Diotima, speaking through Socrates.

> Education turns you around, so that you do not see what you used to see. It also turns you into a free man instead of a servant. Diotima connects the love of particulars with tension, excess, and servitude; the love of a qualitatively uniform "sea" with health, freedom, and creativity. . . . It is a startling and powerful vision. Just try to think it seriously: this body of this wonderful beloved person is *exactly* the same in quality as that person's mind and inner life.

Hawthorne, Susan. "Diotima Speaks Through the Body," *Engendering Origins: Critical Feminist Readings in Plato and Aristotle*. Ed. Bat-Ami Bar On. (Albany: State University of New York Press, 1994), 83–96.

Hawthorne applies feminist theory to analyze the speech of Diotima in *Symposium*, showing how Socrates' retelling of a woman's story to present his ideas on love challenges the other participants in *Symposium* to think about love in a different way.

> Diotima's speech in *The Symposium* makes philosophical use of the female body as a metaphor for understanding the nature of love. The female body and the processes associated with its renewal, change,

and demise become a filter for Diotima's perception of the world. Through her understanding of her own body's function she creates a vision of the world that is distinctively "feminine," and from that vision argues for a particular way of understanding the nature of Eros.

Questions for Discussion

The *Dialogues of Plato* are a collection of independent dialogues, but they also relate to one another in important ways. What themes tie these dialogues together? What stories continue from one dialogue to another?

Have you ever made a decision that goes against what you have been taught to believe? In *Euthyphro*, the title character prosecutes his own father even though he has been taught to honor his parents. Socrates understands Euthyphro's dilemma but disagrees with his decision. Do these difficult choices strengthen or challenge our personal values?

What do you think of Socrates as a character? Is he wise, as he claims? If so, how? Is he funny or foolish at times? How does Plato portray Socrates and what does he want us to think about him?

In *Meno*, Socrates claims that right opinions are as valuable as factual knowledge. Which do you think are more important, facts or opinions? Can you think of current events that show how opinions can be more influential than facts?

Which of the speeches on love in *Symposium* do you find most convincing? Is Socrates right to emphasize the spiritual potential of love over its physical attractions? Is this kind of Platonic love truly possible or is it an unreachable ideal?

The concept of sacrifice in the name of ideals is one of the great themes of literature. In *Crito*, Socrates has an opportunity to escape from prison, yet he chooses to await his execution in order to remain true to his principles. Can you think of other books or movies in which the characters sacrifice their lives or personal safety for the sake of making a point?

One of the main ideas Plato expresses in *Phaedo* is that the world deceives us with false appearances. Which aspects of modern life depend on the creation of an image? Is our society more concerned with image than truth?

In *Apology*, Socrates is charged with corruption and questioning the religious beliefs of his time. What role does religion play in American life? Should religion influence politics today, as it did in Plato's time?

Should Socrates have been convicted of crimes at his trial, depicted in *Apology*? What arguments could he have used to win his case? Do you think his trial was fair?

There are no women in Plato's dialogues, except for a brief appearance by Socrates' wife in *Phaedo* and the priestess Diotima, whose story is told by Socrates in *Symposium*. Why does Plato choose to present philosophical and practical issues only from the perspective of men? What is the effect of this choice?

SUGGESTIONS FOR THE
INTERESTED READER

If you enjoyed reading *Dialogues of Plato,* you might also be interested in the following:

The Clouds by Aristophanes (423 BCE). This comic play makes fun of intellectual life in ancient Athens and is considered one of the best examples of Greek old comedy. It is famous for its satirical and broadly humorous portrayal of Socrates, as mentioned in Plato's *Apology.* The play is available in modern translations.

The Republic by Plato (380–360 BCE). Often considered Plato's masterpiece, *The Republic* continues the tradition of the Platonic dialogue, examining the theory of forms, the immortality of the soul, and other ideas discussed in his earlier dialogues, while also debating the role of government, politics, and philosophy in society.

Nicomachean Ethics by Aristotle (350 BCE). Aristotle, Plato's best-known pupil, built on the foundation of his teacher's philosophy to investigate the pursuit of happiness. In this book, Aristotle analyzes the relationship between happiness and virtue and also defines the doctrine of the "golden mean," the idea that every virtue is a mean between two extreme vices.

On Love by Alain de Botton. This 1993 novel is the first of several philosophical—or philosophy-inspired—works by de Botton. In this novel, the protagonist examines a failed love affair and the nature of love itself (the subject of the *Symposium*) from a wide variety of angles. De Botton achieved widespread acclaim for his later nonfiction works *How Proust Can Change Your Life* (1997) and *The Consolation of Philosophy* (2000).

The Philosopher's Apprentice by James Morrow. This 2008 novel is a science fiction examination of the central questions of the *Meno:* what is virtue, and can virtue be taught? Often satiric and frequently funny, the novel explores the results of a genetic experiment in which three young girls are cloned and "born," at various starting ages, completely without a sense of right or wrong.

BESTSELLING ENRICHED CLASSICS